TOWN DEFENCES IN
ENGLAND AND WALES

TOWN DEFENCES IN ENGLAND AND WALES

An architectural and documentary
study AD 900–1500

HILARY L. TURNER

JOHN BAKER LONDON

© 1971 Hilary L. Turner

First published in 1970 by
John Baker (Publishers) Ltd
5 Royal Opera Arcade
Pall Mall, London SW1

isbn 0 212 98384 9

Printed in Great Britain by
Clarke, Doble & Brendon Ltd

Contents

Illustrations

PLATES

PLANS

MAPS

Acknowledgements are due to the following for permission to reproduce material: the Bodleian Library, Oxford for Plate 1, the Ashmolean Museum, Oxford for Plate 15, the Trustees of the British Museum for Plates 2, 4, 8, Carlisle City Libraries for Plate 3, Mr R. G. Lock and the Museums Department of the City of Southampton for Plate 24. The others are my own copyright.

HILARY L. TURNER

Acknowledgements

The geographical spread of this book has brought me into contact with a great many people who have helped on the work either consciously or unconsciously. To all of them I am most grateful; I owe special thanks to the staff of the Bodleian Library and of the Public Record Office as well as to the many city and county archivists and librarians, town clerks and museum curators who have so willingly answered my queries, brought unknown sources to my notice and provided space in which to study. Information and assistance has been received from many who knew of the work in hand, in particular from Mr Frank Noble and Miss Meriel Jancey of Hereford; Professor S. S. Frere of All Souls College, Oxford; Mr J. T. Smith, Dr E. A. Gee and Mr I. A. Pattison of the Royal Commission on Historical Monuments; and from my supervisor, Mr H. M. Colvin. Many friends have sustained me by their criticism, in particular Dr P. Hyams, Dr D. Palliser, Dr J. R. L. Maddicott and Mr T. G. Hassall; Mrs Barbara Morris drew the plans. Thanks must also go to Mr Martin Biddle, whose enthusiasm has been a great stimulus, and to Mr A. J. Taylor for encouragement to publish.

Lastly, I am most deeply indebted to Mr J. Campbell who gave me the idea for the work, and for his guidance and unflagging interest in seeing it brought to a conclusion.

HILARY L. TURNER
14 January 1970

ABBREVIATIONS

Antiq. Jnl.	Antiquaries Journal.
A.S.C.	*Anglo-Saxon Chronicle*, edited D. Whitelock in *English Historical Documents*, I.
B.A.A.J.	*Journal of the British Archaeological Association.*
B.G.A.S	*Transactions of the Bristol and Gloucestershire Archaeological Association.*
B.M.	British Museum.
Cal. Ch. Rolls	*Calendar of Charter Rolls*, 6 vols., Stationery Office, 1903–1927.
Cal. Close Rolls *C.C.R.*	*Calendar of Close Rolls*, 61 vols., Stationery Office, 1892–1963.
Cal. Inq. Misc.	*Calendar of Inquisitions Miscellaneous*, 6 vols., Stationery Office, 1916–63.
Cal. Lib. Rolls	*Calendar of Liberate Rolls*, 6 vols., Stationery Office, 1917–61.
Cal. Pat. Rolls *C.P.R.*	*Calendar of Patent Rolls*, 54 vols., Stationery Office, 1891–1916.
Coventry Leet Book	*Coventry Leet Book*, ed. M. D. Harris, Early English Text Society, vols. 134–5 (Original Series, 1907–1908).
D.B.	*Domesday Book*, Record Commission, 4 vols., 1783, 1816.
E.E.T.S.	*Early English Text Society.*
Eng. Hist. Rev.	*English Historical Review.*
English Hist. Docs.	*English Historical Documents*, ed. D. Whitelock, volume I, 1955.
F.C.	Field Club.
Hist. Mss. Comm.	Historical Manuscripts Commission.

Jnl.	Journal.
King's Works	*The History of the King's Works*, ed. H. M. Colvin, A. J. Taylor, A. Brown, 3 vols., 1963.
Leland, *Itinerary*	*Itinerary through England and Wales*, ed. L. Toulmin Smith, 5 vols., 1907–10.
Letter Book	*Calendar of the Letter Books of the City of London, A–L*, ed. R. R. Sharpe, 1899–1912.
Lloyd, *History of Wales*	*A History of Wales*, J. E. Lloyd, 2 vols., 1948.
Med. Arch.	Journal of the Society for Medieval Archaeology.
M.P.B.W.	Ministry of Public Buildings and Works.
N.H.	Natural History.
New Towns	*The New Towns of the Middle Ages*, M. Beresford, 1967.
OS	Ordnance Survey.
P.R.O.	Public Record Office.
Procs.	*Proceedings.*
P.S.A.S.	Proceedings of the Society of Antiquaries of Scotland.
R.C.A.M.	Royal Commission on Ancient Monuments.
R.C.H.M.	Royal Commission on Historic Monuments.
Rot. Hund.	*Rotuli Hundredorum*, Record Commission, 2 vols., 1812–1818.
Rot. Litt. Claus.	*Rotuli Litterarum Clausuram*, Record Commission, 2 vols., 1833–44.
Rot. Litt. Pat.	*Rotuli Litterarum Patentium*, Record Commission, 1835.
Rot. Parl.	*Rotuli Parliamentorum*, ed. J. Caley *et al.*, 6 vols., 1767.
Speed	*Theatrum Orbis Terrarum*, J. Speed, 1610.
Trans.	*Transactions.*
V.C.H.	*The Victoria History of the Counties of England.*

Introduction

Town walls are a neglected branch of military architecture, neglected partly because their study has appeared less attractive and less rewarding than the study of castles or abbeys as examples of medieval architectural skill, and partly because it has been considered that there is too little evidence to analyse and on which to base conclusions. But 108 towns were walled in the Middle Ages, and eighty-four preserve at least some remains. Few have been investigated closely, although recently some local archaeological societies have conducted excavations. Much of the material, however, remains unexamined, almost the only work being that of Bryan O'Neil. This study is based on field-work and observation, and has two aims. Firstly, it is an attempt to combine architectural and archaeological evidence with documentary evidence to date the surviving remains of the walls of individual towns. The detailed studies represent those towns where the available material answers the greatest number of questions of general interest. The second aim of the book is to use the local studies to answer such general questions as when walls were built, and for what reasons; how their construction was financed and organized; what architectural and defensive merits the walls possessed.

The book begins with a review of the town fortifications in the tenth century. As an introduction to the stage of development which had been reached, a brief survey of those towns which had been fortified earlier is included. The concern here is less with the physical remains than with the problems connected with the siting and distribution of the fortified towns as revealed in documentary sources, and with the problems of how defences were built and maintained.

The eleventh and twelfth centuries do not seem to have been a period when either the town or its fortifications were considered important. It is possible, however, that a larger number of towns

maintained defences than the documentary evidence reveals, and it
may be that the system of defending, and perhaps also of maintaining and constructing defences, outlined in the Burghal Hidage
continued to function. *Burh-bot,* the duty of maintaining a fortress
and one of those of the *trimoda necessitas,* may have had an existence continued long after the Conquest. There is evidence to suggest
that Maitland's 'garrison theory', and Ballard's extension of it, do
not deserve the scorn of their critics.

The system by which the responsibility for fortifying a town
rested on the surrounding countryside was replaced only in the
early years of the thirteenth century. At this time many towns began
to display an interest in fortifications. At first confined to towns
which had been fortified by either Roman, Anglo-Saxon or Dane,
the interest gradually spread to newer settlements. The need for
defences was considerable, since between 1204 and 1220 England
faced a very real threat of invasion. The need brought into existence
a new tax, the murage toll. A grant of murage was the permission
of the king to levy toll on a specified number of goods coming into
the town for sale, the proceeds of which were to be devoted to the
construction of the walls. The tax was probably more efficient than
the pre-Conquest system of labour, and replaced it because of this,
and because more, and different, towns sought walls, to which the
older system could not be applied. Moreover, the development came
at a time when experiments in taxation were being made, and this
may have been one such among many.

The murage toll, although it was only of local application, has a
history of its own to which no attention has hitherto been paid. It
remained throughout the Middle Ages the most important source
of money for a town which wished to build a wall. Although the
king fixed the terms of the grant, deciding which articles should be
taxed and for how long the grant should remain in force, the town
was responsible for arranging the collection. While this was nomin-
ally under the supervision of the town authorities, it seems to
have been a duty shared by the whole citizenry. Opportunities for
peculation were rife, and when such cases occurred they
could, at the request of the citizens, be investigated by royal
officials.

Eventually it became a widespread practice for groups of people,
for example, the religious, merchants and towns, to obtain exemp-

tion from payment of murage. This, together with the fact that by the early fourteenth century lists of taxable goods had become so long that administration must have been difficult, heralds a change in the character of the tax. It became common for a town to receive permission to assess its inhabitants on the basis of property owned in the town, although the older system never became obsolete.

By the mid-fourteenth century there seems to have been apathy about the maintenance of defences, perhaps because they had served no obvious purpose. However, in the last decades of the century there was a revival of interest, stimulated by the threat of invasion from France. Murage grants were issued in large numbers, but they obviously did not produce sufficient revenue, and many towns received substantial grants from the king in the form of the remission of the fee-farm, part of the proceeds of customs duties, or profits of fines.

The study of the murage tax poses various problems connected with the organization of the work of construction. The amount of money a grant might bring in was limited and unpredictable, and this is reflected in the length of time which it might take to build a wall, and in the quality of the work. The assessment of the architectural and defensive merits of urban fortifications is hampered by the condition of existing remains, only a few of which have escaped alterations. Although a wall was usually well sited as a physical barrier, it might not be very well planned as far as defensive provisions were concerned. The curtain wall was one base from which to attack, as well as being the connection between the mural towers, which were the points from which the main offensive was launched. But the gates were the most important parts of the defences, to which thought was devoted and on which care was lavished. They were the most heavily fortified parts of the circuit, and were provided not only with arrow slits or, later, gunports, but also with machicolations, murder-holes, portcullis, barbican and drawbridge.

Although the basic reason for the existence of a wall was for defence and there is a clear connection between the periods of disturbance and the construction of walls, it is clear that once they were erected they fulfilled other functions. Towers could be lived in; gates, by the nature of their design, could accommodate a room over the arch which could be used for peaceful purposes, for example as a chapel or an assembly room. The gradual relaxation of the military character of gates in the fifteenth century suggests that perhaps they were thought of primarily as being useful for the collection of tolls. The increased trade that the existence of a wall might bring might in some cases, for example Hull, be the reason for its construction. A wall is therefore also an indication of what the town thought it ought to be, and it became a reflection of status; where the seignurial interest was strong the town was unlikely to have a wall. The magnificence of a town wall is an indication of economic prosperity, and its maintenance an indication of the pride of the community.

Some conclusions emerge which possess wider significance in the context of national history than the details of building walls possess alone. One point to emerge is the strength of municipal organization. That a body as amorphous as the medieval city authorities could embark on, and carry through to completion, the large-scale operation of building defences is an important and interesting sidelight on the management of civic affairs. The organization of the work reveals also that many of the inhabitants were involved in the jobs associated with the building and maintenance of the walls, such as the collection of tolls, the scouring of the ditches, the duties of watch and ward, if not in the actual labour.

Secondly, it is interesting that so many towns sought to build walls, since the cost of the operation was considerable and long-continued. It is important also to note the part played by the king. The relations between Town and Crown were good, and co-operation close. It was the king who in the first instance had provided the means to finance the building of walls by the development of the murage grant. Finally, it is interesting that it was the king who controlled the way in which the money for building was raised. At first the burden of murage fell most heavily not on the inhabitants of the town but on those of the countryside. Only when exemption was widespread did the citizens assume responsibility for raising the money through an assessment of property owned within the town. Continuing royal interest is demonstrated by the grants made from royal resources in the late fourteenth century, and clearly the king was as willing to assist the towns to build and maintain their defences as the towns themselves were determined to have them.

CHAPTER ONE

Time and place

Wonderful is this wall of stone, wrecked by fate.
The city buildings crumble, the bold works of the giants decay,
Roofs have caved in, towers collapsed,
Barred gates are gone, gateways have gaping mouth, hoar frost
clings to mortar.[1]

The imagination of this unknown poet was caught by the still visible ruins of a town abandoned after the Roman occupation, and in the tenth century neither the idea nor the sight of a town once walled were strange. The period of the Danish invasions made fortified towns necessary once more, and they were advantageous to the attackers no less than to the defenders. There were needs common to both sides; a base to which the army could rally and from which to make sorties, a base in which non-combatants could seek safety, and finally a base which would at least appear to be sufficiently strong to discourage attack. The two sides, however, waged war in slightly different ways, and these differences are reflected in the date and distribution of the fortified centres Map I). It appears that the Danes for a long time had no settled bases and, instead, preferred guerilla tactics, the lightning strike accompanied by burning and looting. The English, on the other hand, being on the defensive, found it necessary to construct fortifications earlier. Although defences were almost certainly built to answer a specific strategic need, it is unlikely that the settlements to which they were added were deliberately created. By fortifying existing centres a sufficiently comprehensive network of defences could be provided, at least on the English side.

The two documents which provide most of the information about fortified towns in the early tenth century are the *Anglo-Saxon Chronicle* and the Burghal Hidage.[2] Both originate from the English side, and may therefore be concealing much information about the movements of the Danes. The *Chronicle* is the Annual Register of the kingdom of Wessex and conveys information about towns incidental to its main narrative. The Burghal Hidage, dated 911–19, is concerned specifically with towns. It is divided into two parts: first comes a list of towns in the south of England which may be assumed to have been fortified by the English; secondly it is a schedule of the manpower required to defend each town. Its importance for contemporaries lay in the second part, defining the military obligations attached to land surrounding a fortified centre. This document refers only to English towns: the *Chronicle* names towns belonging to both English and Danes. Both sources together make it possible to reconstruct, at least partially, the course of the campaigns between about 870 and 925. They suggest that there were two stages in the fighting. The first was between about 870 and 900 when the English were on the defensive, and the Danes on the offensive; the second, 900-25, in which the roles were reversed. Many of the towns listed in the Burghal Hidage must date from the earlier period, as the document is concerned with towns south of the river Thames, whose fortifications varied from the modest defences of a promontory site, such as Lyng, to large fortresses such as Wallingford. The Danes, on the other hand, if the *Anglo-Saxon Chronicle* can be relied on, worked from temporary bases which may well have been without fortification.

By the time of the second stage, 900–25, the English were in a position to take the offensive, and to carry their campaign into Danish territory. From the *Chronicle* and the Burghal Hidage the English are seen adding to the number of their fortified towns, some of which were sited well within the bounds of territory previously accepted as Danish, while at the same time there is the first mention of fortified towns in Danish possession.

A more detailed study of the distribution of the towns shows that those fortified by the English were defended slightly earlier than those fortified by the Danes, simply because it was not until the English were in a position to take the offensive that the Danes were subjected to any pressing need to defend their capture. In the first phase of the fighting, that of the English defensive actions, the fortified towns are situated south of the Thames; in the second phase the number of towns is smaller, and comprises either the towns extending up the Welsh Marches, or those towns from which the Danes had been expelled, and which were then occupied, and perhaps re-fortified, by the English. The first group comprises the

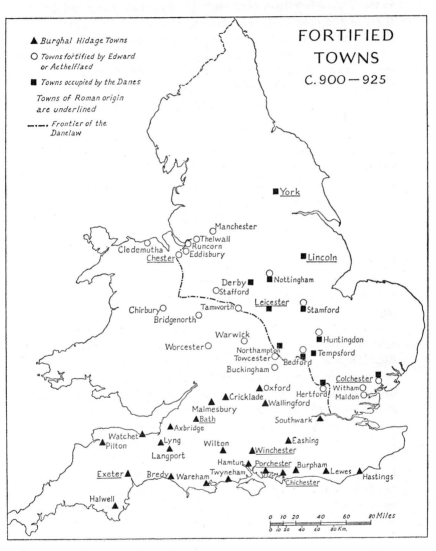

FORTIFIED
TOWNS
C. 900 — 925

▲ *Burghal Hidage Towns*
○ *Towns fortified by Edward or Aethelflaed*
■ *Towns occupied by the Danes*

Towns of Roman origin are underlined

—·—· *Frontier of the Danelaw*

■ <u>York</u>

Manchester
○Thelwall
○Runcorn
Cledemutha ○ ○Eddisbury
<u>Chester</u>

■ <u>Lincoln</u>

Derby■ ○Nottingham
○Stafford
Chirbury○ Tamworth○ <u>Leicester</u>○
Bridgenorth○ ■Stamford

Warwick○
Worcester○ Northampton○ ■Huntingdon
Towcester○ ■Tempsford
Buckingham○ Bedford○

▲Oxford <u>Colchester</u>
▲Cricklade Hertford○ ■Witham○
Malmesbury▲ ▲Wallingford Maldon○
▲<u>Bath</u>
▲Axbridge Southwark ▲

Watchet▲ ▲Lyng Wilton ▲Eashing
Pilton▲ Langport ▲ <u>Winchester</u>
Hamtun▲ <u>Porchester</u> Burpham
<u>Exeter</u>▲ Bredy▲ Wareham Twyneham▲ ▲ ▲Lewes▲
Halwell▲ <u>Chichester</u> Hastings

0 10 20   40   60   80 Miles
0 10 20 40 60 80 Km.

MAP I

burhs listed in the Burghal Hidage, the second those which are said in the *Chronicle* to have been built by Edward the Elder and Aethelflaed in the course of their campaigns against the Danes. While their fortifications may have been the sole reason for the existence of some of these towns others may have been fortified before the tenth century. In this category, obviously, are those of the *burhs* which had been fortified in Roman times. Thus the towns of Exeter, Bath, Winchester, Portchester and Chichester are listed in the Burghal Hidage, and in the *Chronicle* we read that the walls of Chester were repaired in 908, and those of Manchester in 919. Of the seige of Colchester in 917 it is said that the English killed all the people except the men who fled over the wall, and then occupied and re-fortified the town. Yet only a small number of sites were re-used in the tenth century. One reason for this may be that the remains of many of the Roman fortifications were of little value. Many of the towns which had received stone defences would by *c*. 900 have resembled the crumbling state of the ruins as depicted by the poet. But the chief reason must be that the sites of the *burhs* were determined by strategic considerations differing from the pattern of settlement and from the strategic needs of the Roman period.

The third group of towns fortified at this time is made up of towns fortified by the Danes. It is noticeable that much of the Scandinavian settlement of England was urban, and we know from documentary evidence that the Danes had at least seven fortified towns within that part of England under their control, the Danelaw, lying north of the river Thames and east of the Watling Street, namely Nottingham, Derby, Stamford, Northampton, Tempsford, Bedford and Huntingdon, all of whose fortifications they are said to have built themselves.[3] They also held the Roman towns of Lincoln, Leicester, York, and, for a time, Colchester. Many of these towns remained important throughout the Middle Ages, and it is an interesting contrast to the situation south of the Danelaw that only five of the Danelaw towns did not remain fortified places into the later period.

Outside these categories are towns which were probably fortified by 1086, but for which there is no documentary evidence. Archaeological investigation has revealed fortification in the pre-Domesday period at other towns in the Danelaw, amongst them Newark, Thetford, Cambridge and, perhaps, Boston. References to Bury St. Edmunds in the early twelfth century suggest that it was already a fortified town, and its defences may, therefore, have been pre-Conquest. South of the Danelaw, it is hard to believe that London, defended by a stone wall built by the Romans and probably repaired in 886, was over-shadowed by the Saxon *burh* at Southwark. Equally, it is difficult to understand the lack of specific mention of Canterbury and Rochester, to whose Roman defences there are seventh-century references,[4] and which were always important towns. In the west, the existence of fortifications at Worcester is implied by *c*. 899,[5] and at Hereford Harold ordered the construction of gates and bars in 1055 after the town had been sacked by the Welsh.[6] It is possible, however, that these were not the earliest defences. In 1011 Danes besieging Canterbury were said to have been thrown over the walls, but one cannot be certain that this statement is not mere rhetorical flourish.[7] Domesday Book, compiled in 1086, suggests, however, that such fortifications as existed were not necessarily well maintained. Thus at Canterbury it was noted that there were eleven houses in the ditch; similar statements were made about York and Nottingham, but it is possible that at both these places the explanation is not that the fortifications had been neglected, but that the city had expanded beyond the original bounds.[8] At York the eastern line of the Roman fort was clearly too small to contain the settlement,[9] and at Nottingham it is thought that the ditch of the Saxon borough, where it was adjacent to that of the Norman borough on the northern and western sides, had been filled in deliberately.[10]

The period between Domesday Book and the early thirteenth century is a dark one for the history of urban fortifications, as for the history of towns in general. During this period some towns grew and flourished, and began to acquire new liberties; those which did best were usually those in the east. Others, particularly the small *burhs* in the west, appear to have declined. Thus there is no later evidence to show that Runcorn, Thelwall, Eddisbury, Chirbury, Watchet, Lyng, Pilton, Halwell, Bredy, Twyneham, Burpham, Cricklade, or Wareham found any occasion to keep their fortifications in repair beyond the immediate needs of the invasion period. Some towns can have had military value for only a limited period of time, and declined almost immediately after the period of the invasions : others were of importance before the invasions, and continued to be important afterwards. But by 1200 only twenty-two of the forty-eight towns known to have been fortified in 1086 were in a position to repair their earlier defences. If one were to rely on direct written evidence for the town in the twelfth century the conclusion would have to be that towns, even fortified towns, were relatively unimportant. Even the considerable interest in the founding of towns in both England and Wales between 1086 and 1200, did not lead to fortification. Of the 114 foundations, only three are known to have been planned defences from the beginning; Richard's Castle, Pleshey and Castleton.[11] Nevertheless, these figures may be set against the picture of a lack of interest in urban life, given by chroniclers more interested in the castle and its occupants.

For the history of town walls in this period the historian is largely dependent on chronicles, the Pipe Rolls and charters. All are useful, but they provide little more than indirect evidence on the subject. In general, the chronicles give the impression that while castles were important the fortified towns were not. Chronicles in this period are plentiful, and the positive evidence they give can be relied upon. But, although they display considerable interest in describing the fortified towns in the path of Crusading armies, they make little reference to the state of contemporary English towns.[12] This is not to say that there are no references to towns, or to their defences, but to point out that they did not occupy a dominant position in chroniclers' minds. Thus the accounts of the wars of Stephen's reign refer only to towns which we know to have been fortified earlier. The *Gesta Stephani* mention Exeter, Bath, Gloucester, Oxford, and Malmesbury,[13] and the chronicle of John of Worcester mentions Hereford and Worcester.[14] A detailed description of Bristol suggests that it relied on natural defences and on the castle.[15] The chronicles imply that warfare centred on the castle, and an urban castle was, of course, a means of fortifying the town in which it stood, at least as long as town and castle did not have conflicting interests. Occasional references might suggest even that defences of older towns were not being maintained; thus troops entered Worcester in 1140, and Northampton in 1174 without great difficulty.[16] But, as a way of inflicting punishment on a town, the defences of Leicester were razed in 1174, the year of the young Henry's rebellion against his father.[17]

Against this must be placed the additional information which can be gathered from the Pipe Rolls, the accounts of the sheriffs of the counties delivered to the Exchequer. It shows that some towns, again those with fortifications of earlier date, were repairing their defences. Thus Carlisle,[18] Chester,[19] Canterbury,[20] Hereford,[21] and Rochester[22] received allowance for the costs, but no grant suggests repair work after the civil wars, or indeed at any other period of disturbance. Only Southampton, hitherto undefended, received a grant of money large enough to suggest that new work was being undertaken.[23] There is, therefore, some evidence for maintenance, but the Pipe Rolls illustrate clearly the emphasis on the castle and the concentration of effort on building at the castle as opposed to building in the town. The number of references to the castle in a walled town far outnumber those to the wall.

Apart from the towns which were founded with defences in the twelfth century, the only clear reference to any new construction is the confirmation to the abbot of Holme that he should not lose his land, which had been enclosed within the new ditch that the burgesses of Norwich had made without the town after the death of Henry I.[24] In general, however, all that the twelfth-century evidence allows us to say is that while the strategic importance of the fortified town was inferior to that of the castle, town walls did exist, were sometimes repaired, and, in four cases, were built.

The documentary evidence for the twelfth century suggests a decline in interest in towns. It may be misleading, since the limited archaeological evidence available suggests that towns were concerned with their defences, but a lack of interest is not entirely inexplicable, because after 1154 England was not a turbulent country internally. Involvement in foreign warfare made unnecessary any thought of urban fortification at home. Towards the end of the twelfth century, however, increasing political and commercial activity in towns is reflected in chronicles, most specifically in Richard of Devizes' characterization of English towns, and even more strongly in his statement that during the absence of King Richard 'castles were strengthened, towns were fortified and moats were dug'.[25] Moreover, between 1204–1220 England was faced with a double threat of invasion from both France and Wales, more serious and more continuous than any she had faced since the eleventh, even the tenth century. Thus in the early years of the thirteenth century there was renewed stimulus to build defences, creating sufficient pressure to bring about the existence of the murage grant to make them easier to build. The murage grant first appears in 1220.[26] A grant was the licence to levy a toll called 'murage' on goods coming for sale in the town, the proceeds of which were to be applied to the walling of the town. Once the town had obtained the formal permission of the king to levy toll, the onus for the provision of defences was laid on the individual town. From the early thirteenth century onwards a connection between fighting and the provision of defences can be established, at least in a generalized way. The second decade of the century was a time of wars and rumours of war, and it is striking how many grants of timber or money for the improvement of defences are recorded on the Chancery Rolls. In the first instance these were made to towns which already had defences, and it is only after about 1225 that grants were made to enable hitherto unfortified towns to build defences. Thus in 1215 Colchester, Winchester and York received grants of timber;[27] in the case of Winchester it was specifically stated that it was for use in making 'the turrets of the city and to make the wall walks'. Shrewsbury received a grant of timber in 1212,[28] Stafford and Hereford in 1216;[29] Stamford in 1218;[30] Bridgnorth in 1220[31] and Canterbury during the 1220s.[32]

Other towns received gifts of cash. In 1215 John ordered the Exchequer to give £100 to the city of London as a loan towards the cost of walling and fortifying the city.[33] The bailiffs of Hereford in October 1215 were allowed to keep the 100 marks which they had been due to pay to the Exchequer at Michaelmas as the fine which they had made with the king to have their city at farm.[34] In February 1215 the sheriff of Devon was ordered to return to the citizens of Exeter 100 marks of the 300 raised from them by their tallage.[35] In 1221 the citizens of York were allowed £100, the sum for which they had compounded the debts they owed the king.[36] In the same year a writ allowed Jocelin, bishop of Bath, £58 which he had spent on the fortification of Bath in the time of King John.[37] A month later, he was allowed a further £20, apparently in repayment of money spent at the same time.[38] In 1225 the men of Northampton were allowed to keep sixpence from every twenty shillings of rent paid within the borough.[39] Finally, in 1226, fines taken from certain burgesses of Worcester and Oxford for having sold, or attempted to sell, cloth of the wrong width at the fair at Boston were applied to the walling of those towns.[40]

These, however, are all towns where defences already existed, in whatever state of repair. After about 1225 most of the towns which received murage grants were acquiring defences for the first time. A map of the distribution of the grants (map II) shows that they fall chronologically into clear geographical groupings. Of the total of fifty-one grants issued in the thirteenth century, twenty-seven were received by towns in Wales or on the Welsh borders. In addition there were the planned towns of Beaumaris, Conway, Caernarvon, Denbigh, Flint and Rhuddlhan whose walls were financed, not by a murage levy, but by direct royal subsidy. A group in the north of England was fortified against the Scots between 1315 and 1321, consisting of Berwick, Durham, Hartlepool, Lancaster and Richmond. At much the same time defences were built at Tonbridge, Sandwich, Dover and Rye. Of the five towns fortified in the later fourteenth century, three were towns which had been fortified in Roman times and had repaired their defences in the early thirteenth century, and only Plymouth and Salisbury were building defences for the first time. On the other hand, towns which received grants for the first time in the fifteenth century had not been fortified previously. Only a few towns built defences without the help of a murage grant, and in such cases the lord may have provided the money. But whether defences were the result of royal or of seignurial enterprise, few towns of importance were without walls by the end of the fifteenth century.

NOTES

1 'The Ruin', translated by K. Crossley-Holland in *The Battle of Maldon and other Old English Poems*, ed. by Bruce Mitchell 1965.
2 *Anglo-Saxon Chronicle*, ed. D. Whitelock in *English Historical Documents*, I, has been used throughout; the Burghal Hidage is edited in A. J. Robertson, *Anglo-Saxon Charters*, 1939, 246–8; see also N. Brooks, 'The unidentified forts of the Burghal Hidage', *Med. Arch.*, VIII, 74–90.
3 A.S.C., 917, 918, and F. T. Wainwright, 'Aethelflaed Lady of the Mercians', in *Studies presented to Bruce Dickins*, ed. P. Clemoes, 1959, 58–9.
4 W. G. De Gray Birch, *Cartularium Saxonicum*, 1883–92, nos. 5, 3.
5 *English Historical Documents*, ed. D. Whitelock, 1955, I, 498.

6   *Two Saxon Chronicles Parallel,* ed. C. Plummer, 1892, 186.
7   Roger Hoveden, *Chronica (Rolls Series),* I, 75.
8   D.B. I, f. 2; f. 298; f. 280.
9   D. M. Waterman, 'Late Saxon, Viking and Early Medieval Finds from York', *Archaeologia,* 97, 1959, 59-105.
10 R. H. Wildgoose, 'The Defences of the pre-Conquest Borough of Nottingham', *Trans. Thoroton Soc.,* 65, 1961, 19–26.
11 M. Beresford, *New Towns of the Middle Ages,* 1967, 637–44.
12 For example: M. Paris, *Chronica Majora (Rolls Series),* I, 89, 96–100: Benedict Abbas, *Gesta Regis Henrici Secundi (Rolls Series),* II, 127–9, 172–7.
13 *Gesta Stephani,* ed. K. R. Potter, 1955, 22, 39, 40, 43, 47, 63, 92, 153.
14 *Chronicle of John of Worcester,* ed. J. R. H. Weaver, 1908, 48–9, 57.
15 *Gesta Stephani,* 38.
16 *John of Worcester,* 57; Benedict Abbas, *Gesta Regis Henrici Secundi,* I, 69.
17 M. Paris, *Chronica Majora,* II, 289.
18 *Pipe Roll, 31 Henry I,* 140; *Pipe Roll, 11 Henry II,* 54; *Pipe Roll, 2 Richard I,* 49.
19 *Pipe Roll, 7 Henry II,* 35; *Pipe Roll, 8 Henry II,* 20-21.
20 *Pipe Roll, 12 Henry II,* 196.
21 *Pipe Roll, 1 Richard I,* 49.
22 *Pipe Roll, 5 Richard I,* 166.
23 *Pipe Roll, 4 John,* 78–9; *Pipe Roll, 5 John,* 145.
24 *Register of the Abbey of St. Benet of Holme,* ed. J. R. West, (Norfolk Record Society) II, 14.
25 Richard of Devizes, *Chronicle,* ed. J. T. Appleby, 1963, 64–7, 30.
26 *Cal. Pat. Rolls, 1216–25,* 238.
27 *Rot. Litt. Claus.,* I, 193, 240, 195.
28 *Pipe Roll, 14 John,* 90.
29 *Pipe Roll Society,* 31, no. 45; *Rot. Litt. Claus.,* I, 263.
30 *Rot. Litt. Claus.,* I, 370.
31 *Rot. Litt. Claus.,* I, 421.
32 W. Somner, *Antiquities of Canterbury,* 1640, 10.
33 *Pipe Roll Society,* 31, no. 15.
34 *Rot. Litt. Claus.,* I., 231.
35 *Rot. Litt. Claus.,* I, 186.
36 *Rot. Litt. Claus.,* I, 456.
37 *Rot. Litt. Claus.,* I, 454.
38 *Rot. Litt. Claus.,* I, 456.
39 *Rot. Litt. Claus.,* II, 66.
40 *Rot. Litt. Claus.,* II, 131, 135.

Towns fortified between

■ 1220 — 1250
▲ 1251 — 1299
○ 1300 — 1349
◇ 1350 — 1400
● 1401 — 1520

Towns without grants are
underlined; e.g.... <u>Beverley</u>

DISTRIBUTION
OF FIRST
MURAGE GRANTS

○Berwick

○<u>Alnwick</u> ●
<u>Warkworth</u>·

Newcastle ▲

■Carlisle

Durham○

<u>Penrith</u> ○

●Hartlepool

○Richmond

■Scarborough

○Lancaster

■York
<u>Beverley</u>·
<u>Hull</u> ○

·<u>Stockport</u>
<u>Castleton</u>

Grimsby ▲

○<u>Conway</u> ▲ Flint·
<u>Caernarvon</u>○ <u>Denbigh</u> ●<u>Ruthyn</u>   ■Chester
<u>Rhuddlan</u>

■Lincoln

○Overton
▲Oswestry

·<u>Newark</u>
■Nottingham   ○<u>Boston</u>

■Stafford

<u>Aberystwyth</u>▲
<u>Dolforwyn</u>· ▲Montgomery
Clun▲
Knighton▲ ■Ludlow
<u>Rhayader</u>· ▲Radnor ·<u>Richard's Castle</u>

Shrewsbury■

Leicester ▲

▲Stamford

■King's Lynn
Norwich▲
Yarmouth▲

▲Bridgenorth

○Coventry
○Warwick

<u>Thetford</u>·
·<u>Cambridge</u>
Southwold·
Dunwich▲

<u>Cardigan</u>▲
·<u>Haverfordwest</u> Carmarthen■
<u>Pembroke</u>○ ▲<u>Dryslwyn</u>·
Tenby○ ▲Swansea

Hay·■
·<u>Brecon</u>
Crickhowell·
Monmouth▲

■Hereford

■Northampton

Framlingham▲
Ipswich·

■Gloucester

Colchester◇
·Harwich

Abergavenny▲
·Kidwelly
<u>Cowbridge</u>·
<u>Cardiff</u>·
<u>Chepstow</u>·

·<u>Malmesbury</u>

■Oxford

London■

○<u>Rochester</u>■
<u>Bristol</u>■
◇Bath

·<u>Barnstaple</u>

Ilfracombe●

Tonbridge○ Canterbury◇ ○<u>Sand-
wich</u>

▲Bridgewater
Taunton·
Salisbury◇

■Winchester

○Dover

Rye○
Winchelsea○
▲Lewes
<u>Hastings</u>

·<u>Launceston</u>

■Exeter
Totnes▲

Southampton○
Melcombe·
Poole●

·Chichester Arundel▲

Plymouth◇

Portsmouth○

0 10 20   40   60   80 Miles
0 10 20   40   60   80 Km.

MAP II

CHAPTER TWO

Ways and means

The way in which the building of a wall was organised and financed varies from period to period. From before the Conquest until the late twelfth century, although the evidence is largely inferential, it seems clear that the obligation to maintain a wall was vested in the land in the vicinity of the defences, and was a duty incumbent upon those owning the land. In the early thirteenth century this system was disintegrating and developing into a new pattern : instead of the duty belonging to local men, and being little more than a labour service, it became a financial exaction levied on those who sought to sell goods in the town. This in its turn became unsatisfactory, for a number of reasons, and a new system was introduced, so that the money was provided by those who had lands or rents within the town. Walls were constructed first by service from lands, then by money and finally by money raised from lands.

The first phase of this cycle is set out in the Burghal Hidage. It seems probable that this document was drawn up not simply as a catalogue of fortified towns, but was also recording, or perhaps even establishing, the system by which town defences were to be built and maintained. Having stated how many hides were assigned to each town, the second part of the document lays out a table for reckoning how much land was required for the defence of the town, and how many men were needed. 'For the maintenance and defence of an acre's breadth of wall sixteen hides are required. If every hide is represented by one man, then every pole of wall can be manned by four men. Then for the maintenance of twenty poles of wall eighty hides are required and for a furlong one hundred and sixty hides are required by the same reckoning as I have stated above.'[1]

It seems clear that some sort of general obligation to maintain *burhs* was recognized in the later Anglo-Saxon period. The laws of Athelstan (924–39) commanded that all *burhs* were to be repaired at

Rogation-tide (the three days before Ascension Day), and this command was re-iterated by Aethelred (979–1013) and Cnut (1016–35).[2] No details are given of how the responsibility for the work was to be organised. This fact, together with the repetition of the obligation, suggests that the method was clearly established and universally understood. It suggests also that it was universally applicable. Later, Domesday Book affords information as to how, in certain cases, the duty of maintaining fortifications was apportioned by 1065. Thus at Chester the sheriff had the right to summon one man from each hide in the county to repair the walls of Chester;[3] at York eighty-four carucates beyond the walls were 'in the king's three works with the citizens';[4] and at Oxford there were 721 geld-paying houses and 229 called mural mansions because in return for wall repair they were quit of all royal custom except fyrd service.[5] It was largely on the basis of these instances that Maitland advanced his 'garrison theory'. He contended that the duty of maintaining the bulwark of the county's borough was incumbent on the magnates of the county, and that they discharged it by keeping haws in the borough and burgesses in those haws.[6] The houses, and the inhabitants, which were said in Domesday to belong to outlying manors, were appurtenances of this system.

This theory, although it has come in for much harsh criticism,[7] has not yet been countered effectively. It may still prove possible to link arrangements noted in Domesday Book with the Burghal Hidage, and the link between the responsibility for wall-work and land suggests that the list of boroughs with contributory properties compiled by Ballard may not be so absurd as his critics have made out.[8] There is also some twelfth-century evidence to show that a legal obligation to repair the wall of a town was in existence, and the reason for the silence of documents may therefore be that such a system was functioning throughout the period, though there was no occasion to record its workings. The Domesday system of Chester can be traced in the general obligation on the inhabitants of a town or county to maintain the town wall, an obligation which in some cases was still enforced. At Bury St. Edmunds the charter of 1121–38 states that 'if the ditch by which the town is surrounded ought to be repaired, if the knights of the abbey and the free sokemen work there, then the burgesses shall work there . . . because that work is not more incumbent on the burgesses than on the knights'.[9]

At Ipswich in 1204 the king ordered the ditch of the town to be made; it was done 'with the aid of the whole neighbourhood and of the county of Cambridge'.[10] At Wallingford, on the other hand, the burgesses were made quit of 'work on the castles and on the walls . . . from all customs and servile work'.[11] These examples demonstrate the continuance of the Domesday system throughout the twelfth century. Only at the end of the century are the beginnings of change revealed. In the charter to Hereford granted in 1189 the imposition of a toll was given preference over the exaction of labour services implied in earlier charters; the townsmen were given the town at farm provided that they attended to its fortifications.[12] The burden of providing defences was thus put firmly onto the townsmen, probably for the first time. No details of how the work was to be achieved were laid down, but it seems possible that the king's insistence on the importance of the fortifications implies that he was giving up a measure of control. Land could only be freed from the duty of *burh-bot*, the repair of town fortifications, by the intervention of the king, since the duty was one of the inalienable royal rights; if indeed the duty of fortification rested on the land in general, the novelty of the arrangements at Hereford was that the king was handing responsibility for the defences to the townsmen, and commanding them to organise work on their defences themselves. Their task was later eased by the development of the murage grant, a tax levied by the town whose proceeds were to be spent on the walls. In granting permission to levy murage the king was to a certain extent gaining a measure of control he had not enjoyed for a long time. It is unlikely that he had been able to enforce the performance of labour services vested in the land, whereas he alone could give or withhold a grant of murage. Royal control over murage grants ensured that fortifications could be built if necessary, and such control was gained at no cost to the king, since the murage toll tapped sources which would not in any case have come to the Exchequer.

The advent of the murage grant represents the second stage in the development of the sources of finance for building walls. The grant was the licence to levy a toll, called 'murage', on goods coming for sale in the town, the proceeds of which were to be applied to the walling of the town. Throughout the Middle Ages it remained the chief source of income for a town wishing to build fortifications. To some extent the grant was probably the systematisation of the grants of cash or timber which had up till then been issued on an *ad hoc* basis. It was fairly clearly an innovation in 1220 when it is first found on the Patent Rolls.[13] The grant may also have been the answer to the problem of how to supply a large number of towns all making demands for money simultaneously, and in need of a sufficient supply to enable them to undertake a sustained programme of work. Its advent must have expedited, at least initially, the desire and achievement of fortifications for a town.

Once the murage grant had been evolved there developed a need to keep records. There are two classes of records useful for the study of the finances of town walls. First there are the records of the central government on which the murage grant was recorded : usually it is to be found on the Patent Rolls, and it is therefore possible to find out from central sources on what occasions a town sought permission to levy murage. Additional information may be derived from other Chancery records, the Close Rolls, and from the Exchequer in the Liberate Rolls, the Pipe Rolls and the Memoranda Rolls. Each of these enrolments provides useful evidence for the sources of money for walls. Secondly there are the accounts kept by the towns themselves : these sub-divide into several groups. The most frequently found are the accounts of the bailiffs, in which scattered references to wall-building enable us to deduce the stages in which the wall was built, or when some part of it was repaired. Then there may be rolls concerned with murage alone : some record receipts and expenses, others record only receipts. Such records, however, have not survived for the earlier period, and much of our information, both about the construction of walls and, more specifically about the murage tax, is derived from the central records.

Murage was a tax with only local application, although references to it are scattered throughout the records of the Exchequer and of the royal courts, so that murage was clearly a subject which came to the notice of many royal officials in a variety of contexts. Murage grants quickly became the accepted method by which to fortify a town. The grant, however, is no more than a formal permission to levy money with the intention that it should be applied to the construction of defences, and the grants themselves rarely reveal much about the construction of the wall. The date at which a murage grant was first received can be used as only a rough guide to the date at which construction was first started, and it is only when there is a check, such as the records of the town officials, or, less pleasantly, an investigation into suspected cases of embezzlement, that the grants can be used as an indication of progress.

Nevertheless the tax has a history of its own which has not hitherto been investigated.[14] Murage was only ever granted after an application to the king, but there were several ways in which this permission might be obtained. It is noticeable that the earliest grants were usually made when the king was near the town concerned, and one must suppose that a deputation of the men of the town presented themselves before the itinerant court to make known their needs. Later there are occasional entries in accounts for payment for someone riding to ask for the renewal of a grant.[15] Alternatively someone else might intercede on behalf of the townsmen. The men of Hereford in 1271 obtained a grant at the instance of Richard de Hereford, king's clerk;[16] the men of Stamford in 1265 at the instance of their lord, John de Warenne, earl of Surrey.[17] A grant might also be given on the information of a royal official, as for example at York in 1299, on the information of the treasurer.[18] Later in the century some petitions were presented in parliament. The Londoners in 1279 apparently had asked for permission to levy murage on wines and in the memorandum is written 'that the murage the Londoners seek to take on wines, they shall take after a delay of two years'.[19] Petitions for the right to levy murage did not have to go before parliament. This was probably exceptional procedure; they more often took the form of a petition to the king and Council. Some of the petitions have been preserved, but they are of little value, being no more than bald statements of the request without any indication of their date.[20]

The Londoners' petition of 1279 had been granted, but a second, presented in the October parliament of 1290, was refused.[21] The terse words 'the king does not recognize the necessity' provided an illustration of Maitland's comment that 'such grants were not to be had as a matter of course'. And even the king in granting murage had to take established rights into account. In the case of Durham, where episcopal jurisdiction cut out the king's right to act within its limits, a petition in parliament from those asking that the king's permission should be given to the bishop to allow murage to be levied was answered with the words 'Inform the bishop of Durham that with the assent of his council the king allows the bishop to levy murage for the enclosing of the city'.[22] A later murage grant to the city in 1337 is phrased in the same terms.[23] In 1338, following a grant made to the men of Harwich, the men of Ipswich complained that the king had had no right to make such a grant because 'the port of Orwell ought to belong, and has belonged to their town and that none but their bailiffs and ministers ought to make distraints or attachments, or levy toll or other custom there'. This claim of the burgesses of Ipswich forced the king to revoke the grant within a month.[24] By 1352, however, some compromise seems to have been reached between the two parties and Harwich received a grant both then and in subsequent years.[25] Similarly, in 1410, because he had infringed the rights of the bishop of Durham at Hartlepool, Henry IV was forced to revoke a grant he had made in 1400.[26]

The initiative to start proceedings to obtain a grant of murage lay with the town, but the responsibility for the terms of the grant seems to have rested with the king. At first grants were issued sparingly, and on very limited conditions. Grants state that murage could be levied only once a week,[27] and the first grants were made only for one year. This quickly lengthened into periods varying from three to five years, and the grant could always be renewed when it expired. By the middle of the thirteenth century the average length of a grant was five years, lengthening to seven by 1300. It was rare to have a grant for a period longer than this until after *c.* 1350 when ten years became the standard. There are, of course, exceptions to this; for example a grant to the men of Oswestry in 1283 gave them the right to levy murage for twenty years.[28] And as at first the time limit was short so also was the list of articles which could be taxed, and the rates were low (see Appendix A). Gradually, however, the list of taxable articles lengthened and the lists of the early fourteenth century reached formidable lengths. The decision to increase the number of articles taxed rather than the amounts payable must have meant the tax became impractical to administer and may even have meant a falling off in the profits. It may have been this which led to an alternative method of raising money, namely the assessing of property in a town. Writs authorizing this procedure begin to appear in the early years of the fourteenth century, and coincide

c

with the time at which the lists of taxable wares were at their longest and a period when there is a decline in the number of grants issued.

This increase in the number of taxable goods, together with the increase in the length of the term of the grant, opened the way to two abuses. The first was that of levying too much, the second that of diverting the proceeds. Both began to attract public attention at much the same time, about 1270. The first abuse caused the author of the *Mirror of Justices* to observe that 'all those that take murage or other kind of custom to a greater amount than is right fall into the sin of larceny'.[29] In an attempt to check this abuse a paragraph was devoted to murage in the Statute of Westminster I, 1275, within the section which deals with 'those that take outrageous toll'.[30] Here it was laid down that 'if the citizens or burgesses in receipt of such a grant levy murage otherwise than as it was granted unto them, they shall lose their grant for ever, and shall be grievously amerced to the king'. This clause may have resulted from cases when the jurors involved in the inquests of 1274–5 were asked about the tolls levied. In Scarborough they replied that the burgesses had taken the toll for two years longer than the term allowed, adding that they had been levying it on both merchants and non-merchants, and also on every ship and every boat. The jurors completed their statement by saying that not even a third of the money collected had been applied to the walls. The last grant had been in 1268 for three years.[31] The case of Scarborough was not an isolated one for at the time of the *Quo Warranto* inquests other examples of the abuse of murage monies were discovered. At Stamford and Lincoln the collectors were accused of taking the stone bought for the town to their own use, and at Bath there were complaints that the existing walls were being used as quarries for building stone.[32]

The second abuse to which murage was open was that of diversion of the proceeds, either by the collectors before the money reached the communal coffers, or later, by the corporation. The fact that on occasion the town might receive a royal command to devote the money to other uses cannot have encouraged them to maintain high standards of honesty. For example at Bristol in 1276 the wages of the supervisor of the works at the castle were to be paid out of the issues of murage.[33] Between 1267 and 1275 the constable of the castle had received the money for work done at the castle,[34] and some seventy years later the profits from the tax were to be applied to the making of a new quay.[35] Similar illustrations can be found at Southampton and Newcastle.[36] A study of both the Chancery and the local borough records suggests that the system of collection was easy to abuse, but it is not entirely fair to suppose, as one might from examining only the Chancery records, that the collectors alone were responsible for peculation. Murage was clearly a convenient source of revenue for a town to tap, and in the absence of any very close check on the finances the medieval corporation clearly felt no special obligation to apply the proceeds solely to the construction or maintenance of the walls. Evidence of this practice implies that a grant of murage need not, after a certain period of time, mean that the defences were in need of repair. The longer the period for which a grant continues the more suspect must be the uses to which the money was put, and there are several cases in town accounts where the amount of money collected can be seen to have been spent on anything but the walls.[37]

This then was the fault of the corporation. But the system by which the money was collected was both complex and chaotic, and practice varied from town to town. Inevitably in the circumstances where both deliberative and executive functions were combined in the town council and were not separated as now, and where there were no paid officials to carry out the decisions of the council, the citizens themselves became involved in the duties of collection. This made it possible for money to be diverted from its proper use since it passed through many hands. A grant to Worcester in 1236 suggests that it is making an innovation in the method of collection when it says 'with this addition, that Peter Colle and John Fraunceys, burgesses of Worcester, be appointed to collect it, and Ralph Felagh and Alexander Draper be appointed to receive it from them by tally and apply it to the work of the wall, and that both parties answer at the king's command for the money received from the same custom'.[38] The sheriff was ordered to take the oaths of the four burgesses concerned. At Chester the first grant (of 1249) specifically states that it was to be collected by two men of the town and deposited in the abbey.[39] The abbot was to have one key of the chest, the two collectors another one each.

In Newcastle in 1350 the two collectors were to be appointed by common assent in the Guildhall, which suggests that they too were burgesses.[40] In 1307 the citizens of Exeter petitioned the king and council to issue a commission to investigate the accounts of the mayor and bailiffs, though whether this was because they suspected the authorities or their deputies of embezzlement is not known.[41]

Elsewhere there were more complex arrangements for collection. For example at Shrewsbury, where there is a long series of rolls recording both receipts and expenses, it is seen that the collectors might change every week. This system probably began with the intention of preventing embezzlement, but Shrewsbury had five gates to man, and with a different person acting as collector every week one may well wonder what proportion of the toll ever reached the common chest. Moreover, the number of people employed— the same name rarely occurs twice in any one roll—suggests that the whole town must have been involved in the collection of the tax. This in itself suggests that the opportunities for embezzlement were high.

At London responsibility for the collection of the tax was farmed out to one person for a specific period. In 1308, for example, it appears very clearly from the Letter Books that the City had been divided up into areas and each was granted by the mayor, aldermen, sheriffs and chamberlains of the City either to an individual or to two men for an agreed sum, to be paid in fixed monthly sums.[42] In 1310 two ironmongers, Roger Hosbond and John Dod, were elected wardens of the murage issuing from the whole City, and were sworn before the Mayor and Commonalty diligently to cause the money to be collected, and faithfully expended on the walls.[43] Yet in 1317 a writ was sent to the mayor and sheriffs ordering them to permit Edmund Windsor, king's sergeant, to collect the murage granted four days previously, and to send him a transcript of the said customs.[44] Clearly then the king felt that some profit was to be made from the tax, and that it was sufficiently high to be useful as a way of rewarding his servants.

As a preliminary check against the embezzlement of funds some early grants had laid down that the money was to be applied by view and testimony of a specified person, presumed to be responsible and above suspicion, for example the constable of the castle at Hereford (1238),[45] or the constable and the abbot of St. Peter's at Gloucester (1265).[46] This was the same system by which a check had been kept on a sheriff spending money on royal works, but as happened with the sheriff the similar check on the towns' collectors had also disappeared by the mid-thirteenth century. From this time on we find the petitions of townsmen that the king should appoint someone to audit the accounts. Thus in Lincoln in 1267 the discovery of a case of the misappropriation of murage resulted in a request for royal help to investigate the matter.[47] In Newcastle in 1272 the farmers of murage had to render their accounts before William Kirkton and William Lilleburn who had been appointed as auditors by the king,[48] and in 1280 before Thomas Normanvill, the king's escheator north of the Trent.[49] Nottingham enlisted royal help in 1279,[50] and commissions of oyer and terminer for the purpose of auditing accounts continued to be issued until the late years of the fourteenth century, dying out only when the many towns then in receipt of government aid had to render accounts to the Exchequer. Those towns which did not obtain grants from the fee-farm or from customs duties often reverted to the system of accounting either to the local abbot, as in Shrewsbury in 1428,[51] or their fellow burgesses, as at Hereford in 1426,[52] who after auditing the accounts of the mayor were to send them to Chancery.

Concomitant with the desire for the right to levy murage and for proper control over the money raised was the desire to be free from any obligation to pay the toll to others. The spread of exemption from payment of the toll was a privilege extended to many classes of people very quickly. The first section of the community to have been favoured in this way were ecclesiastical communities and their servants. In 1321–2 the archbishop of York petitioned parliament to uphold the general resolution of the Council of Vienne (1311–12) stating that all people of the Holy Church ought to be quit of toll in all places on the goods and chattels destined for their own use.[53] It must have been the existence of this decree which prevented the bailiffs of Coventry assessing the religious for any contributions towards the cost of the walls in 1365,[54] although in the early thirteenth century the king had been able to order the bishop of Exeter not to oppose the levy of the tax.[55]

But ecclesiastics did not for long remain the only privileged group. Exemptions are common in the Charter rolls from about 1240 onwards, either to individuals, perhaps kings' servants or messengers, to great lords and their tenants, to the men of the manors of ancient demesne, to foreign merchants and finally to townsmen. The latter were the slowest group to get the right to be exempt from the payment of tolls to other towns, though presumably not to their own town.

The first town to be given this privilege was Carmarthen, in 1233,[56] when the first murage grant was received, and at the same time the citizens were specifically exempted from payment of murage at Bristol. The men of York were freed in 1254.[57] In 1260 York and Lincoln made an agreement not to charge toll of each others' citizens.[58] This is the first of such reciprocal arrangements which some towns negotiated,[59] which must have caused many arguments at the gates. The Letter Books of London, one of the few collections of the daily business of a town we possess, are full of cases where the claim to such a privilege was tested, for example with the men of Norwich.[60] Even if towns did not negotiate specific agreements amongst themselves each town was apparently responsible for knowing whether a claim to exemption was genuine or false, and in the few extant records of this sort the leaves contain transcribed lists of exempt towns, for example in the *Port Books* of Southampton and in the *Little Red Book* of Bristol.[61] But even towns were slow to claim the privilege of exemption, and it is only in the early decades of the fourteenth century that the number of such exemptions reaches noticeable proportions. It seems that towns did not have to claim specific exemption from the payment of murage in the same way as an individual, but were covered by the general clause of exemption from the payment of tolls written into their charter. By the early decades of the fourteenth century such exemptions covered many towns.

That exemption from the payment of murage was probably a concession worth obtaining is suggested by the complaints of declining trade in consequence of the levying of the tax, which, though not frequent, are known from various places at different dates. The Londoners made the complaint in 1319, the men of Portsmouth in 1344, and those of Coventry in 1370, although in the last case it was stated that the merchants of the town were to be assessed instead.[62] For a time the taking of murage in these towns was suspended, though the right was always resumed at a later date.

The wide spread of exemption from the payment of murage even by the middle of the fourteenth century leads one to wonder who remained to pay the tax, and suggests that the profit which could be made from the tax was dwindling. These facts together with the abuses to which the tax was open and its clumsy development herald a change in its character.

In the early years of the fourteenth century a new form of wording begins to appear. A petition of the bailiffs and citizens of Norwich in 1308 was concluded by giving them permission to 'distrain as may be just for the repairs of the said walls proportionately to their said tenements according to the tallage reasonably assessed or in future to be assessed by you upon them, all, both strangers and inhabitants, having tenements in this city'.[63] This very clearly suggests that money for the repair of the defences was no longer supplied entirely from the levy of murage, but had become an assessment on property within the town. This form of phraseology appears more and more frequently throughout the fourteenth century, though it never altogether replaces the earlier form of murage grant. Some towns for a time had the later form of the grant, and then reverted to the earlier form, which may perhaps be an indication of work being done on the defences as distinct from mere maintenance at much less cost. The newer wording is also the key to explaining entries such as the one found in the London Letter Books in 1321, where it is written that 'in the presence of the Mayor and Aldermen the Commonalty were asked if they agreed to murage being levied',[64] even though this was at a time when the city already had permission to levy murage. It reveals that the tax at this time was held to be the responsibility of the citizens and not of itinerant merchants.

The newer phraseology does, however, lead to yet further difficulties in using the accounts. At some towns there are indications either from the town accounts or from commissions of inquiry that murage was levied continuously, whether the town was in receipt of a currently valid grant or not. In theory there was a check on this in London since the old grant was supposed to be given up in return for the new authorization. Whether this procedure was very strictly adhered to is doubtful, though the men of Totnes in

1355 were honest enough to surrender their grant on the grounds that nothing was being done.[65] But where accounts show murage was being levied continuously, there is always the possibility that it was levied under the terms of assessment on the inhabitants of a town. The receipts may be a perfectly legal levy, although there is no record in the Patent Rolls of specific authorization. In some cases, however, the town concerned did have permission to assess its inhabitants, and it may be that once the assessment had been fixed it was levied every year as a primitive form of rates. This form of levying murage is almost certainly the explanation of the murage rolls or books found in Winchester, Canterbury, Coventry and Chester which do not record details of payment gate by gate as in the Hereford or Shrewsbury accounts, but in which small sums of money are recorded ward by ward, even at Winchester, street by street. The lack of a specific authorization for the levy may often obscure the fact that building was in progress.

Whatever the complications of murage it seems that by the middle of the fourteenth century the murage grant of the early thirteenth century had outlived its usefulness, and was in need of replacement. One alternative method, that of assessing the inhabitants, had already been implemented, and throughout the century other expedients were used.[66] Sources of revenue for wall-building therefore become more varied, and less standardized, and amongst those most commonly tapped were the profits from judicial fines, the fee-farm of a town and customs duties. The expiration of the truce of Brétigny in 1369, and the almost continuous warfare between France and England from that year until 1389, gave a fillip to the need to find new sources of revenue. The documents reflect a growing fear of invasion, a fear which is mirrored in the scale of provisions made for the defence of towns.

Two petitions from the commons in parliament reveal the extent of the panic, and the need that was felt for increased fortification. In 1369 the commons asked that all castles, abbeys, priories, cities, towns and boroughs should be surveyed and put in order 'since the damage of the wars is apparent from day to day'; and that walls, ditches and gates should be duly repaired.[67] Two years later they asked that everyone in England should be allowed to make a fort or fortress, walls and crenellated towers or battlements as he pleased, and that burgesses and citizens of every town should have permission to enclose or strengthen their ditches and walls, notwithstanding any statute to the contrary.[68] The petition of 1369 clearly had its effects for in that year a large number of commissions to inspect and repair walls and ditches was issued.[69] While the crisis was at its height ecclesiastics were asked for contributions towards the defences despite the decree of the Council of Vienne,[70] and the urgency of the moment is well expressed when the king wrote to the men of Canterbury in 1387 ordering them to re-elect to office two bailiffs who were said to have lent all their power and diligence to fortifying the city, and who the king believed would continue to hasten the work because of the peril daily threatening.[71]

Taxing the inhabitants to pay for their own defences had been the obvious way for the government to provide for the defence of the realm without itself incurring any extra financial burdens, but by the late fourteenth century it was no longer the most effective way of obtaining money. These years were a time of economic difficulty, and pleas regarding the poverty of the inhabitants of the towns begin to appear. Much new work followed the petition of 1369 which received a favourable answer, though that of 1371 apparently received none, but it was almost certainly the threat of invasion coupled with pleas of poverty from the towns which stimulated the central government to tap new sources for the building of defences.

By the year of the Good Parliament, 1376, and in the following three years, fear of invasion had greatly increased. It was justifiable, especially in the months following the expiry of the two years' truce with France in June 1377. In the parliaments of these years several petitions from towns whose mayors had already received orders to strengthen their fortifications were heard. In 1376 the men of Southampton for example went back, whether consciously or not, to an old method of financing building operations and asked that the king should pardon them part of the fee-farm of their town; not only were they unable to pay the full amount but, because of heavy financial burdens, the town was only half inhabited and consequently even less able to raise sufficient money to meet all their costs. The immediate answer was that the king would consider their plea.[72] It was not until December 1377 that their arrears were pardoned (though as far as the possibility of applying this money to the walls was concerned this was probably of little practical value) and they were pardoned further payments to the Exchequer for two years.[73] Though few towns were ever pardoned either the whole or a part of their fee-farm for long periods they might receive part of the money towards the cost of fortifications as Southampton did twice, in 1377 and again in 1400,[74] and Yarmouth in 1457.[75] In the parliament of 1376 the mayor, bailiffs and commonalty of Winchester had sought financial aid, suggesting that it should come either from the fee-farm of the town, or from the custom of ulnage.[76] The immediate result of this request was only permission to levy contributions on the inhabitants.[77] The request for money from the fee-farm was never granted, although in 1389 they received a grant of £20 annually for five years from the ulnage, so that the Exchequer did have to provide some measure of assistance.[78]

In the parliament of 1379 the men of Rye petitioned for a grant from the fines levied by the Justices of the Peace in the county of Sussex to help them repair the walls of the town after the damage done by the French raiders in the summer of 1377.[79] It seems that no answer was made to this petition but we have the accounts of John Melton presented to the Exchequer in 1384–5,[80] and we know therefore that some help was given from the receipts on taxes payable on fish. Earlier, between 1372 and 1375, they had already received some money from the profits of the bailiwick of the town and £8 from the yearly rent of the issues of the manor of Iden.[81] Similar grants from the fines, ransoms, amercements, issues and other profits from the cognizance of pleas were later granted to the men of Newcastle in 1403,[82] and of Carlisle in 1410.[83] The walls of Northampton in 1404 became, as those of Rye had done, a charge on the farm of a manor and a grant of £40 yearly for six years from the fee-farm of the manor of Kingsthorpe, Northants, was received.[84]

Most interesting of the grants of money towards the cost of fortifications made in these years, and in a context broader than the development of murage, is the series of grants made to the burgesses of Colchester. In December 1382 they were exempted from sending any of their number to parliament for five years, so that they could apply to the cost of walling the town the money which would otherwise have paid the expenses of their representatives. On the expiration of their exemption in 1388 the burgesses renewed their privilege, and continued to do so until 1410.[85]

From the reign of Richard II onwards therefore the sources for murage money are more varied. It had been necessary to tap more than local resources during the threat of invasion, and, the precedent once set, it was probably difficult to reverse. The effect of these financial innovations is to increase the documentary sources for the study of town walls, since all towns in receipt of money which would otherwise have gone to the Exchequer had to render accounts there.[86]

The fifteenth century was not a time when many towns began to build defences for the first time, but repair work was carried out in many places, sometimes to a considerable extent. The documentary evidence shows that several new sources of finance were found. Thus it became common in the fifteenth century for a sea-port town to receive a grant from customs duties towards expenses. Such was the case at Southampton in 1417 and 1478,[87] Winchelsea in 1414,[88] Sandwich in 1461,[89] Plymouth in 1463[90] and Newcastle in 1484.[91] Newcastle, perhaps because of its specially vulnerable position on the Scottish border, received special treatment in the early years of the century frequently being pardoned the payment of subsidies granted in parliament.[92] Shrewsbury was similarly excused in 1407.[93] Other towns received a licence to receive lands in mortmain, whose revenues were to be used to offset the cost of the defences. Grants of this kind were made to Norwich in 1392,[94] Canterbury in 1409,[95] Coventry in 1417 and 1423,[96] and Winchester in 1440.[97]

Throughout the century murage grants taxing goods for sale continued to be issued, though to a decreasing number of towns. Those towns which did still levy murage in this way are found renewing their grants with regularity, and eventually most of them turned their grants into a right lasting either for some long period of years, fifty in the case of Winchester in 1441,[98] sixty for Bristol in 1446[99] or, even into a perpetual right, as the men of York did in 1449, and those of Newcastle in 1484.[100] And, although we have no record of the authorization, Coventry was still collecting murage in 1650[101] and Chester in 1818[102] if the persistence in the one case of a murage book, in the other of murage rolls is anything to go by. Murage grants were amongst the exemption clauses of the Acts of Resumption of 1450 and 1451,[103] and grants to Southampton were specifically exempted in that of 1482.[104] The habit of levying murage thus persisted for a long time, and when the sporadic fighting of the Wars of the Roses began those towns which were not in immediate possession of a grant were still able to obtain permission to reconstruct their defences, at least by way of taxing their inhabitants.

NOTES

1 Quoted from A. J. Robertson, *Anglo-Saxon Charters*, 1939, 246–8.
2 II Athelstan, 13; V Aethelred 26, I; VI Aethelred 32, 3; II Cnut 10 and 65; F. L. Attenborough, *The Laws of the Earliest English Kings*, 1922.
3 D.B. I, f. 262b.
4 D.B. I, f. 230.
5 D.B. I, f. 154, and C. Stephenson, *Borough and Town*, 1933, 102.
6 W. Maitland, *Domesday Book and Beyond*, 1897, 189.
7 J. Tait, *Eng. Hist. Rev.* XII, 1897, 775; C. Petit-Dutaillis, *Studies Supplementary to Stubbs Constitutional History*, 1908, I, 78–83; J. H. Round in commenting on the Domesday Survey in *V.C.H. Surrey, Herts, Essex, Berks.*, and *Hereford*.
8 M. Bateson, *Eng. Hist. Rev.*, XX, 1905, 143–7.
9 A. Ballard, *British Borough Charters*, 1913, I, 93.
10 Ipswich Borough Records, Little Domesday.
11 A. Ballard, *British Borough Charters*, 1913, I, 94.
12 *Hist. Mss. Comm.* 31, 284.
13 *Cal. Pat. Rolls, 1216–25*, 238.
14 N. Neilson, *Customary Rents and Services*, 1910, 141–2; W. S. Holdsworth, *History of English Law*, third ed. 1923, II 393; F. Pollock and W. Maitland, *History of English Law*, second ed. 1898, I, 662.
15 For example at Ludlow, 1317-18.
16 *Cal. Pat. Rolls, 1266–72*, 584.
17 *Cal. Pat. Rolls, 1258–66*, 469.
18 *Cal. Pat. Rolls, 1292–1301*, 481.
19 *Rotuli Parliamentorum Anglie Hactenus Inediti 1279–1373*, H. G. Richardson and G. O. Sayles, *Camden Society*, I, 1935, 4.
20 P.R.O.   SC/8/157/e7820;   SC/8/204/e10186;   SC/8/319/e404; SC/8/327/e854; SC/8/346/e1365.
21 *Rot. Parl.*, I, 55.
22 *Rot. Parl.*, I, 302.
23 *Cal. Pat. Rolls, 1334–8*, 387.
24 *Cal. Pat. Rolls, 1338–40*, 109.
25 *Cal. Pat. Rolls, 1350–54*, 317.
26 *Cal. Pat. Rolls, 1399–1401*, 355, is the grant revoked in *Cal. Pat. Rolls, 1408–13*, 264.
27 *Cal. Pat. Rolls, 1216–25*, 499.
28 *Cal. Pat. Rolls, 1281–92*, 108.
29 *Mirror of Justices*, cap. X, ed. W. J. Whittaker, *Selden Society*, VII, 26.
30 *Statutes of the Realm*, I, 34.

31 *Rot. Hund.,* I, 108; *Cal. Pat. Rolls, 1266–72,* 254.
32 *Rot. Hund.,* I, 314–15, 357; 322, 398–9. Miss Neilson's reference to the word *muragium* as meaning the actual stone used in the work is unique, *Rot. Hund.,* I, 322; *Rot. Hund.,* II, 123, 132–3.
33 *Cal. Pat. Rolls, 1272–81,* 186.
34 *Cal. Pat. Rolls, 1266–72,* 59.
35 *Cal. Pat. Rolls, 1345–8,* 285.
36 *Cal. Pat. Rolls, 1281–92,* 229; *Cal. Close Rolls, 1272–9,* 546.
37 For example, at Ludlow in 1299–1300 and 1313–14.
38 *Cal. Pat. Rolls, 1232–47,* 155.
39 *Cal. Pat. Rolls, 1247–58,* 49.
40 *Cal. Pat. Rolls, 1348–50,* 556.
41 *Cal. Pat. Rolls, 1301–07,* 544.
42 *Letter Book C,* 161–3; the same arrangements were made in 1302, (*Ibid.,* 107); 1329 (*Ibid.,* E, 237); 1332 (*Ibid.,* 273); 1338 (*Ibid.,* F, 24); 1342, (*Ibid.,* 81).
43 *Letter Book D,* 231.
44 *Cal. Pat. Rolls, 1313–17,* 655.
45 *Cal. Pat. Rolls, 1232–47,* 224.
46 *Cal. Pat. Rolls, 1258–66,* 428.
47 *Cal. Pat. Rolls, 1266–72,* 270.
48 *Cal. Pat. Rolls, 1266–72,* 667.
49 *Cal. Pat. Rolls, 1272–81,* 373–4.
50 *Cal. Pat. Rolls, 1272–81,* 318.
51 *Cal. Pat. Rolls, 1422–9,* 519.
52 *Cal. Pat. Rolls, 1422–9,* 336.
53 *Rot. Parl.,* I, 392.
54 *Cal. Close Rolls, 1364–8,* 165.
55 *Cal. Pat. Rolls, 1216–25,* 514.
56 *Cal. Close Rolls, 1231–4,* 199.
57 *Cal. Close Rolls, 1253–4,* 15.
58 *Cal. Close Rolls, 1259–61,* 39.
59 For example Southampton and Salisbury, *The Oak Book,* ed. P. Studer, 1910–11, II, 18; Nottingham and Lincoln, 1485, W. H. Stevenson, *Records of the Borough of Nottingham,* 1882, II, 349; Grimsby and Southwold, quoted in *Hist. Mss. Comm.,* 37, 14th Rep., 250.
60 1340—*Letter Book F,* 44, and Norwich, Liber Albus, f. 23.
   1377—*Letter Book H,* 53, and Norwich, Liber Albus, f. 23.
61 *Southampton Record Society;* and *Little Red Book,* ed. F. B. Bickley, 1900.
62 London, *Cal. Pat. Rolls, 1317–21,* 347.
   Portsmouth, *Cal. Pat. Rolls, 1343–5,* 322.
   Coventry, *Cal. Pat. Rolls, 1367–70,* 369.
63 Quoted from the Book of Pleas, f. 64d, printed in W. Hudson and J. C. Tingey, *Records of the City of Norwich,* 1906–10, 325–7.
64 *Letter Book E,* 146–7.
65 *Cal. Pat. Rolls, 1354–8,* 243.
66 In London, for example, in 1365 the fines from the improper sales of sweet wines in the city and suburbs were allocated to the repair of the walls and ditches, *Cal. Close Rolls, 1364–8,* 176–7.
67 *Rot. Parl.,* II, 300.
68 *Rot. Parl.,* II, 307.

69 Bath, *Cal. Pat. Rolls, 1367–70,* 277; Winchester, *Cal. Pat. Rolls, 1367–70,* 246; Southampton, *Cal. Pat. Rolls, 1367–70,* 229-230; and Lincoln, *Cal. Pat. Rolls, 1367–70,* 271.
70 *Cal. Pat. Rolls, 1374–7,* 502; *Rot. Parl.,* III, 20.
71 *Cal. Close Rolls, 1385–9,* 342.
72 *Rot. Parl.,* II, 346.
73 *Cal. Pat. Rolls, 1377–81,* 76.
74 Quoted from T. Madox, *Firma Burgi,* 1726, 290.
75 *Cal. Pat. Rolls, 1452–61,* 387.
76 *Rot. Parl.,* II, 346.
77 *Cal. Pat. Rolls, 1377–81,* 111.
78 *Cal. Pat. Rolls, 1388–92,* 115.
79 *Rot. Parl.,* III, 70; *Anonimalle Chronicle,* ed. V. H. Galbraith, 1927, 107; *Chronicon Anglie (Rolls Series),* 151–2.
80 P.R.O. E 364/31 m.A.
81 *Cal. Pat. Rolls, 1370–74,* 203.
82 *Cal. Pat. Rolls, 1401–5,* 255.
83 *Cal. Pat. Rolls, 1409–13,* 192.
84 *Cal. Pat. Rolls, 1399–1401,* 322; *Cal. Pat. Rolls, 1401–5,* 333.
85 *Cal. Pat. Rolls, 1381–5,* 214; it was renewed in 1388, *Ibid.,* 1385–9, 505; 1394, *Ibid.,* 1391–6, 379; 1404, *Ibid.,* 1401–5, 355; 1410, *Ibid.,* 1408–1413, 199.
86 The accounts are now to be found in the P.R.O., E 101, or E 364.
87 *Cal. Pat. Rolls, 1416–22,* 109; *Cal. Pat. Rolls, 1401–1405,* 333.
88 *Cal. Pat. Rolls, 1413–16,* 273.
89 *Cal. Pat. Rolls, 1461–7,* 63.
90 *Cal. Pat. Rolls, 1461–7,* 269.
91 *Cal. Pat. Rolls, 1476–85,* 509.
92 *Cal. Pat. Rolls, 1401–5,* 372, 465; *Ibid.,* 1405–8, 411; *Ibid.,* 1413–16, 273, 381; *Ibid.,* 1416–22, 343.
93 *Rot. Parl.,* III, 618-619.
94 *Cal. Pat. Rolls, 1391–6,* 121.
95 *Cal. Pat. Rolls, 1408–13,* 104.
96 *Cal. Pat. Rolls, 1416–22,* 105, and *Hist. Mss. Comm.,* 47th Rep., 118.
97 *Cal. Pat. Rolls, 1436–41,* 400.
98 *Cal. Pat. Rolls, 1436–41,* 507, 531.
99 *Cal. Pat. Rolls, 1441–46,* 416.
100 York—*Cal. Pat. Rolls, 1446–52,* 221.
     Newcastle—*Cal. Pat. Rolls, 1476–85,* 509.
101 *Hist. Mss. Comm.,* 47, 15th Rep., 106.
102 *Hist. Mss. Comm.,* 7, 8th Rep., 369.
103 *Rot. Parl.,* V, 185, 219.
104 *Rot. Parl.,* VI, 201.

CHAPTER THREE

Cost and construction

The building of a town wall was essentially a local affair. More often than not the money to finance the operation had been raised locally; the decision to build at all was a local decision, taken by the community and its representatives, rather than one imposed from above, although in some cases the murage grant was obtained by the lord on behalf of his burgesses, who might otherwise have gone without a wall. Labour was recruited in the neighbourhood, and materials were often bought locally; thus quarries at Thevesdale supplied stone for York, and on the Isle of Wight for Southampton.[1] Overall supervision was usually entrusted to local masons, although there are exceptions. At Conway and Caernarvon, for example, the king's master builder, Master James of St. George, planned and executed the works, and at Canterbury Master Henry Yevele planned and directed the building of the West gate. Such considerations are relevant to a discussion of the cost of construction, the organization of the work and the length of time such an operation occupied.

The attempt to answer these questions reveals the deficiencies of the sources. Many of the extant city accounts start only after the greater part of the work had been completed; most record the amounts spent with only vague details of the expenditure on men and materials. Occasionally there is a detailed account, as for example for the Cow Tower at Norwich, for the building of the North Bar at Beverley,[2] or for the repair of a section of the wall between King's gate and South gate in Winchester, and some impression of the effort involved can be obtained. In a few cases a more specific entry was made from which a more detailed estimate of the cost of sections of the wall or the ditch can be made. Thus at Yarmouth in 1336–7 two masons were paid £8 5s 7d for the construction of eleven rods to a height of sixteen feet (4·88 m.).[3] At Berwick in 1360 Henry of Holme and three other masons were paid at a rate of £5 6s 8d per rod of wall seventeen feet thick at the base, eight feet thick at the top and thirty-five feet high.[4] In 1374 thirty-nine royal perches of the city wall at Winchester cost 13s 4d per perch.[5] At Canterbury in 1391–2 eighteen perches and a new tower cost £192,[6] while at Coventry in 1430 fourteen and a half perches and half a round tower were built for £77 13s 4d.[7] More rarely still, there are contracts between the city and a mason in which definite specifications were laid down. At Chester in 1322 John Helpeston was engaged to build the Water Tower for £100, and it was to be ten and a half ells wide, twenty-four ells high and 4 ells thick.[8] At York in 1345 Master Thomas Staunton was to build twenty perches of wall, each six ells long and six ells high, at a cost of seven pounds of silver per ell.[9] Where such diverse measurements are used it is difficult to assess relative costs with accuracy.

It is clear, however, that wall-building was not a cheap operation. A summary of the amounts collected from the levy of murage and of the amounts spent reveal several points (see Appendix B). Firstly the receipts show considerable variations, and it would have been almost impossible for a town to budget its building programme. The procedure seems to have been to start without knowing the amount of money that would be available, in the hope that work would not be brought to a halt, rather than wait until funds had accumulated. The documents give no answer to the related questions of what happened if more was spent than was received, or if more was received than was necessary. But one point stands out very clearly. The murage toll brought in very small sums in relation to the money needed to build anything substantial. Admittedly many of the walls had been completed before accounts are extant, but when substantial amounts were required at the end of the fourteenth century, special grants had to be made from central sources. The total cost of walling Caernarvon (see Appendix B), or the £300 estimated to be necessary for repairs at Carlisle in 1344,[10] provide some idea of the sums needed to wall relatively small areas, and comparison of these figures with the amounts spent by other towns raises the question whether the murage grant could ever have provided sufficient money to meet the costs. The fact that the amounts raised were so small is undoubtedly one of the reasons why the grants were continued for so long. Although it seems inevitable that in many cases the town must have incurred a debt, yet there is no trace amongst the town archives that this was so. Similarly, when a town had received a grant from the Exchequer, and overspent the amount, it seems that it was simply written off.[11] In other cases it is possible that work came to a halt. This raises the question of how the work of building the walls was done.

In some cases the work was contracted out to a mason. Thus Robert Hertanger contracted to build the South gate at King's Lynn for £100 in 1416; the same gate was rebuilt in 1520 by Nicholas Hermer of East Dereham and Thomas Hermer of Burwell.[12] The terms of the contracts in these cases are not known, but at York the contract with Master Thomas Staunton stated that he would supply the men, while the City would supply the materials. At Chester, on the other hand, John Helpeston was responsible for the supply of both men and materials. Most commonly, the bailiffs themselves might be in charge of the work, either on the less spectacular work of building the curtain wall or on the more impressive parts such as the gates. Thus William Rolleston, merchant, and the eleven other members of the town council supervised the building of the North Bar at Beverley,[13] and at Coventry the chamberlains were in charge of the repair of Hill Street gate in 1423.[14] The records of other towns show that the corporation kept control of the operation in their own hands, and some of the workmen were employed year after year, for example, Simon Frost at King's Lynn. At Exeter the supervisors, Richard Whyte and John Holm, directed the work between 1384 and 1388, although the names of the workmen are different. The system must therefore have been to hire whoever came forward. On the occasions when the king had ordered a town to repair its fortifications, workmen might be obtained under a royal licence to impress. This method of obtaining labour was used for only a short time, between 1369 and 1386, and in only a few towns amongst them Canterbury, Southampton, Winchester and Sandwich.[15] All these were towns in receipt of grants from the Exchequer, and in which, because of the fear of invasion, the king seems to have taken a special interest.

The fact that control was usually the responsibility of the individual town has some bearing on the question of how long it took to build a wall. Local organisation was not always very efficient, and the difficulties would have been increased by the

D

monetary problems. Moreover, the continuation of a grant of murage does not necessarily imply that building was in progress. Thus, it is necessary to do more than note the dates of the first and last murage grants, for although in some cases these may define periods of building activity, in other examples further documentary evidence shows that although murage was being levied little or no work was in progress. Thus there are the accounts where only a small fraction of the money raised was spent on the walls, and where the money was spent instead on miscellaneous expenses. Other evidence suggests that there was rarely any urgency felt about the need for a speedy building programme. At Southampton the walls may have been ruinous before the attack of 1338; they were certainly in ruins afterwards, but no action was taken to repair them until 1363, and the work was probably not completed until the 1370s or later. At Rye, although the town had received permission to levy murage from 1329 until 1353, the walls were said in 1369 to be unfinished. At Alnwick the first murage grant dates from 1434, but the work was still incomplete in 1474. At Winchelsea the area first enclosed proved to be greater than the town required; in 1380 a commission was set up to discover how the town could best be fortified, but work began on a reduced circuit only in 1415. At Canterbury several sections of the wall can be dated very exactly and show that much was achieved in a relatively short time, but there was a considerable time lag before the whole circuit had been completed, and at Coventry the circuit took nearly 180 years to complete.[16] Evidence suggests that at Newcastle the defences were completed between 1265 and 1318, and at Norwich between 1297 and 1343, but these examples also represent a fairly long time span. Comparison with the time taken at Caernarvon, where much of the work had been completed in two years,[17] shows how much was gained from the existence of an unlimited supply of money readily available. Such problems must be borne in mind when reviewing the structural remains, and in assessing their effectiveness.

NOTES

1 *Cal. Pat. Rolls, 1321–24*, 233; *Ibid.*, 1399–1401, 239.
2 A. F. Leach, 'The Building of Beverley Bar', *Trans. of East Riding Antiq. Soc.*, IV, 1896, 26–37.

3   H. Swinden, *Antiquities of Great Yarmouth*, 1772, 81.
4   P.R.O. E 101/482/27.
5   Pipe Roll of the Bishop of Winchester, Hants Record Office, 159–382, m. 35d.
6   P.R.O. E 364/27 m.D.
7   *Coventry Leet Book*, 136.
8   B. M. Harleian Mss. 2046, 26b; printed L. F. Salzman, *Building in England down to 1540*, 1952, 428–9.
9   First Register of Freemen, ff.351–3, York City Library.
10   P.R.O. C 145/152 (4). The estimate had increased to £500 by 1348, C 145/161 (3).
11   There is no trace amongst the records that any attempt was made to recover the money.
12   H. J. Hillen, *History of King's Lynn*, 1907, 760–61.
13   A. F. Leach, 'The Building of Beverley Bar', *Trans. East Riding Antiq. Soc.*, IV, 1896, 26–37.
14   *Coventry Leet Book*, 57–8.
15   Thus such licences were received by Southampton in 1369 and 1374; Winchester in 1369 and 1385; Canterbury in 1378 and 1380. But they were also received by towns not receiving subsidies: Oxford in 1371; Exeter, Hull and Salisbury in 1377; Chichester in 1385; Newcastle and Sandwich in 1386. References in the Patent Rolls.
16   E. Gooder. 'The Walls of Coventry', *Trans. Birmingham Arch. Soc.*, 81, 88–99.
17   J. G. Edwards, 'Edward I's Castle Building in Wales', *Procs. of British Academy*, XXXII, 71.

CHAPTER FOUR

Planning and building

The development of town defences was a natural progression from the provision of a ditch behind which was an earth rampart, sometimes crowned by a timber palisade, sometimes fronted by a slight stone wall, to a more complex circuit of towers and heavily defended gates linked by strong stone curtain walling.

For information about the appearance of the pre-Conquest towns we are dependent on the *Anglo-Saxon Chronicle* and on archaeological evidence. The differences in appearance between English and Danish towns are not likely to have been considerable, and what we know about towns fortified by the English is likely to be applicable to those in the Danelaw. The laconic entries in the *Chronicle* 'that he caused the *burh* to be fortified' convey the impression that the fortifications of towns cannot have been much more elaborate than a ditch and earthen bank; Towcester alone is said to have been provided with a stone wall. The brevity of the entries, however, conceals the advantage enjoyed by some towns, in that they had Roman defences, even if the value of these must have varied considerably. Excavation has shown that when in the thirteenth century some of these towns rebuilt their fortifications, work had often to start from the level of the Roman footings.[2] At Exeter, on the other hand, Roman work still stands in many places to a height of twenty feet (6·1 m.), and on one stretch a small section has been claimed as the repair work carried out by Athelstan.[3] But for the most part, pre-Conquest defences were of timber surmounting an earth rampart, itself protected by one or more ditches. The rampart was in most cases built up from the earth thrown up from the cutting of the ditch and often bound together with alternating layers of turf. Sometimes, however, the earth was brought from a distance, as at Hereford, or the bank might be built up from blocks of spade-cut clay, as at Warwick. Further strength might be derived from a timber interlacing, either using upright posts round which the bank was packed, or, more casually, by an interlacing of boughs and twigs. At Lydford and Tamworth vertical holes have survived, presumably to support a timber palisade and rampart walk above the bank while the alternate layers of earth and turf stood unsupported. While in the early stages timber defences were most common, later, stone came to be used, either to form a revetment in front or behind the bank, or, less frequently, on the top of the bank. But throughout the period fortifications remained simple rather than complex structures and, so far, none of the towns first fortified at this time has been found to contain towers or turrets within the circuit; gateways were probably simple rectangular structures rising only a little higher than the surrounding enceinte. Nevertheless they may have incorporated such features; as yet excavation has not been sufficiently comprehensive for the possibility to be ignored. The nature of the prevailing warfare obviated any necessity for a complex series of defences, such as became necessary to deflect artillery missiles or even to prevent the too near approach of the battering ram or mangonel of the later Middle Ages. These defences seem to have been constructed to repel hand-to-hand fighting rather than missile attacks of any sort, so that there was little need to provide the means from which to aim projectiles at the attacker while at the same time keeping as much as possible of one's own defences beyond the reach of his missiles. Lydford alone is an example where the defences might have been planned to be effective against missiles; out of the triple ring of ditches the outer row is a shallow, comparatively insubstantial work, which, although too wide to be easily jumped, is not inherently defensive in character. It would, however, serve to trip an advancing attacker, giving the defenders time to loose one volley, and, while the attackers scrambled out of the first ditch only to be caught in the next, time to prepare a second. Only when one of the towns fortified by the Romans was used is the picture different; the unbastioned towns, such as Winchester, were not perhaps so impressive as the Saxon shore fort of Portchester with its ring of bastions still in a moderate state of repair, but each of the Roman towns whose defences were re-used had this in common, namely that they were fortified in stone; none of those which had wooden fortifications in the fourth century survived to be incorporated into the pattern of tenth-century defence. This avoidance of stone in the provision of defences must not be taken to mean that the defences were flimsy and incapable of withstanding attack; timber defences, intricately woven together, made a barrier as strong as anything bound with mortar. It was the natural building medium of the age, easy to obtain, and more readily replaceable than stone.

Reliance on earth and timber defences only gradually gave way to dependence on stone, and there was never an absolutely complete change. Ditches and earth banks, sometimes surmounted by a timber palisade, was the only protection enjoyed by some towns until the late Middle Ages. It should not be assumed that they were a rough and ready means of defence; the depth of the ditch at Sandwich and the steep slope of the bank offers even now a considerable obstacle, but in view of the relatively early transition from timber to stone defences it is interesting that a bank and palisade should still have been considered sufficient protection until the late fourteenth century and even into the fifteenth. Thus at Southampton in 1363 jurors considered that a wall of stone *or* earth would be sufficient to repel attack,[4] and at Salisbury in 1377 the citizens petitioned successfully to enclose the city with a ditch.[5] Coventry and Sandwich seem to have begun to replace their earthen defences with stone walls only in the fifteenth century. In other towns, however, the change to the use of stone in preference to timber came much earlier. This may reflect prosperity or the existence of the proprietary interests rather than a feeling that timber defences were deficient in any way. Some had probably begun by repairing earlier fortifications. Shrewsbury, for example, received grants of timber in 1212 and 1220,[6] but by 1242 a stone wall had been completed since the king ordered that the townsmen should give the stone which remained from the town wall to the Friars Preacher.[7] Oxford was also given timber between 1229 and 1233,[8] but in 1244 a licence to the Friars Minor ordered them to build a wall crenellated like the rest of the wall of the town.[9] Excavation at Hereford suggests the same pattern of development, and certainly by the time of the Barons' Wars part of the defences were in stone. But in other cases, such as Montgomery, the timber defences begun in 1267 were being replaced in stone by 1279–80. It is probably safe to assume therefore that the construction of defences in stone had become common by the mid-thirteenth century.

In many cases, however, it is probably true that ditches and earth banks were little more than passive measures of defence, and to a large extent the development of defences in stone is to be explained not only by an increasing acceptance of stone as the natural building material, but also because of developments in weapons against which the town might expect to have to defend itself.

The town wall was probably the only defence the citizens enjoyed against possible hostilities. They had no parallel to the keep in a castle to which they could retire if things went badly. Once the enemy had got past the town wall, those inside were at his mercy. The wall had therefore to play both an offensive and a defensive role, and it was conceived not only as a barrier to attack, but also as an active part of the defences.

Its mere presence might defend the city against the attack of a timid or lethargic enemy, but it had also to be so constructed that the offensive could be mounted against more active besiegers. Because it was a single line of defence the town wall could far less afford to have weak spots than a bailey wall, and, while some factors governed the siting of both, there are others of which particular care was taken in the case of a town wall.

It is rare to find that there is no connection between the town defences and those of the castle. Norwich, where the castle is situated in the centre of the town, and Chepstow, where it is separated from the town by a steep valley, are the exceptions rather than the rule. Usually the castle occupied the highest point in the town, and the town defences would connect with it, as, for example, at Arundel and Totnes, because of this. Taking advantage of the ground, the castle might project beyond the wall, as at Carlisle and Shrewsbury. At Ludlow, Canterbury and Southampton the castle stood within the circuit and the two shared a common line of defence.

The outline of the walls is almost always either rectangular or roughly circular. Their alignment avoided awkward re-entrant angles, except at Newcastle where such an angle was forced on the planners by the inclusion of the suburb of Pandon. Similarly, care was taken to avoid a wall being overlooked from higher ground outside its line, and there is evidence of such careful siting at Chepstow. At Winchester the same problem was overcome because of the existence of a horn-shaped earth-work defending a suburb on the higher slope beyond the west wall.[10] Tactical requirements could, however, lead to the exclusion of suburbs. At Oxford, for example, no attempt was made to include the settlement beyond the East gate when a stone wall was built on the line of the earlier fortifications. Any extension would have had to cross marshy, badly drained land.

The stone wall, however, was not always the first defence which the town possessed. Where earlier defences were replaced or renewed the line was usually that of the earlier defences. This is especially true of Roman towns, where there are extensions of the walls only at York, Lincoln, Chester and London. Where Saxon timber defences were replaced there are at least three cases where the stone fortification represents an extension of the earlier pre-Conquest line, namely at Hereford,[11] Worcester[12] and Nottingham.[13] But when a wall was built for the first time after 1200, few towns did more than enclose an already built-up area, and only at Bristol,[14] Coventry[15] and Scarborough[16] is there any evidence to suggest that the walls were re-aligned to include expansion not allowed for in the earliest plan. In some cases the walls were planned to run through already existing buildings which had to be pulled down to make way for it. For example, the course taken by the north wall at Newcastle involved the destruction of property of the bishop of Carlisle, for which the townsmen were ordered to pay compensation.[17]

The ease with which the wall could be reached from within the town was also a factor to be taken into consideration when the alignment of the walls was planned. Frequently the line of the *pomerium*, the road behind the walls from which the towers could be approached by the defenders and along which supplies could travel, perhaps more speedily and with less interruption than along the wall walk, is to be traced in many towns (e.g. Norwich, Oak Lane; Southampton, Cuckoo Lane; Shrewsbury, Behind the Walls).

Finally the thickness to which the wall was built should be considered, although it is a factor which differs from town to town probably in relation to the availability of men, money and materials. It may vary within one circuit if the construction of the wall was spread over a long period of time, for example at Canterbury, Southampton and Norwich. Its thickness varied also with the nature of the terrain, though there is no consistency from town to town in the approach to a similar problem. Thus on the precipitous cliffs of Denbigh the breadth increased; on the slope of Carrow Hill at Norwich it was halved, and the wall walk was never built; at Newcastle, at the descent into Pandon Dene, the thickness remains consistent with that of the wall above it.

If, however, the line of the walls could not be fitted into the lie of the ground, or if its contours offered no advantages, the ditch afforded additional protection. Thus along certain sections of the wall at Newcastle where the slope of the ground was inconsiderable a ditch was dug; at Exeter the north side of the town was protected by the fall of the cliff, but on the south side there was a ditch. The ditch at Newcastle is said to have been sixty-six feet (15·29 m.) wide and fifteen feet (4·57 m.) deep, [18] and at Chichester it was fifty feet (15·29 m.) wide.[19] The width of the ditch and of the berm on which the wall stood is clearly an important measure of their usefulness. It prevented archers, and, later, gunners from coming too close to the base of the walls and towers, and from approaching the blind spots of the defences. It was also a protection against mining and sapping operations and against scaling ladders. Throughout the Middle Ages the importance attached to a ditch is attested by the frequency with which it was ordered that it should be scoured and cleansed, and at London the alderman in charge of each ward was frequently enjoined to see that the inhabitants, on whom the duty fell, performed their functions.[20]

Earth banks and ditches, however, were little more than passive measures of defence. The stone wall had features which enabled the townsmen to take a more aggressive stand against attack, although it is not easy to give a composite picture of the architectural styles and developments in the town wall as military architecture. The limitations of the documentary evidence when it is used to establish the date of masonry work are considerable. The ruined and incomplete state of many town walls means that there are questions relating to their development and evolution, and to the way in which they could be used defensively, which must be left unanswered, both generally and in relation to individual towns. Nevertheless, despite the difficulties, it is worthwhile examining separately the features which make up a town wall, the towers, the curtain wall and the gates, and to reach at least some assessment of their merits.

Probably the most important features were the mural towers or turrets from which missiles could be discharged. Town walls often include many such towers. At Newcastle, where the circuit of the walls is approximately two miles, there were twenty-four towers; Southampton had twenty-nine in a circumference of 1 mile 221 yards; Hereford, seventeen in 1 mile 40 yards; Yarmouth, sixteen in 1 mile 478 yards. Within any one circuit the mural towers are not always of the same plan (see fig. 1). Some of those of Southampton are square, the others half-round; York shows a similar mixture. Even where the towers are fairly uniform in plan as, for example, at Newcastle and Canterbury, each tower does not necessarily have the same internal arrangements. The obvious explanation for such small differences, that the towers were of different dates, does not always apply. The towers on the west walls at Newcastle, built simultaneously, demonstrate this point. It may be that the differences represent minor improvements, the significance of which is now lost. But they also suggest that there was rarely any coherent plan behind the construction of the defences, and that a variety of plans might be used only for convenience sake. The mixture of designs makes it difficult to assign an exact date to the use of any one plan. It is, however, possible to establish a sequence of tower plans.

The earliest towers are shallow half-round projections which protrude only a relatively short distance beyond the line of the wall, and which present a fairly broad face to frontal attack. Such is the one bastion remaining on the walls of Hereford, *c.* 1260. The next development is that of the D-shaped tower, found on the walls of Conway and Caernarvon, *c.* 1285 (plate 34), Yarmouth, four-teenth century (plate 19), Newcastle *c.* 1290 (plate 9), and Canterbury *c.* 1390 (plate 22). The D-shaped tower is found in the walls of all these towns which were built between 1260 and 1390. After that date it drops out of use. It projected further from the wall, its furthest point being perhaps twenty to twenty-five feet (6·1–7·62 m.) in front of the wall, but its diameter was only about twenty feet (6·1 m.) as opposed to the thirty feet (9·14 m.) of the Hereford type. Therefore, while exposing a smaller area to attacking fire, it was also better positioned to give flanking cover to the walls. It may also be that this shape of tower could be used to turn the wall through an obtuse angle more easily than any other, and this may in part explain its longevity. The only improvement on this type, the horseshoe shaped tower, in which the walls of the

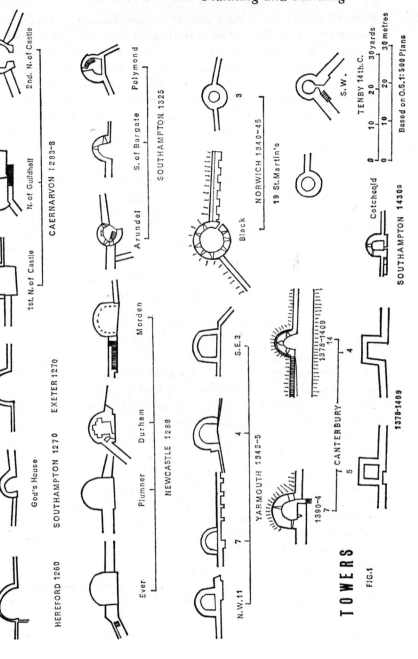

TOWERS

FIG.1

tower closest to the curtain wall were bent inwards, is found in town walls only at Southampton (Catchcold Tower) in the fifteenth century. The horseshoe plan may have been a development of the circular towers such as those which straddled the fourteenth-century walls at Norwich, for example the Black Tower (plate 17), rather than of the D-shaped tower. The square tower is also of late fourteenth or fifteenth century date. Examples are found at Canterbury and Southampton. In both Exeter and Denbigh, there is a five-sided tower (plate 40).

The variety of designs makes it possible to trace the development of defensive ideas underlying the different plans but it is less easy to link the sequence with a set of rigid dates within which any one plan was employed to the exclusion of others. An apparently early plan might continue to be built for a long period of time, and even, as at Canterbury, simultaneously with the building of towers on a different plan. The difficulties of trying to schematize the development of mural towers are similar to those encountered in trying to classify into date-tight compartments the evolution of the castle keep. It may also be the case that it is unnecessary to draw a distinction between the round and the square tower, and to attempt to lay any great significance on the change from one to the other. In assessing the defensive merits of one plan over another the important point to stress is the extent to which a tower projected beyond the wall. Towers of a bold projection enabled the defenders to discharge enfilading fire from advantageous positions. They enabled the besieged to conduct an active defence. While round towers are less vulnerable to bombardment and mining, and provide a better field of fire, square towers may have been more convenient for the operation of medieval artillery. This could well explain why in the fifteenth century more square towers were built than round. It is probably more important to study the disposition of the towers and their relation to the wall, and to study the weapons against which they were designed, than to try to establish an exactly dated sequence of plans.[21]

The importance of the relation of the towers to the defensive strength of the wall is best seen by a detailed study of the defences of several towns. No other town defences in Great Britain equal the considered design of those of Conway and Caernarvon. They were carefully planned and were built within a short period by specialized engineers. 'The plan was to create a barrier of masonry so strong that it could not be breached, and which, while presenting a continuous front to the enemy without, was so sectioned within as automatically to isolate any scaling party that might succeed in obtaining a foothold on its summit. Each of the flanking towers was so designed as to act as a circuit-breaker between one section and the next, continuity of the wall walk across the towers' open gorges being maintained only by a simple plank bridge which could easily be removed or destroyed by the defenders.'[22] If the bridges were removed then each tower became a self-contained unit of defence, the stone steps from street level to wall walk being under cover from the tower.

This is the first, and indeed the only occasion in which there is any sophistication in the urban defences of Great Britain. By way of comparison with the arrangements of Conway and Caernarvon it is instructive to consider in other towns the relation of the tower and the wall walk, both of which were clearly important parts of fortifications. Sufficient remains of the walls at Canterbury, Chepstow, Chester, Newcastle, Norwich, Oxford, Southampton and Yarmouth for an investigation of the trick of 'sectioning off' the defences, but it is difficult to show that the principles employed at Conway had any wider influence.

The underlying idea was, however, foreshadowed at Oxford, at the north-east angle tower. The wall walk was carried round the roof of the tower, which is open-gorged. The same device of lifting the walk round the tower is found at Chepstow. The fortifications of both towns are earlier than those of Conway, and although in practice the raising of the walk prevents any isolation of the tower from the rest of the defences, the removal of the stairs, and the continuation of the walk only by a plank would have come close to the arrangements of Conway.

At Newcastle, where the walls were built in the late thirteenth century, the relationship between tower and wall walk is difficult to decide since now the wall does not stand to its full height. The walk appears to have passed over the towers at roof level at the Ever and Herber towers where external stone stairs remain, and through the tower at the Durham tower at first floor level (plate 9), making isolation impossible. At Norwich, the similar passage of the wall walk through the tower, thereby making isolation impossible, is demonstrated both at the West Boom tower and at the tower by St. Benedict's gates. Both towers can be dated to the middle years of the fourteenth century. At Yarmouth also, where the walls are of similar date, the walk probably passed through the D-shaped towers.

At Canterbury, despite differences in date between the two kinds of half-round tower, the wall walk appears to be continuous. Neither type is earlier than the late fourteenth century. The tower in the War Memorial Garden has suffered reconstruction but seems to show that the wall walk passed across the tower at the level of the second chamber which had a doorway onto it, and that from the walk an external flight of stone steps led to the roof of the tower. The towers in the south-east quarter of the town (plate 22), built as open-gorged towers, now have the wall walk running past at the level of the first floor. This is similar to the thirteenth-century arrangements at Chester, where at both King Charles' and Bone-waldesthorne's towers the walk passes the tower at an angle which makes it impossible that the two were very closely connected (plate 32).

At Southampton almost every development of the wall walk is illustrated. To the north of God's House gate is a half-round open-gorged tower where the wall walk was clearly made continuous by a plank; this tower was dated by O'Neil to the end of the thirteenth century, by analogy with Conway and Caernarvon.[23] At the north-west angle the Arundel tower is a complete drum tower and the wall walk is carried up to the roof level, and there ends. The nature of the ground makes it logical that it should start again from the base of the tower. Slightly to the south, at Catchcold tower, dated to the early years of the fifteenth century it bypasses the firing chamber and passes over the roof of the tower.

Thus with the single exception of the tower to the north of God's House gate at Southampton the ideas underlying the defences of Conway do not seem to have been adopted elsewhere. The explanation can hardly be that local masons were not competent to copy them, but simply that they did not know of them, and were working in isolation. The wall walk in general, therefore, served only two purposes. In addition to being the means of communication between the towers it also had a part to play in the defence of the walls. Its importance as the means of communication between the towers is revealed by the lack of provision of stairs in towers, a fact which incidentally stresses their lack of isolation. At Conway and Caernarvon the tower was reached by a stair alongside it (fig. 1). At Hereford, Chepstow, Oxford, Southampton, Chester and Canterbury (fig. 1) access was from the wall walk alone. Each of these towers (except Chester) was open-backed, and in some, for example, at Canterbury, timber staging with a ladder to the upper floor must have provided the platform from which to use the upper gunports. But in other cases it is less easy to decide how a tower was approached. Thus at Yarmouth there is no trace of an internal stair. It may be that the tower was divided into two separate parts; a ground floor entrance to a basement chamber, from which there was no access to the floors above. These could have been reached from the wall walk at first floor level, and by a wooden stair to the second floor. A similar arrangement, with the emphasis on the wall walk as the chief means of entering a tower, is demonstrated at Norwich in the boom tower and at the tower by St. Stephen's Street. At the Black tower, from which the wall walk departs, a brick stair was built into the thickness of the tower wall providing access both to the wall walk and to the upper floors in the tower. At Newcastle, at the Durham, Heber, Morden and Ever towers, a stone stair connected the wall walk to the lower chamber (fig. 1).

Its second use was in the defensive role of the walls. It formed a base from which volleys of arrows could be fired, and additional protection for the defenders was provided by crenellation. Although only a few sections survive, notably at Norwich, Conway, Caernarvon, Tenby and Newcastle, documentary evidence suggests that crenellation was a general practice. At Oxford in 1244 the Friars Minor were ordered to build their wall and crenellate it like the wall of the city.[24] An indenture made in 1266 between the Prior and Convent of St. Swithun at Winchester and the townsmen stated that the Convent was to be responsible for the section wall between King's Gate and Southgate, and that it was to be battlemented.[25] In the fifteenth century a man at Canterbury rented a piece of land which ran under the walls for the length of sixteen crenellations.[26] At Berwick, between 1392 and 1395, stone was bought for crenellations,[27] and there is a similar entry in accounts for Sandwich in 1471.[28] Although it is not common, there are occasions when crenellation was specifically mentioned in the grant of murage; it can be taken to mean no more than a general permission to fortify.[29] In a grant to Winchelsea in 1415 permission was given 'to build a wall and to crenellate, tower and embattle it', and here a more emphatic meaning is probably to be understood.[30] In only a few cases was a licence to crenellate issued separately.[31]

Some walls were more effective in allowing the defenders to take offensive action than were others. Most walls had towers which served as heavily defended points of counter-attack, but there were great variations in the strength of the defences of the curtain wall. In some towns little use was made of the curtain-walling as a means of defence except to carry the wall walk and as a barrier to easy entry to the city. In such towns defence had to be conducted from the top of the walls. At the places where the walls were crenellated the defenders were protected by the merlons. In favourable circumstances crenellation gave a bowman a wide field of vision and fire; but when he was under fire he must often have been limited to the oblique angle open to him when he was sheltering behind a merlon. It would be quite impossible for defenders on the summit of a sheer curtain wall to command its base and this, as much as any additional reasons of further protection, made a ditch necessary.

But in the walls of some towns were two rows of slits. The upper row was used from the wall walk, the lower from ground level. This is the case, for example, at King's Lynn, Norwich, Yarmouth (plate 18), Tenby and Denbigh. In each of these places the wall walk is carried on arches spanning the embrasures which shelter the lower line of slits. The date of four of these walls is comparable : Denbigh is earlier, and the reason for the appearance of the feature here is explicable topographically. It occurs in only a short section, between the Countess tower and the Goblin tower, where the ground falls steeply away from the base of the wall. The upper row was presumably intended to command dead ground at the base of the wall.

The offensive uses of the wall walk could be enhanced by the use of bretasches. There are occasional references to these in accounts. Thus at Berwick in 1344-5,[32] and at Carlisle in 1348 when they were said to be broken down, [33] definite orders were given for their provision. Structural evidence suggests that they may also have been employed at Norwich on the section of the wall at Carrow Hill, and at Chepstow, where there are regular lines of square holes passing through the walls. The corbel tables on the towers at Newcastle would also have been used in this way (plate 9).

The curtain wall, therefore, might constitute more than a mere physical barrier to the defence of a town. Nevertheless, defence depended principally upon the opportunities for attack provided by towers. Arrow slits, especially when they were inserted into towers, had advantages for a bowman over the crenellated wall walk, although their use in towers by no means diminished their use in the intervening curtain wall. The enclosing wall of the tower gave the bowman greatly increased protection, though at the same time it must have hampered him. Firstly, his field of vision was greatly reduced in width by the slit; the position from which he had to discharge his arrows was more uncomfortable. In the *garrites* of Newcastle there is a slight recess in the wall behind the slit into which the archer's drawing arm fitted since the passage of the *garrite* is only 2 feet 11 inches wide.[34] Arrow slits are never sufficiently numerous to have permitted the discharge of heavy volleys from the walls. Even in the towers there are usually only three, one facing in each direction. Secondly, unless the slit splayed out at the base as in the fish-tail slits in the Grey Mare's Tail tower at Warkworth Castle, and in the Durham and Herber towers at Newcastle, the archer was even less able to command the base of the wall than he would have been on the wall walk. Lastly, the development of the cross-type slit with four circular openings at the end of each arm of the cross must have made accommodation more uncomfortable and increased difficulties of firing from the embrasure when it was occupied by four men, although it presumably had the advantage of giving a more concentrated field of fire.

The gradual development of fire-arms in the later Middle Ages is reflected in the provision of gunports in town walls to accommodate the new weapons. Because its development comes late, examples are found chiefly in towns where construction is later than the mid-fourteenth century; few towns inserted gunports into earlier walls. Most surviving examples can be dated from documentary evidence, but it is difficult to trace much development in their design largely because of lack of knowledge to determine with what sort or size of weapon their use was intended.[35] The external appearance of a gunport is that of a circular hole topped by a vertical slit. Inside the tower was a splayed embrasure on which to rest the

E

barrel of the gun. The earliest example, in the west walls of Southampton, was dated by O'Neil to *c.* 1360.[36] The opening is five to six inches (0·127–0·162 m.) in diameter and the length of the slit about forty-four inches (1·12 m.). At the West gate in Canterbury, dateable to *c.* 1380, the diameter is ten inches (0·254 m.) and the length of the slit thirty-four inches (0·834 m.). By 1418, the conjectured date of the Catchcold tower at Southampton, both hole and slit measured eleven inches (0·279 m.), and at King's Lynn, in the South gate of 1520, there is no slit and the diameter of the hole is ten inches (0.279 m.). Three significant changes in the development of the gunport might be sought : firstly, the increase of the width of the circular hole to accommodate larger guns; secondly, a more widely splayed hole, to provide greater manoeuvrability and a wider field of fire; and thirdly, a decrease in the length of the embrasure, to permit of guns being mounted on wooden trunnions rather than resting their full weight on the solid bed of the embrasure. But none of these changes occurs; the only noticeable change is in the reduction of the length of the slit, which probably occurred naturally as builders departed from the ideas of arrow fire and considered more closely the nature of gun fire.

Guns had certain disadvantages in use. They could not be manoeuvred either as quickly or as easily as bows. Their line of fire was limited to a straight line, and would therefore be easy to avoid. Nor was their range as great or as accurate as that which could be achieved by a well-trained bowman. But, on the other hand, they possessed a certain psychological value. In some cases gunports appear to have been arranged with more care than the disposition of arrow slits. It has been demonstrated that the gunports in the western arcade at Southampton had a very wide field of covering fire, and left no area of wall uncovered. Similar evidence of planning is noted at the West gate of Canterbury.[37] At the south-west angle of the defences at Canterbury the gunports are placed at different heights in alternate towers, presumably with the provision of more effective cross-fire in mind. Yet the use of cannon cannot have been a serious threat to the safety of either the attackers or the beseiged, although it is clear that the possession of guns was common.

Towers from which weapons could be best deployed, because of their greater numbers and consequent greater flexibility and possibility of variation in the matter of internal arrangements, obviously bore the brunt of attack. But gateways also had an important part to play in defence, besides having other roles to fulfil. They are perhaps the most sophisticated element in urban defences, and it is unfortunate that so many should have been destroyed. Where they have survived they are also the parts of the defences which were most frequently rebuilt, so that it is often difficult to assign a single date, or to disentangle the different building periods.

The importance of the gate is demonstrated by the fact that in several towns the gates were in stone before any other part of the defences. Such was the situation at Norwich, where excavation has shown that St. Benedict's gates were erected slightly earlier than the stone wall which abuts against them.[38] The same may also be true at Newcastle in 1246 when the sheriff was ordered to repair the gate.[39] At Beverley the North Bar stood always as a brick gateway in the middle of earth banks. Similarly at Sandwich, the gates were stone structures breaking the circuit of timber palisades or large dykes until the fifteenth century.

More care seems to have been given to gates than to any other features. They were re-modelled to match new military techniques and new fashions, and it is possible to trace a more definite evolution in design than is visible in other features (see fig. 2.). The earliest gates appear to have been rectangular structures, a single passageway between two guard chambers. Such, for example, is the suggested reconstruction of the Bargate at Southampton in its earliest form,[40] and of the Burgess gate in Denbigh. The design of the gates of Conway and Caernarvon improved on this, by adding projecting half-round towers onto the front face of the rectangle (plate 36). By the middle of the fourteenth century the principles of design had changed entirely, and the round tower was normal. Thus at Rye the Langate consists of two circular towers flanking a passageway with only a small space above the arch and almost no extension of the structure on the inside of the defences (plate 23). At Winchelsea the Landgate (plate 30) consists of four circular towers linked together by short stretches of curtain walling, again without provision of space above the gateway. Prints show that gates at Yarmouth and Exeter, known to have been built in the mid-fourteenth century, developed the schemes used at Rye and Winchelsea. The circular flanking towers were retained, but they were moved further from the central passageway, and, inside the walls, at first floor level a

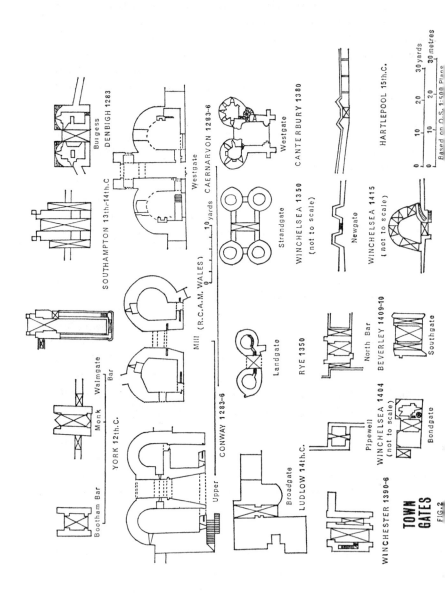

TOWN GATES

FIG.2

chamber projected backwards, providing greater room for purposes other than the purely military one of housing the winding gear of the portcullis. For example, at Southampton the room was used as the Guildhall; at Caernarvon, as the Exchequer. The conjunction of circular towers and a room behind seems to have been fairly common in the fourteenth century as far as it is possible to judge from the much rebuilt gates at Totnes and Ludlow, and from the prints of St. Stephen's gates, Norwich.[41]

The conjunction of the circular towers with the squared hind-chamber reaches its most developed form in the Bargate at Southampton and, more obviously, at the West gate at Canterbury, dated to *c*. 1380 (plate 20). In both cases the towers have been placed to round off the square corners of the chamber on its external face, adding to the defensive strength of the gate without diminishing the space available in the chamber behind the line of the walls. But even at the time at which Canterbury gate was designed, the square or rectangular plan had once more come into its own, and the West gate at Winchester, built *c*. 1390, reverts to this plan (plate 31). From this time on it seems that flanking towers were out of fashion and gates were once again plain rectangular structures. There is the gate defending the bridge at Warkworth, dated to 1400 (plate 10); Pipewell Gate at Winchelsea, dated 1404–1405; the North Bar at Beverley, dated to 1409–1410 (plate 6); and the South gate at King's Lynn as rebuilt in 1520 (plate 16). The three exceptions to this scheme of development are the Bondgate at Alnwick, the New gate at Winchelsea and Sandwell gate at Hartlepool. The external face of the Bondgate (plate 5), presents two slightly projecting three-sided towers standing on a square base plinth. At Winchelsea also there are three-sided flanking towers, but the gate is little more than a masonry barrier placed across the road into the town. Its interior face was completely open, and the embrasures from which it would have been defended can be seen clearly. At Hartlepool twin triangular towers flank the central arch.

The re-emergence of the square plan is susceptible of several interpretations. The most obvious, and that used to explain the appearance of the square mural tower, the change in weapons from bows to cannon, scarcely seems to apply when it is realized that the West gates of both Canterbury and Winchester were designed nearly simultaneously, one round in plan, the other square. Moreover, few, if indeed any, of the gates built after this date seem to have had any provision for the firing of cannon, so that no consistency in the application of the principle can be discerned. A more accurate explanation may be the progressive relaxation of the military character of the gates, noticeable in the fifteenth century. Most of the examples listed above show that they become less defensible structures, not only in plan but also in the provision made for active defence. At the end of the fourteenth century the gate had reached the highest point of its development, and some significance should probably be attached to the fact that it was at that time that many of the towns which possess the most impressive gates were in receipt of large grants of money from the Exchequer. Not only was the gate at its largest and most massive, but it had been provided with the maximum provisions for defence. It could mount a heavy fusillade of arrow or gun fire. Attackers had then to get through the heavy wooden doors of the gate, and they might be attacked meanwhile from above from a machicolated parapet. This could be used either to shower missiles on those attacking the gate, or, more practically, to pour water on fires lit against the doors. The parapet is a feature which appears only on gates of this period, for example at the West gates of Canterbury and Winchester, the Bargate at Southampton and the Land gate at Rye (plates 20, 31 and 27, 23), although it is a feature commonly found in castles. Apart from its use on gates it is found only at the Catchcold tower at Southampton and at the south-east corner tower at Tenby.

The gate might derive additional protection from the existence of a barbican. Remains survive at the Upper Gate, Conway, and at Walmgate Bar at York (plate 12). At Newcastle the drawings of G. B. Richardson show that at least the Newgate was protected in this way.[42] In the ordinances for safeguarding the city of London in 1377 it was laid down that the gates were to have portcullises and chains, and to have barbicans in front.[43] From the gate, control was exercised over either the drawbridge, such as existed at Canterbury where the holes through which its chains passed can still be seen, or over the 'turning bridge' (*pons versatilis*) such as is known to have existed at Newcastle.

By the end of the fourteenth century the external face of the gate might present a formidable obstacle to attack. But if the besiegers successfully forced an entry, there was rarely anything to prevent the whole gate from passing under their control. Frequently it was possible to move directly from the guard chambers to the upper floors, and from there on to the walls. Thus at Canterbury and Winchester the stair rose from the guard chamber to the upper levels. At Warkworth, although the guard chamber was on one side of the gate with no means of communication to the upper room, the stair was on the other, quite undefended. Others, however, were stronger units of defence. The Upper Gate at Conway reveals very complex arrangements to prevent attackers easily gaining control over the whole structure.[44] Easy communication was also blocked at the Burgess gate at Denbigh and in the West Gate at Southampton, where there seems to have been no connection between the guard rooms and the upper floors, and in the Land gate at Rye there was a stair in only one of the flanking towers. The South gate at Tenby is a design unique amongst urban gate plans, where the attackers, if they overcame the first wall, a kind of primitive barbican, would be trapped within a semi-circular wall from which they could be attacked and still have the main entrance to overcome.

Gates, though often impressive, were not therefore the heavily defensible structures they appear to be. The relation of the gate to the wall is important, and the distance from which it projects beyond the line of the wall is perhaps an indication of the degree to which it was regarded as a focal point for defence. Some gates were clearly intended to assist sallies, whereas others, less prominent, might do no more than hold off a beseiging force for a short time; still others, one feels, might be capable of neither of these things and were intended more as barriers which could not be passed without first paying toll. It may even be the case that by the end of the fourteenth century the gate had ceased to be regarded as important primarily in a military context and had become simply a display of civic wealth and status, decked with the trappings of fortification.

Town defences, then, do not exhibit the skilled design of English castles. To what extent the builder of town walls might know of, or copy, the defensive tricks of the castle is a point which can never be established finally. Comparison of gate or tower plans suggests little exchange of ideas or knowledge of each other's work. The fact that the building of a town wall was so essentially a local affair goes a long way to explain the deficiencies of urban defences, and explains the absence of sophistication. The contrast is the more pointed when the work of Master James of St. George at Conway or Master Henry Yevele at Canterbury is contrasted with the standard of work produced by the local masons. Moreover, the fact that a town wall might not always serve a purpose exclusively military, so that a certain relaxation of military necessities could be permitted, goes far to explain why striking developments and refinements are neither found nor to be expected in town defences.

NOTES

1 *Anglo-Saxon Chronicle*, s.a. 917.
2 B. Cuncliffe, 'Winchester City Wall', *Procs. Hants. Field Club*, XXII, 1962, 51–81.
3 I am grateful to Lady Aileen Fox for this information.
4 *Cal. Inq. Misc.*, III, no. 425, 154.
5 *Rot. Parl.*, III, 255.
6 *Pipe Roll, 14 John*, 90; *Rot. Litt. Claus.*, I, 417.
7 *Cal. Close Rolls, 1237–42*, 403.
8 *Cal. Close Rolls, 1227–31*, 268; *Cal. Close Rolls, 1227–31*, 527; *Cal. Close Rolls, 1231–4*, 276.
9 *Cal. Pat. Rolls, 1232–47*, 447.
10 Martin Biddle, 'Excavations at Winchester, 1966', *Antiquaries Journal*, XLVII, 1967, 251–79.
11 I am indebted to Mr. Frank Noble for this information.
12 D. R. Shearer, 'Dating the City Wall by Excavation', *Trans. Worcester Archaeological Society*, XXXVI, 1959, 62.
13 R. H. Wildgoose, 'The Defences of the pre-Conquest Borough of Nottingham', *Trans. of Thoroton Society*, 65, 1961, 21.
14 W. F. Whittard, *Bristol and its adjoining Counties*, 1955, fig. 23.
15 *Medieval Archaeology*, V, 1961, 325.
16 M. Andrews, *The Story of Old Scarborough*, 1947, 34–7.
17 *Cal. Close Rolls, 1318–23*, 54.
18 J. Brand, *History and Antiquities of the town of Newcastle upon Tyne*, 1789, I, 6.
19 *Cal. Pat. Rolls, 1377–81*, 72.
20 *Letter Book E*, 146–7 and *passim*.
21 The ideas underlying this paragraph were suggested by reading J. R. Hale 'The Early Development of the Bastion', in *Europe in the Middle Ages*, ed. J. R. Hale, J. R. L. Highfield and B. Smalley, 1965, 474–5; and J. A. Thompson, *Crusader Castles*, 1957, 48–50.
22 A. J. Taylor, *Conway Castle and Town Walls*, 32.
23 O'Neil, *Southampton Town Wall*, 254.
24 *Cal. Pat. Rolls, 1232–47*, 447.
25 Quoted from W. H. Jacobs, *The West gate of Winchester*, 1905.
26 *Hist. Mss. Comm.*, 9th Rep., 140.
27 P.R.O. E 101/483/5.
28 P.R.O. E 101/468/28.

29   Southwold, *Cal. Pat. Rolls, 1258–66,* 108; Hull, *Cal. Pat. Rolls, 1321–4,* 7; Rye, *Cal. Pat. Rolls, 1367–70,* 224.
30   *Cal. Pat. Rolls, 1413–16,* 368–9.
31   Penrith, *Cal. Pat. Rolls, 1345–8,* 69; Salisbury, *Cal. Pat. Rolls, 1370–74,* 220.
32   P.R.O. E 101/482/26.
33   P.R.O. C 145/161 (3).
34   *Arch. Aeliana,* fourth series, XI, 1934, 8; *'garrite'* is an old French word meaning watch-tower, and is used by Brand to describe those on the walls of Newcastle upon Tyne.
35   See O'Neil, *Castles and Cannon,* 18–19.
36   O'Neil, *Southampton Town Wall,* 256.
37   D. F. Renn, 'The Southampton Arcade', *Med. Arch.,* VIII, 1964, 226–8.
38   J. G. Hurst, 'Excavations at St. Benedict's Gates, Norwich, 1951 and 1953', *Norfolk Archaeology,* XXXI, 1955, 32–6.
39   *Cal. Lib. Rolls,* 1240–45, 85.
40   R. M. D. Lucas, 'Architectural Notes on Bargate', *Procs. Hants. Field Club,* IV, 1898–1903, 131–6.
41   Robert Fitch, *Views of the Gates of Norwich,* 1861.
42   The drawings are deposited in the Newcastle City Library.
43   *Letter Book H,* 64.
44   A. J. Taylor, *Conway Castle and Town Walls,* 39–40.

CHAPTER FIVE

Walls and wars

The geographical grouping of walled towns shows a clear relation to the wars of the English kings, and to the periods of political and military disturbance which the country suffered during the Middle Ages. The evidence for the provision of walls is drawn from government records and from contemporary or near contemporary chronicle sources. The attempt to link the two sources is an attempt to discover not only against what enemies and against what kind of attack town walls were built, but also to discover to what extent the defences were effective, and in what light they were regarded by contemporaries.

The first noticeable connection between unrest and the construction of walls is in the period of disturbance preceding and following the sealing of Magna Carta, 1215-25. Some part of this interest in defences may have to be ascribed to the fact that there are better documents, but it is also true that a connection between towns receiving grants and the areas of disturbance can be traced. Thus York and Colchester received grants of timber in April 1215,[1] and Winchester in December.[2] London and Exeter received cash grants, London, significantly, in May.[3] The bailiffs of Cambridge were to be allowed the costs of fortifying their town in November 1215.[4] Stamford received a grant of timber in 1218.[5] On the Welsh Marches Shrewsbury received a grant of timber in 1212,[6] Hereford in 1216[7] and Bridgnorth in 1220.[8] Murage grants were first recorded in 1220 and became common after 1225, probably because the fear of attack made several towns, especially those which had defences from an earlier date, take steps towards renewing their fortifications. Yet the castle was still the important unit of defence, and it, rather than the town, was the centre which the armies sought to control. Since it was also the point on which landed power was based, control of the castle could mean control of the lordship and of its resources. The emphasis on the castle is stressed in the chronicles by the graphic descriptions of the sieges of the castles of Lincoln, Newark, Bedford and Rochester.[9] These were all places where the town had had earlier defences, but little importance seems to have been attached to them. Similarly of Northampton, which also possessed defences of Saxon date, Walter of Coventry wrote that 'the armed barons, turned back to Northampton . . . and the gates were closed, and guards were stationed both at the gates and on the walls. They began to lay siege to the castle which lay within the town, but it was in vain, since they had no artillery.'[10] While it was relatively easy to capture the town, the capture of the castle was a more difficult operation.

In the early thirteenth century the first murage grants were received only by towns which had been fortified earlier, presumably because other towns were not sufficiently important or in sufficient danger to need protection. By the time of the next period of unrest, that caused by the Welsh wars of the thirteenth century, the situation had changed and few of the many towns to receive grants had been fortified earlier (c.f. Maps I, II).

It may seem surprising on a first glance at the map of the distribution of murage grants that so many small towns on the borders of Wales should have been in receipt of murage. Closer study reveals that the walls were erected as a protection against attack by the Welsh, but it is surprising to find that in many cases a town had been attacked and sacked on several occasions before any thought was given to providing it with defences. Thus the town and castle at Carmarthen were sacked in 1214 and again in 1231, but there was no grant of murage until 1233.[11] Similarly, the castle and town of Haverfordwest were attacked and burnt in 1219–20, but there was no effort to wall the town until 1264.[12] Kidwelly, attacked in 1231, did not receive a grant until 1280.[13] At Montgomery, where a castle had been built in 1221,[14] there were attacks on the settlement in 1231 and again in 1257, but the town had no protection other than that afforded by the castle until the building of the first defences after 1267.[15] There were other towns in the area which remained unwalled, and which were dependent on the castle for protection for a long time, such as Cardigan, Swansea and Cardiff. There is only one instance, Hay on Wye, where the town was attacked in 1231 and where a grant was obtained the following year.[16]

Yet there were other towns in the area which were never attacked but which nonetheless received murage grants. For a long time the important strategical factor would have been the possession of strong points on which to base the campaigns, and it would not have mattered whether the base was a castle or a walled town. The distinction between the fortified and the unfortified towns may lie in the importance attached to them as military bases. When a town was dependent on the castle the defence of the town was not considered of primary importance, but when the town itself was considered as a military base then it was walled. Thus the construction of Montgomery castle could precede the building of the walls by as much as forty-three years. Chronicles repeat with monotony the fact that towns and castles were burnt, but the damage may not have been extensive. As the wars continued it may have become a matter of pride amongst the Marcher lords that their towns should be walled. By the time of the Edwardian campaigns most of the Marcher towns were defended. The greatest building enterprise in the area was the fortification of Flint and Rhuddlan, used as bases in the campaigns, which were fortified only with a timber palisade, and of Conway and Caernarvon. These towns, constructed to hold and maintain the English position in Wales, enjoyed the protection of the most sophisticated stone defences in the country. While their first purpose was to protect the inhabitants, they must also have had the effect of emphasising English status and prestige.

The lesson of the Welsh Wars seems to be that walls were considered a useful if not an indispensable element of protection, but the contrast with the events of the Barons' Wars raises the question of how far they could ever act as a useful and effective barrier against attack. A few towns obtained grants during the course of the revolt, but so little is known about the loyalties of towns that it is difficult, though tempting, to link these grants with localized outbreaks of fighting. Thus towns as far apart as Yarmouth, Chichester, Totnes, Southampton and Grimsby received grants between 1260 and 1265, Yarmouth specifically that it might remain loyal to the king. Coventry and Sandwich made some efforts to provide defences for themselves, although they did not receive murage. Of the other towns most heavily involved, however, most already had fortifications, but these did not always succeed in repelling attack. For instance Robert Ferrars, earl of Derby, was resisted by the citizens of Worcester who manned the walls and gates, but he succeeded nevertheless in entering the city through the castle.[17] At Winchester in May 1264 the troops of Simon de Montfort the younger entered and burnt part of the city, despite the existence of fortifications which we know to have been in good repair.[18] At Gloucester in 1265 the army of Henry III and the Lord Edward captured the town after only one day's fighting, but another two passed before they captured the castle.[19] In other places, however, the picture is not so clear. In the attack on Northampton it may only have been the treachery of the prior who showed the royal army a weak place in the fortifications near his property which lost the city for Simon de Montfort.[20] The description of the attack on Rochester in 1264 suggests that the walls proved to be a considerable obstacle, since the chronicler noted that Earl Simon did not succeed in entering the city on the first day of the fighting.[21] Of London we read first in 1263 that the city was fortified and defended with iron chains across the streets,[22] and then that in 1265 the king's men who 'occupied the fortifications, tore up all the barriers and iron chains, which were remarkably effective for the defence of every open space and narrow street'.[23] The degree to which defences were effective is not therefore easy to assess. The fact that some towns took the trouble to obtain a grant suggests that the protection of a wall was at least considered desirable, even if some of the towns already fortified gained little protection.

In the aftermath of the wars, during the period in which there was still a certain amount of skirmishing on the part of the rebel leaders who preferred to carry on the war rather than submit to terms, a few towns asked for permission to levy murage. Thus Lewes received its first grant in 1266 at the instance of its lord, earl de Warenne.[24] In East Anglia, a much disturbed area since the rebel band called the Disinherited had their headquarters in the Isle of Ely from which they made frequent sorties to harass the countryside, we read that they 'invaded the Marsh land and even attacked [King's] Lynn in Easter Week, but retreated, their plans frustrated by the manful resistance of the townsmen'.[25] The presumption must be that at the time the town had no wall since soon afterwards the townsmen decided that discretion was the better part of valour, and in May they accepted their first murage grant.[26]

By the early fourteenth century one area demonstrates still more strongly the acceptance of walls as a feature of a town. In the second decade of the fourteenth century the northern Marches of England suffered many raids from the Scots. In 1312 they burnt Corbridge, Hexham and Darlington, and raided Hartlepool and Durham.[27] In 1314 there was a raid on the county of Richmond, and the towns of Brough, Appleby and Kirkoswald were burnt also.[28] It is, therefore, scarcely surprising to find a large number of murage grants issued in these years. Berwick and Richmond received grants in 1313,[29] although there is some evidence to suggest that orders at least had been given for the fortifications of Berwick earlier.[30] Durham and Hartlepool, the latter plundered in June 1315,[31] received grants the same year,[32] and Lancaster the next. The effects of the raids on Newcastle, some part of whose walls had already been constructed, was to hasten their completion. But what a wall might mean in time of siege is vividly portrayed in a vignette of the initial letter of the charter granted to Carlisle in the following year, 1315 (plate 3), and is amplified by a chronicler's description :[34]

> the King of Scotland . . . came to Carlisle, invested the city and besieged it for ten days, trampling down the crops, wasting the suburbs. . . . On every day of the siege they assaulted one of the three gates of the city, sometimes all three at once; but never without loss, because there were discharged on them from the walls such dense volleys of darts and arrows, likewise stones, that they asked one another whether stones bred and multiplied within the walls. Now on the fifth day of the siege they set up a machine for casting stones next the church of the Holy Trinity, where their king stationed himself, and they cast great stones continually against the Caldew gate (west) and against the wall, but they did little or no injury to those within except that they killed one man. But there were seven or eight similar machines within the city, besides other engines of war, which are called springalds, for discharging long darts, and staves with sockets for casting stones, which caused great fear and damage to those outside. Meanwhile, however, the Scots set up a certain great *berefrai* like a kind of tower, which was considerably higher than the city walls. On perceiving this, the carpenters of the city erected upon the tower of the wall against which that engine must come if it had ever reached the wall a wooden tower loftier than the other; but neither that engine nor any other ever did reach the wall, because, when it was being drawn on wheels over the wet and swampy ground, having stuck there through its own weight, it could neither be taken any further nor do any harm.
>
> Moreover the Scots had made many long ladders, which they brought

with them for scaling the wall in different places simultaneously; also a sow for mining the town wall had they been able; but neither sow nor ladders availed them aught. Also they made long bridges of logs running upon wheels, such as being swiftly and strongly drawn upon ropes might reach across the width of the moat. But during all the time the Scots were on the ground neither the bundle sufficed to fill the moat, nor those wooden bridges to cross the ditch, but sank to the depths by their own weight.

Howbeit on the ninth day of the siege, when all the engines were ready, they delivered a general assault on the city gates and upon the whole circuit of the wall, attacking manfully, while the citizens defended themselves just as manfully, and they did the same the next day. The Scots also resorted to the same stratagem whereby they had taken Edinburgh castle . . . and they set up long ladders and the bowmen . . . shot their arrows thickly to prevent anyone showing his head above the wall. But . . . they met with such resistance there as threw them to the ground with their ladders so that there and elsewhere round the wall some were killed, others taken prisoner and others wounded; yet throughout the siege no Englishman was killed save one man struck by an arrow and the above, and few were wounded.

On the eleventh day, whether they had heard the English were approaching, to relieve, or whether they despaired of success, the Scots marched off in confusion to their own country, leaving behind them all their engines of war aforesaid.

A siege such as that was not likely to calm fears, and the alarm caused by the incursions had not diminished by 1321; in that year the citizens of Hull received a grant of murage,[35] and the citizens of Beverley sent a petition to parliament asking that they should be allowed to wall their town.[36] That their fear was justifiable is proved by the events of the next year when the Scots, having burnt Ripon, marched on to York and Beverley where they were bought off by the burgesses and canons, and did no damage.[37] The same procedure was employed at Richmond in 1316.[38] Perhaps for smaller towns there was no great necessity for going to the trouble of providing defences, but for larger and richer towns a wall would provide protection and might prove cheaper than constant levies for ransom money.

Carlisle and Penrith came under attack in 1345,[39] and this is perhaps the reason why the state of the defences at Carlisle caused so much concern in 1348.[40] The attack also explains the murage grant to Penrith in 1349.[41] In this period the emphasis of war in England seems to be shifting from the sieges of castles towards plundering and raiding so that it was more advantageous for the town to have some kind of defences.

The events of further fighting in the later fourteenth and fifteenth centuries reveal similar strategy. In the course of the Hundred Years War the French made many raids on coastal towns; in this kind of 'tip and run' warfare one would expect the existence of a wall to afford a considerable degree of protection. That a wall was felt to be useful is suggested by the fact that the raids made by the French tended to stimulate construction or repair work in the towns likely to be attacked, and in which, although murage had been granted, it is clear that little had been achieved beforehand. Thus the attack on Southampton in 1338 forced the townsmen into completing their defences, and the same pattern is repeated after the burning of Rye in 1377, of Winchelsea in 1380 and of Sandwich in 1457.

The deterrent effect of the existence of a wall came to be fully appreciated in the course of the Wars of the Roses. Even the briefest study of the marches and countermarches of these years shows that the armies confined themselves to the main roads, and avoided large towns as far as they could. With one or two exceptions their pitched battles were fought away from towns. This is not to say that towns escaped all effects of the Wars. Ludlow, an important political and military centre, was sacked in 1459,[42] despite its walls; Grantham, Stamford, Peterborough, Huntingdon and Royston, towns on the main road south, were plundered by Margaret's forces in 1461.[43] Significantly perhaps, only one of these, Stamford, had walls. Several towns were still levying murage, and work on the defences is recorded both in important towns and in those which felt themselves to be involved. Thus the ditches at Shrewsbury were cleaned in 1461,[44] at Southampton in 1460,[45] at Worcester in 1459[46] and at Norwich in 1458.[47] The gates were mended at Beverley in 1460,[48] and at Salisbury in 1455[49] £20 was bequeathed to the Mayor and Commonalty for 'the making of barres about the city'. Throughout the century Coventry and Sandwich were engaged in re-building timber defences in stone. On the part of the older towns there was considerable interest in maintaining defences which by this time had been shown to have considerable value. Five towns built walls for the first time. Two, Barnstaple and Poole, were ports, which might be expected to want some protection against pirate raids.

Three were perhaps encouraged to fortify themselves by continued fighting. Thus Ruthyn obtained a grant in 1407,[50] and Alnwick in 1434.[51] Warkworth, dominated by its castle, needed little protection other than the gate defending the bridgehead built about 1400, and never received a grant of murage. Once again there is a connection between a period of unrest and the building of fortifications.

Although a direct and immediate connection between the incidence of disturbances and the construction of walls can be established in only a few cases, an appreciation of their potential value is clear throughout the Middle Ages. Whether or not they were directly attacked a general feeling of panic, as much as any specific cause for alarm, could stir people into taking action.

There was widespread fear at the end of the fourteenth century, and its consequences are seen, not in chronicles, but in the official records of the government. It is at this time that four towns with defences dating from Roman times first repaired in the early thirteenth centry, began again to interest themselves in their fortifications. The bailiffs at Bath were ordered to repair the walls in 1369;[52] those of Canterbury in 1363.[53] Colchester received murage, albeit in an unusual form, in 1382[54] and Rochester's defences were repaired between 1396 and 1399.[55] It has already been mentioned that the expiry of the truce of Brétigny produced a flood of orders to towns commanding them to repair their defences, as a result of the petition to parliament in 1369 asking that every fortified place in England should be given orders to put itself into a state of repair. There was at that time no reason to expect attack other than the fact that the truce had expired. Later, murage grants show that rumours caused a town to receive orders to repair its defences, as for example at Exeter in 1377, when it was stated that 'the king had learnt that his enemies of France and others adherent to them purpose to invade the realm . . . and to attack the same city'.[56] Similarly, as has already been noted, the king intervened in municipal elections at Canterbury in 1387 to secure the return of two bailiffs whom he could trust to continue the work of walling the city, 'because of the peril he saw daily threatening'.[57] There was clearly a feeling that even if danger were not imminent a town ought to be prepared to resist attack, and at Canterbury in 1403 the king again had to urge the townsmen to continue the work of walling the town, having learnt that the bailiffs were neglecting

F

their duty and 'were not mindful of the damage and peril which would befall the city and the parts adjacent if war were to be moved between the king and his adversaries'.[58] The words neither represent a commonly used Chancery formula, nor reflect upon the actual condition of the defences. But in the case of Canterbury it is not surprising to find that the king was more anxious than the citizens that the town should be walled, since it was an excellent point at which to check the advance on London should a French force succeed in landing on the south coast.

From Gloucester there is an even clearer indication that it was the king rather than the citizens who felt they should enjoy the protection of defences. In 1360 they were ordered to repair their fortifications 'without delay, the truce with the king's adversaries of France or other colourable excuse notwithstanding; as the king lately . . . hearing that the walls and towers were ruinous whereby damage and peril as well to the town as to the parts adjacent might probably happen in the king's absence by invasion of his enemies, ordered the bailiffs to cause the same to be repaired. And though they caused the greater part to be repaired accordingly, yet that for a truce has been proclaimed . . . they are not caring for the repair of that which remains, whereat the king is much surprised; and because it is advisable that the town should be well fortified in time of peace as of war.'[59]

Each of these cases carries with it a strong suggestion that the maintenance of defences was a burden which the citizens would willingly have avoided had the king not insisted on its necessity. The benefits of defences were clearly not considered to be so great as to justify their maintenance even at a time when attack threatened. There is evidence to show that a wall had to serve an immediate military purpose to justify expenditure on it. At King's Lynn, where an attack on the town had caused the citizens to obtain a murage grant, charges were brought against some of the citizens who 'having houses and other buildings adjoining the wall pierced it and pulled it down' only ten years later.[60] It is clear in other cases too that the attitude to defences changed in time of peace; some towns asked for permission to cease levying murage because it kept traders away from the town. There was a general feeling that walls were an item on which the town could economize,[61] and by the end of the fourteenth century many towns were admitting only a grudging financial responsibility for their defences. In the last decades of the century several towns claimed that they were too impoverished to pay for repairs to their walls, and received heavy subsidies from the Exchequer to persuade them to build or to complete parts of the circuit. Despite their alleged poverty towns such as Southampton, Rye and Winchester not only overspent the grants they received, but they made no effort to cut their spending on other things. There had clearly been a decline in interest in the defences which only a substantial grant of money could revive.

Despite such resentment, displayed, it is true, only at a time when because of the Black Death it is possible that the towns were really least able to support additional financial burdens, it is clear that provision for the defence of towns was taken seriously throughout the Middle Ages. Such provisions can be considered under two main heads, firstly the provision of manpower, demanded from the individual inhabitants of the town, and secondly the provision of weapons at the expense of the whole town. Even when there was no threat of attack towns made some attempt to observe the system of Watch and Ward laid down in 1252.[62] Between Ascension Day and Michaelmas Day watch was to be kept from sunset to sunrise in every city, borough and town of England. No details of how the duties were to be distributed were laid down, and there is little trace of regular appointments to the Watch in city archives. At Southampton in 1339 Thomas, the precentor of the church of St. Mary, was responsible for finding two armed men and two archers for the watches on the walls.[63] The records of the individual assessment for the duty, together with the fines for non-performance, are preserved for Bridgwater in 1417 and 1437.[64] But it is possible that the duty devolved automatically on the inhabitants of the wards, and required no special organisation, in the same way that in some towns responsibility for the maintenance of the walls was apportioned. Thus at London the custody of the city was apportioned in 1309 on the basis of ward boundaries, and repairs and guard duties were linked and assigned on the same basis in 1377, 1379 and 1381.[65] Norwich and York had similar arrangements.[66]

At Stamford Leland noted that 'there were seven principal towers or wards . . . to each of which were certain free-holders in the town allotted to make watch and ward in time of need'.[67] At Shrewsbury there survives a list of the foot soldiers and the bowmen in two divisions of the town under the command of four constables whose duty it was to defend the town in case of attack.[68] The presence of a wall would make much easier the execution of the provisions of the statute, and must have made the safe-keeping of a city a much less arduous task.

The arrangements for providing men continued in force even after a communal responsibility for the provision of weapons was assumed, a responsibility perhaps forced on the town because of the greater expense of artillery weapons and because they were of little value for the defence of a single person; and unlike the weapons required by the Statute of Watch and Ward, were not likely to be in the possession of an individual. The possession of guns by towns, however, was common. London had 'six instruments of latone usually called "gonnes" and five roleres to the same, also pellets of lead for the same instruments, which weigh four hundred weight and a half'.[69] Southampton corporation bought a gun for 5s 8d in 1382, and in 1468 there is a detailed list of the guns belonging to each tower in the circuit.[70] A similar list exists for Norwich for 1386, when a record was made of the assessment owed by each man in the wards towards their cost,[71] and there are references to guns at King's Lynn in the same year. Canterbury owned guns from at least 1403; in that year the guns were taken to the West gate, and two stone cutters were paid to make round stones for them. Some were repaired in 1449–50, and others were bought in 1460–61, when they were brought from Whitstable.[72] Rye and Exeter also had guns,[73] and at Coventry in 1451 it was ordained that 'there should be made four guns of brass : two greater called serpentines and two smaller. Every gun should have three chambers.' In 1471 the Leet Book records the delivery to Chesilmore gate of 'a gun and two chambers, a handgun and thirty-two pelettes; to Robert Onley a serpentine gun and a staffe gun and a chamber to a gun; to John Wylgrys a great gun and a chamber, a staffe gun and a bag'.[74]

Such provisions suggest that some care was taken to ensure that a town wall should be an effective barrier to easy entry. It is difficult to decide whether the fact that they were so rarely put to the test is a tribute to their actual value or merely to their deterrent potential.

NOTES

1 *Rot. Litt. Claus.*, I, 195, 193.
2 *Rot. Litt. Claus.*, I, 240.
3 *Close Roll for 1215, Pipe Roll Soc.*, XXXI, no. 15, 132.
   Rot. Litt. Claus., I, 186.
4 *Rot. Litt. Claus.*, I, 234.
5 *Rot. Litt. Claus.*, I, 370.
6 *Pipe Roll John 14*, 90.
7 *Rot. Litt. Claus.*, I, 263.
8 *Rot. Litt. Claus.*, I, 421.
9 Ralph Coggeshalle, *Chronicon Anglicanum (Rolls Series)*, 175, for the
   siege of Rochester; the others are described by M. Paris, *Chronica
   Majora (Rolls Series)*, III, 18–20, 33, 85–8.
10 Walter of Coventry, *Memoriale (Rolls Series)*, II, 219.
11 *Annales Cambriae (Rolls Series)*, 71; Lloyd, *History of Wales*, 674;
   Cal. Close Rolls, 1231–4, 199.
12 *Annales Cambriae (Rolls Series)*, 74; *Cal. Pat. Rolls, 1258–66*, 348.
13 Lloyd, *History of Wales*, 674; *Cal. Pat. Rolls, 1272–81*, 418.
14 M. Paris, *Chronica Majora (Rolls Series)*, III, 64.
15 Lloyd, *History of Wales*, 674; *Annales Cambriae (Rolls Series)*, 93;
   Cal. Pat. Rolls, 1266–72, 106.
16 Lloyd, *History of Wales*, 674; *Cal. Pat. Rolls, 1225–32*, 477.
17 *Flores Historiarum (Rolls Series)*, II, 487.
18 *Annales Monastici, De Waverleia et Wintonia (Rolls Series)*, 101.
19 *Annales Monastici, De Wintonia et Waverleia (Rolls Series)*, 362.
20 *Annales Monastici, De Dunstaplia (Rolls Series)*, 229–30; *Gervase of
   Canterbury (Rolls Series)*, II, 234.
21 *Flores Historiarum (Rolls Series)*, 489–90.
22 *Gervase of Canterbury (Rolls Series)*, 234.
23 *Chronicle of Bury St. Edmunds*, ed. A. Grandison, Nelson's Medieval
   Texts, 1965, 32.
24 *Cal. Pat. Rolls, 1258–66*, 590.
25 *Chronicle of Bury St. Edmunds*, Nelson's Medieval Texts, 34.
26 *Cal. Pat. Rolls, 1258–66*, 596.
27 *Lanercost Chronicle*, ed. J. Stevenson (Bannantyne Club, 1839),
   219–20.
28 *Lanercost Chronicle*, 228–9.
29 *Cal. Pat. Rolls, 1313–17*, 35–6; *Cal. Pat. Rolls, 1307–13*, 555.
30 The *Lanercost Chronicle* states that Edward had come to the town in
   1310, 'which town the king of England had caused to be enclosed with
   a strong high wall and ditch' (214). The statement is supported by
   Cal. Close Rolls, 1288–96, 477, and the *Chronicle of Walter of
   Guisborough*, ed. H. Rothwell (*Camden Soc.*, LXXXIX, 1957), 275.
31 *Lanercost Chronicle*, 230.
32 *Cal. Pat. Rolls, 1313–17*, 347; *Rot Parl.*, I, 302.
33 *Cal. Pat. Rolls, 1313–17*, 512.
34 *Lanercost Chronicle*, 230–32.
35 *Cal. Pat. Rolls, 1321–4*, 7.
36 *Rot. Parl.*, I, 394.
37 *Adam Murimuth (Rolls Series)*, 37–8.

38 *Lanercost Chronicle,* 233.
39 T. Walsingham, *Historia Anglicana (Rolls Series),* I, 266.
40 *Rot. Parl.,* II, 218; P.R.O. C 145/161 (3).
41 *Cal. Pat. Rolls, 1345–8,* 66.
42 J. Whethamstede, *Registrum Abbatiae (Rolls Series),* I, 342–5.
43 J. H. Ramsay, *Lancaster and York,* 1892, II, 243.
44 *Cal. Pat. Rolls, 1452–61,* 657.
45 *Cal. Pat. Rolls, 1452–61,* 602.
46 *Cal. Pat. Rolls, 1452–61,* 528.
47 *Cal. Pat. Rolls, 1452–61,* 441.
48 Quoted from G. Poulson, *Beverlac,* 1829, 229–30.
49 Quoted from *Hist. Mss. Comm.,* 55, Various Colls., IV, 203.
50 *Cal. Pat. Rolls, 1405–1408,* 375.
51 *Cal. Pat. Rolls, 1429–36,* 345.
52 *Cal. Pat. Rolls, 1367–70,* 230.
53 *Cal. Pat. Rolls, 1361–4,* 373.
54 *Cal. Pat. Rolls, 1381–5,* 214; see Gazetteer.
55 *Cal. Pat. Rolls, 1396–9,* 137; *Cal. Pat. Rolls, 1399–1401,* 379.
56 *Cal. Pat. Rolls, 1374–7,* 476.
57 *Cal. Close Rolls, 1385–9,* 342.
58 *Cal. Close Rolls, 1402–1405,* 194–5.
59 *Cal. Close Rolls, 1360–64,* 43.
60 *Cal. Pat. Rolls, 1272–81,* 238.
61 London, *Cal. Pat. Rolls, 1317–21,* 347.
    Portsmouth, *Cal. Pat. Rolls, 1343–5,* 322.
    Coventry, *Cal. Pat. Rolls, 1367–70,* 369.
62 *Foedera,* I, 281.
63 *Cal. Close Rolls, 1339–41,* 215.
64 *Bridgwater Borough Archives,* ed. T. Dilks (*Somerset Record Society,* LVIII, 1945), 57–9, 118–20.
65 *Letter Book D,* 212; *Ibid.,* F, 57; *Ibid.,* H, 64, 127–8, 171–3.
66 R. Howlett, 'Norwich Artillery in the Fourteenth Century', *Norfolk Archaeology,* XVI, 46–75; see pp. 111–12.
67 Leland, *Itinerary,* V, 5.
68 *Hist. Mss. Comm.,* 47th Report, 41.
69 *Letter Book F,* 1.
70 T. Rogers, *History of Prices,* 1866, II, 559; *V. C. H. Hants,* III, 497.
71 R. Howlett, 'Norwich Artillery in the Fourteenth Century', *Norfolk Archaeology,* XVI, 46–75; earlier, Richard Spynk had provided springalds for the gates, F. Blomefield, *History of the County of Norfolk,* 1806, IV, pt. i, 86–7; *Red Register,* ed. H. Ingleby, 1919, II, 27.
72 *Hist. Mss. Comm.,* 5th Report, 138, 140.
73 *Hist. Mss. Comm.,* 5th Report, 490–92; Exeter Receivers' Accounts, 1460–61.
74 *Coventry Leet Book,* ed. M. D. Harris, *E.E.T.S.* Orig. Series, 134–5, 260, 363–4.

CHAPTER SIX

Embattled majesty

It is probably true to say that the primary purpose of a wall was defensive, that it was built for this purpose and was regarded principally in this light. Times of peace, however, might cause the townsmen to feel some resentment against the financial burden imposed by the up-keep of the wall: they might even feel sufficiently secure (or sufficiently resentful) to neglect it completely, certainly to the extent that orders for the removal of dirt and filth, even buildings, from the ditch were common in the late fourteenth century. Many, however, recognized that walls were a protection not only in times of unrest but were also a protection against attackers less organized than armies. It was not necessary to experience a siege before appreciating the benefits of walled protection; far lesser alarms and rumours of disturbance would cause the city authorities to order the closing of all the gates, even during the day, and insistence on the strict observation of the provisions of the Statute of Watch and Ward. Thus at London in September 1297 the mayor and aldermen ordered that the gates were to be well guarded by day and night,[1] and in 1312 they laid down the means for the protection of the City during the 'coming time of parliament', and sent special instructions to the gatekeepers.[2] In 1381 the gates of London were closed against the peasants, who entered the city only because two of the aldermen opened the gates to them,[3] whereas at Norwich the closed gates at least kept the peasants outside the city. At Norwich in 1399 the Council ordered strict watch to be kept at the gates during the time of the deposition of Richard II.[4] The qualities of the two serjeants in charge of each of the London gates were that they should be 'skilful men, fluent of speech, to keep a good watch upon persons coming in and going out so that no evil might befall the city'.[5] The existence of a wall would enable the city authorities to keep a closer check on the movements of people in and out of the town, an important consideration when freedom of movement without guarantees was restricted, and when legal status could be determined by place of residence. A wall was also protection against plague or infected persons entering the city, and at London the gatekeepers were sworn to turn lepers away from the city.[6] Walls were therefore useful as a protection against less serious commotion than war, and their presence was a useful barrier against casual raiders. Walls did not have to fulfil a military role in the narrowest sense of the word : their use in a wider context of protection was not over-looked.

While it is also clear that walls were put to uses far removed from the military considerations which had brought them into existence, there is some evidence to suggest that from the beginning some parts of the defences had been considered to have a dual purpose. By the nature of their design, gates had space over the arch, and from an early period this was put to a variety of peaceful uses. The most common was that of the chapel above the gate, and there are examples of this at Southampton, Exeter and Winchester. At Caernarvon the Exchequer was housed above the east gate, and at Southampton the room above Bar gate served as the Guildhall. In 1311 the gates of London were used to accommodate the Templars, held as prisoners.[7] The non-military uses of a gate are reflected in the non-defensive characteristics of the internal face of the gate, which was built to admit light rather than for defence; and, in the fifteenth century, even the external face was not as heavily fortified as it had been in the fourteenth century, and a gradual relaxation of the defensive characteristics indicates that gates served purposes other than purely military.

Few walls incorporated features which were not entirely for defence; the sole surviving exception is the row of privies built into the wall at Conway (plate 37), a slightly different proposition from the single latrine incorporated in towers at Newcastle and Tenby. But a wall might change character and become less exclusively military almost as soon as it was built. It might be pierced for the passage of drains or aqueducts as happened at Carlisle in 1238,[8] or gates to the friaries built outside the walls might be driven through a wall only recently constructed. Thus at Shrewsbury and Worcester permission was given to the Friars Minor to pierce the wall for a postern.[9] Still further relaxation of the military nature of defences is suggested by the leasing of mural towers to private individuals.

This practice is found early in the thirteenth century, and it may have begun with the aim of defraying some of the costs of construction and maintenance. The tenant had to undertake to keep the tower in repair and to allow the bailiffs of the city free access to it in time of war. In the meantime the city not only saved the money which it would otherwise have had to spend on the up-keep of the tower, but also enjoyed the rents. But the practice must have made the nature of the wall less defensive; the inhabitants inevitably made changes to make the towers into dwelling places. Thus in London, Alexander Swerford was allowed the free use of a turret near Ludgate in 1235 with permission to construct in it such buildings as he pleased.[10] At Gloucester the school of theology attached to the Friars Minor was held in one of the towers, rented annually from the bailiffs for sixpence.[11] On London's wall, from the thirteenth century onwards two, and perhaps four, towers were inhabited regularly by hermits.[12] Later evidence suggests that the leasing of towers and of the rooms above the gates was common practice from 1305 onwards.[13] By the end of the century most of the gates were leased out. Leases similar to those of London are found at Leicester in the mid-fourteenth century and at Norwich at the end of the century.[14]

Such uses must to some extent explain why towns continued throughout the Middle Ages to spend money on the maintenance of their defences. Whether or not such peaceful uses were considered when the initial decision to build a wall was taken is not certain. There is little evidence to show that considerations other than military influenced the construction of a wall, but one of the other possible reasons, the benefit to trade, must be considered.

Two petitions suggest that trade was one of the prime considerations which influenced the decision to build a wall. In 1321 the townsmen of Hull sought permission to wall the town saying that if the town were more secure trade would come there from both England and abroad.[15] They added, as though it were of secondary importance, that they would have protection from the Scots. A similar petition, setting forth the political and commercial advantages the town would enjoy if it were walled, was submitted to Edward II by the men of Beaumaris.[16] This is the only evidence to support the theory that walls were in some cases erected not for defensive reasons, but because they were commercially advantageous. Not only did the existence of a wall encourage trade to come to a town because it was protected, but it prevented people entering the town at any point other than the gates, thereby avoiding payment of tolls due to the city. Tolls, not the wall may, therefore, be the real grievance which caused the strangers of the county to present the citizens of Norwich at the sheriff's tourn because its construction had obstructed the entries to the city which the country folk were accustomed to use.[17]

An indirect piece of evidence to support the contention that the desire to stimulate trade was one of the motives behind the building of walls is the fact that many of the smaller towns obtained their murage grants through the interest of their lord. In many cases it would be he who would benefit from the amount of money which could more easily be collected at the gates, and so many towns may have been walled for the sake of increased trading profits. That the possession of walls could result in increased trade seems to be the explanation for the building of town walls in some cases. At Cowbridge the enclosed area is only thirty-three acres, and the town is situated not in a defensive position, but on the line of a main road; thus as there seems to be no question of defence the walls must have served to regulate ingress and egress and to facilitate the collection of tolls.

The economic advantages to be gained from the possession of a wall could therefore be an explanation for their construction. But to some extent the wall is a reflection of the fortunes and prosperity of the towns. The desire for independence on the part of the towns was not manifested only at the end of the twelfth century. Citizens continued to want a greater degree of control over their own affairs throughout the Middle Ages, and with civic pride is linked the existence and maintenance of fortifications. A wall was the physical expression of the legal separation of the town from the countryside, and what one town had, another must have envied. In much the same way as in the nineteenth century town halls were erected to ornament the newly important towns of the West Riding, so walls were built in the Middle Ages. Thus it was pride as much as considerations of defensive strength which dictated that in the later Middle Ages money should be spent on ever more splendid gates, or on remodelling the parts of the fortifications most likely to attract attention.

That reasons of municipal independence and civic pride were indeed reasons for building defences is shown by comparison of the general characteristics of walled and unwalled towns. Of the 249 in possession of charters by 1520, 108 were walled. Amongst these were the most important commercial centres of the land, independent of all control. The explanation for the lack of defences in those towns which were not walled lies partly in the fact that they were not as large or as prosperous as the others, and partly in the question of ownership. Thus one large group of towns which were not fortified, although for strategic reasons they might be expected to have had defences, were those which were under ecclesiastical lordship.[18] Of the forty-six towns owned by the church only eight were walled : Beverley, Bury St. Edmund's, Bath, Hartlepool, Newark, Lynn and Salisbury. In fact four had been walled by their over-lord; Bath was of Roman, Bury and Newark of pre-Conquest, foundation. The eighth, Taunton, is said to have had defences in the twelfth century which were never rebuilt in stone. The other large group of unfortified towns were those which had been founded deliberately by various classes of overlords. Only ten were planned with defences, six by Edward I and four in connection with a castle to which the town was clearly no more than an appendage. Towns deliberately founded tended to stay under seigneurial control, and the fact that many remained unwalled suggests that there is a clear connection between proprietary interests and lack of fortifications. It was not considered desirable for a town under the control of a lord to have defences.

In the course of time, however, thirty-eight planned towns were given, or acquired walls. As happened at Cowbridge, the lord came to realize that a wall could work to his advantage, and would make the collection of tolls easier, as we have seen. Alternatively the town might be freed from its over-lord, and begin to construct a wall. This is true of Coventry, for example, in the mid-fourteenth century, where the wall was not begun until the town became independent. At Hull it was on the initiative of the townsmen in the early fourteenth century that the walls were built. Other towns planted in the thirteenth century received a charter giving them a blanket permission to provide fortifications; the charters of Salisbury and Montgomery envisaged that the town would be walled.[19] Clearly it was felt that a wall was something which enhanced the dignity of urban status, and the idea was fully developed by the end of the thirteenth century when the wall was considered a necessary part of a town. This is surely the significance which attaches to the story of Edward I beginning the building of the fortifications of Berwick by wheeling a barrow of earth to the top of the bank.[20] Conway and Caernarvon, also founded by Edward, demonstrate the same point. The walls were built not only for protection against the Welsh, but also to impress them with English power and prestige.

The town wall served many purposes. It was primarily the means of defence against attack and a protection against civil disturbances. This was the reason which in most cases had brought the wall into existence. It was then found to have secondary police uses as a means of controlling the movements of individuals and of keeping a check on the ingress and egress of travellers. The collection of tolls was simplified, and the measure of safety given to markets by being 'within the gates' was an additional stimulus to trade. The towers let as dwelling houses brought in useful rents and were maintained without additional expense to the corporation; the gate chambers might provide a town hall, a prison or a chapel.

But town walls brought to the medieval mind more than these practical advantages, more than status and prestige in worldly affairs. It is interesting to imagine what importance the town wall had for people of the Middle Ages. Many towns preserve remains which, impressive even now in their ruined state, must once have been one of the most striking features of the medieval town. Indeed the town wall became the symbol of great cities and is represented in art as their most distinctive feature. In the thirteenth-century seal of the Barons of London part of the city is seen over the wall which predominates in the foreground; in the fifteenth century, Canterbury cathedral is depicted with the wall of the city taking equal prominence. Colchester and Shrewsbury also portrayed the town wall on their seals.[21] In manuscripts too the wall is pictured in the illustrations of a city (plate 2). Such illustrations were rarely the representation of an actual wall, but were usually stylized drawings. Closely scrutinized, however, these miniatures show all the defensive features of an actual wall.

In literature also the wall is the first feature to be described. One literary form, more common on the Continent than in England, was the description of cities based on the writer's own observations or on classical geography.[22] Only three such descriptions of English towns are extant. In Fitzstephen's description of London, which was based on the author's own knowledge, the walls are mentioned only in passing, and it was clearly felt that they were a natural adjunct of a great city.[23] Secondly, there is a late twelfth-century description of Chester.[24] This is based neither on classical sources nor on observation, and 'much is mere verbiage, and metaphor and allegory are worked to death' in an attempt to endow the walls with mystical virtues. Lastly, there is the mid-twelfth-century description of Durham, which is perhaps the most accurate of the descriptions of English towns and the most matter of fact.[25] The author describes the nature of the site briefly, and goes on to amplify his statement without exaggeration of the details. The impression left is that of a town strongly fortified by both art and nature. Such descriptions are in no way reliable architecturally, and they make no attempt to be accurate stone by stone descriptions, but they are interesting because they show that walls were accepted as part of a town. In other cases the literary model required far greater exaggeration of the truth. The description of Carthage in Aeneas, for example, sums up the contemporary feeling of what a wall should be.[26]

Only a few made any attempt to portray a wall as it might really appear (plate 1). The description of the foundation of Troy[27] draws a recognizable picture of a wall :

> And at the corner of every wall was set
> A crowne of gold with riche stones fret
> That stone full bright against the sonneshene,
> And every tour bretexed was so clene
> Of chose stone (that were not thi asondre)
> That to behold it was a very wonder.
> Therto this city compassed enviroun
> Had sexe gatis to entre into toun.
> The first of al and most principal
> Of mighty building allone peereless
> Was by the king called Dardanydes
> Strong and mighty both in war and peace
> With square toures set on every side
> At whos corners of verray pomp and pride
> The workmen hav with stern and fel visages
> Of rich entaille set up gret ymages
> Wrought out of stone.

The emphasis, however, is always on the strength of the walls, and, as in the oath of the shipmasters of the great fleet of Spain who swore to hold against all men as firmly as stone lies on stone in the wall of the town of Dover,[28] this was perhaps the attribute which medieval man appreciated most, whatever the allegorical or imaginative possibilities the poets might attribute to the walls.

NOTES

1 Quoted from H. T. Riley, *Memorials of London*, 1868, 35–6.
2 *Letter Book D*, 292.
3 B. Wilkinson, 'The Peasants Revolt of 1381', *Speculum*, 1940, XV, 12–35.
4 F. Blomefield, *History of the County of Norfolk*, 1806, IV, 115.
5 *Letter Book C*, 85.
6 *Letter Book H*, 9.
7 *Cal. Close Rolls, 1307–13*, 308.
8 *Cal. Close Rolls, 1237–42*, 53–4.
9 *Cal. Close Rolls, 1242–7*, 445; *Cal. Close Rolls, 1227–31*, 566–7.
10 *Cal. Pat. Rolls, 1232–47*, 106.
11 *Cal. Close Rolls, 1242–7*, 447.
12 Rotha M. Clay, *The Hermits and Anchorites of England*, 1914, 66–8.
13 *Letter Book C*, 143, 152; *Ibid.*, E, 39, 49, 84; *Ibid.*, G, 327; *Ibid.*, H, 2, 15, 97, 208, 288, 433.
14 M. Bateson, *Records of the Borough of Leicester*, 1899–1901, II, 55–7, 259, 265; Norwich City Archives, 1378–9 *et passim*.
15 *Rot. Parl.*, II, 385.
16 Quoted from E. A. Lewis, *The Medieval Boroughs of Snowdonia*, 1912, 102.
17 Quoted from W. Hudson and J. C. Tingey, *Records of the City of Norwich*, 1906–1910, I, 59.
18 The figures are taken from Sir W. Savage, *The Making of our Towns*, 1952, 94.
19 *Cal. Ch. Rolls*, I, 10; *Sarum Charters and Documents*, 175–8 *(Rolls Series)*.
20 *The Chronicle of Walter of Guisborough*, ed. H. Rothwell *(Camden Soc., 1957)*, 275.
21 *Catalogue of Seals in the Department of Manuscripts in the British Museum*, W. de G. Birch, 1892, II.
22 J. K. Hyde, 'Medieval Descriptions of Cities', *Bulletin John Rylands Library*, 48, 1966, 308–340.
23 *Materials for the History of Thomas Becket (Rolls Series)*, III, 2–13.
24 *De Laude Cestrie*, ed. M. V. Taylor, *Trans. Lancs. and Cheshire Hist. Soc.*, LXIV, 1912.
25 *Dialogi Laurentii Dunelmensis Monachi et Prioris*, ed. J. Raine, Surtees Soc. 70, 1880.
26 G. D. West, 'The Description of Towns in Old French Verse', *French Studies*, XI, 1957, 50–59.
27 Lydgate, Troy Book II.
28 *Cal. Inq. Misc.*, IV, 57.

GAZETTEER

PART I

The North

York is the only town where a continuous history of fortification from the Roman period seems probable; other settlements, despite the turbulence of the late tenth and eleventh centuries, were apparently undefended. The allegorical poem, the *Dialogi Laurentii*, describes Durham as a strongly fortified centre by the middle years of the twelfth century, and on the western coast it was perhaps matched by Carlisle. Scarborough and Newcastle began to build defences in the thirteenth century, and the frequency of Scottish raids in the second and third decades of the fourteenth century impelled seven towns to seek the means to protect themselves against further incursions. A further two towns, Alnwick and Warkworth, both closely connected with the Percy family and thus likely to be involved in warfare, were fortified in the fifteenth century.

ALNWICK   Only murage grant 1434 (*CPR*, 345). From 1452, £20 was to be received from customs duties annually for 30 years (G. Tate, *History of Alnwick*, 1866, 238). William, bishop of Norwich, left £10 towards the cost in 1449, and further permission to raise money was received in 1474 (Tate, 240–41). Although this suggests that the building of the walls may have been a long-drawn out process, the dating of the Bondgate can be more closely fixed, since in 1450 Matthew, the mason of Alnwick abbey, was paid £1 10s for carving the stone lion over the archway, now much weathered (illustrated in C. H. Hartshorne, *Illustrations of Alnwick, Prudhoe and Warkworth*, 1857, 84). In the same year £17 17s 2d was spent on the gate itself (Alnwick Mss CVIII.l.e.). The wall can be traced on the line of Hotspur Street and the Green Batt to the site of the former Clayport gate, and thence along Dispensary Street to Pottergate. The present structure is an eighteenth-century re-building of the medieval gate. The walls then ran down Northumberland Street and turned east to cross Narrow gate where there was a small tower

(OS 1st ed. 25). They then merged with the castle defences, from whose southern side a short spur wall may have run as far as Bondgate (G. Skelly, *Procs. of the Soc. of Antiquaries of Newcastle on Tyne*, VIII, 1897–8, 19; M. R. G. Conzen, *Trans. of Institute of British Geographers*, 27, 1-48).

Bondgate is built of large blocks of ashlar, and consists of a single four-centred arch flanked by two rectangular chambers. Portcullis grooves remain in front of the entrance to each chamber, which was centrally placed in the archway. Twin towers, three storeys high, project in front of the arch, built on square plinths with the corners canted off at a height of about two feet; the divisions between the floor levels are clearly marked by two string courses which are continuous across the southern face of the gate. Crenellations are now missing, but that they once existed is suggested by the stone corbels which now project above the arch. One small window in each end face lit the lower rooms; the middle chambers had three small slits each, but the top floor may have been unlit on the southern side; the present slit may be a modern insertion. On the interior face the windows are larger; one, centrally placed and presumably lighting the space above the arch, is of two lights; on the eastern side is a mullioned four-pane window, perhaps enlarged from the original two lights. The western tower was apparently lit only by a slit, perhaps because the stair rose from the chamber below at this point. The two windows of the top floor are now blocked (plate 5).

The abutment of the wall is still visible on the western side, six feet wide and standing about fifteen feet high, the level of the first string course.

BERWICK   First murage grant 1313 (*CPR*, 36). Other grants and allowances were intermittent throughout the fourteenth century (Appendices B & C, and see also *The King's Works*).

The extent of pre-Edwardian defences is not known, but possibly the earth-work known as the Spades Mire is to be regarded in this light (K. G. White, *PSAS*, xcvi, 355-60). Much of the fourteenth-century circuit was destroyed in the new construction of the sixteenth-century, but these later fortifications excluded the medieval wall on the north-west, and the earlier work remains at the Bell tower, which stands on a wide bank above a ditch. The north-east corner and the eastern line of the medieval defences can still be traced although a certain amount of levelling and infilling was carried out in the seventeenth century. The medieval wall formed the defence of the area known as the Lower Town until the early eighteenth-century, but it is now lost. None of the original entrances to the town survives. (I. Macivor, *Antiq. Jnl.*, XLV, 64-96.)

A plan of the medieval defences is in B. M. Cotton Augustus, I (ii), 14.

BEVERLEY No murage grants. A petition to parliament in 1321–2 indicates a desire to wall the town, but the reply was that the king wanted to study the charters and to consult the archbishop of York (*Rot. Parl.*, I, 394) and no more is known of the proposals. In 1371, when a commission of array was issued to 'provide against the dangers which may happen to the town, and to the inhabitants by reason of the defect of the fortifications' the suggestion is that the town was not very strongly defended (*CPR*, 101). The initial impetus to wall the town might have followed an attack by a Scots raiding party in 1321 (*Adam Murimuth, Rolls Series*, 37-8), and there are references to gates and ditches in the Beverley cartulary from the early fourteenth-century (quoted in J. J. Sheahan, *The Town of Beverley*, 1856, 36), and intermittent references to the upkeep of bars in the town accounts in the fourteenth and fifteenth-centuries (A. F. Leach, *Beverley Town Documents*, Selden Society, XIV, 31; G. Poulson, *Beverlac*, 1829).

The North Bar, the only town gateway to be built in brick still extant, was constructed between 1409–1410 at a cost of £97 17s 4½d the work being carried out under the direction of William Rolleston and other members of the town council. It is a square structure, single arched and built in three stages. Portcullis grooves and wooden folding doors remain. The north face is buttressed, with two recesses and a modern window. The south face displays three recesses below a gabled string course, and two small windows above it. Two slight buttresses rise to the much restored parapets. The chamber above the arch, in which was housed the machinery to raise and lower the portcullis, was probably reached from the wall or perhaps by an external stair; there were no guard chambers from which an internal stair might rise (J. Bilson, *Trans. East Riding Antiq. Soc.*, IV, 1896, 38-39; A. F. Leach, *Ibid*, 26-27). Plate 6.

Leland wrote that he could not see that the town had ever been walled (*Itinerary*, V, 39) and certainly all that now remains to be seen is a bank and ditch. Its course can be traced west from North Bar along York Road and the western line runs past Westwood Hospital to the site of Newbegin Bar across Westwood Road. From there the ditch continued south on the line of Sloe Lane, turning east along Rutt Lane, and being preserved in the line of the municipal boundary as far as England's Springs. From this point its course is no longer clear because of housing. Poulson wrote that the defences were connected with the Walkergate drains (in the south-east corner) and could be seen easily only in the grounds of the present St. Mary's Manor house, and thence returned to the North Bar. The four other bars in the circuit have been destroyed.

CARLISLE The documentary evidence shows an almost continuous picture of construction. Rufus visited the town in 1092, and is said to have 'set up the walls' (*Two Saxon Chronicles Parallel*, ed. C. Plummer, I, 227), and in 1122 Henry I ordered the city to be fortified with 'castle and towers' (Symeon of Durham, *Historia Regum, Rolls Series, II*, 267). The Pipe Roll of 1130 records the expenditure of £14 16s 6d (*Pipe Roll 31 Henry I*, 140) which is probably to be connected with Henry's command, and makes Carlisle one of the earliest towns in England to be fortified after the Conquest. Further work was in progress when in 1164 10s 6d was spent on the gates (*Pipe Roll 11 Henry II*, 54), and in 1190 when 19s 5d was spent on the gates and on a granary (*Pipe Roll 2 Richard I*, 49).

The first murage grant was received in 1232 (*CPR*, 483). Grants were almost continuous throughout the thirteenth century (Appendix C), but less frequent in the fourteenth century when alternative means to provide the money for defences had to be found. The constable of the castle in 1324 was commanded to carry out the repairs which the king had ordered to the walls (*CPR*, 406) and in 1331 the payment of £40 of the fee farm of the city was pardoned 'in consideration of the damage sustained by the frequent comings of the Scots' (*CCR*, 194). By 1344 it was estimated that £300 was still needed to repair the damage; by 1348 the estimate was £500 (*Cal. Inq. Misc.*, II, no. 1093, & III, no. 3; P.R.O. C 145/152 [4] & 161 [3]). The citizens sent a petition to parliament asking for help, saying that six perches of the wall were on the point of collapse, and part had already fallen (*Rot. Parl.* II, 218). It is perhaps significant that in 1345 there had been a commission of audit into the murage accounts (*CPR*, 587). Despite the petition the only record of repair is the account of William of Windsor, who spent £162 11s 4½d on repairs to both castle and town walls in 1367–8 (P.R.O. E 364/3, m.G). The wording of a second petition in 1376 suggests that the defences were still in a very bad condition; it stated that the gates could not be closed, nor the bridges raised, and that the number of citizens had so diminished that they could scarce defend a quarter of the city (*Rot. Parl.* II, 345). No answer was received until after a third petition had been submitted in 1379 (*Rot. Parl.* III, 63-4) in which it was said that the repair of the city was not the king's responsibility, but that he would cause orders to be given to those whose responsibility it was. In case 1386–7 £80 was spent on materials, in 1390 £139 3s 10d (P.R.O. E 101/483/3, E 364/26 m.B, E 364/29 m.G). In 1395 £60 was spent on the walls of both the town and the castle (P.R.O. E 364/30 m.F, 1395). In 1399 £200 was assigned for the same purposes, but there is no record to show that anything was done (P.R.O. E 404/15/99).

In 1409 the citizens were still complaining that their defences were ruinous, and they received an annual grant of £13 for ten years for repairs (*CPR*, 40), and a grant of the fines and the profits of justice towards the general cost of defence in 1410 (*CPR*, 192). In 1421 the defects in the buildings of the castle and in the town walls were surveyed by William Stapilton and Christopher Boynton, and in the next year £286 16s 8¾d was spent in repairs (*CPR*, 408; P.R.O. E 364 m.B). In 1438 an annual grant of £80 from the fee farm was received for three years, on condition that a sum equal to the fee farm was spent in the first year. The overseer of the works, John Skipton, had already spent £80 on the materials, and ready shaped stones were waiting to be used (*CPR*, 538).

The walls enclosed an area of forty-five acres. Their course is known from a plan in the Cotton Augustus manuscript, (B. M. Cotton Augustus I (i) 13) (plate 4) and from Speed's plan of 1610. There were three gates in the circuit: Caldew gate to the north-west, Richard gate to the east and Bocher gate to the south. None of these now survives, but prints in the Castle Museum show that they were simple rectangular single arched structures.

From the north-east side of the castle the wall ran along West

Tower Street and East Tower Street, where it turned south on the line of Lowther Street to the Citadel. From that point the wall has disappeared, but it can be seen again from a promenade below the line of the street, West Walls. It returned to join the castle defences on the line of Devonshire Walk.

Little of the fabric of the walls remains. A short section is visible by the car park in Bitts Park off Finkle Street. The section is about fifty-five feet (16.76 m.) long, standing to a height of about five feet (1·52 m.) (*Trans. Cumb. & Westm. Antiq. & Arch. Soc.*, N.S. XVI, 1916, 291). The northern, exterior side represents the top courses of the wall protecting the wall walk since excavation showed that earth has accumulated only to a depth of about nine feet (2.74 m.). Excavation against the interior face showed an accumulation of fourteen feet (4.27 m.), an amount sufficient to bury the parapet walk. The condition of the masonry was said to be excellent, and was dated to the twelfth century (*Trans. Cumb. & Westm. Antiq. & Arch. Soc.*, N.S. LXII, 1962, 326–7). It is certainly very different from the masonry visible in the West Walls, being of smaller, more regularly sized blocks. On the southern side of the street, West Walls, the wall can be viewed for a length of about eight hundred feet (243.84 m.). The masonry is of local sandstone cut into large and irregularly sized rectangular blocks. Much of the work in this section is patching, and the wall no longer remains to its original height. The crenellations have disappeared, and many stones in the double chamfered base plinth have been replaced. By the steps the plinth consists only of a single chamfer. Possibly this section was in existence by 1238 when the Friars Preacher had permission to breach the wall to bring an aqueduct to their property which stood near the junction of Blackfriars Street with Victoria Viaduct (*CPR*, 53–4).

The siege of the town, described in the Lanercost Chronicle (ed. J. Stevenson, 1839, 230–32) is illustrated in a vignette in the initial letter of the charter of 1315, (plate 3).

DURHAM   Murage was granted twice, in 1315 (*Rot. Parl.* I, 302) and in 1337 (*CPR*, 387), perhaps for the enclosing of the town north of the castle from the North gate across Clay path to the River Wear by Walkergate, and thence south to Bridge gate and the castle. The cathedral precinct and the town lying south of the castle may have

been walled by Bishop Ranulph Flambard (1099–1128), their course
lying along Broken Walls and Prebends Walk to Water gate and
returning to the castle below the line of South and North Bailey.
Kingsgate stood at the bottom of Bow Street, where a short stretch
of masonry remains, and North gate at the top of Sadler Street.
These were the fortifications described in the poem the *Dialogi
Laurentii*, not stone by stone but as an impressive whole (ed. J.
Raine, *Surtees Soc.* 70, 1880).

HARTLEPOOL   First murage grant was in 1315 (*CPR*, 347), and
there were other intermittent grants until the early fourteenth century. The fortifications are portrayed on Dromeslawer's drawing
(no date) (B. M. Hatfield Mss. f. 4) but it is difficult to relate this
to the modern street plan. Sandwell gate, on Town Wall, alone
remains. The upper stages of the structure cannot be reconstructed,
but it seems probable that the gate was intended for use as a watergate rather than as a purely defensive work, since it opens onto the
shore. It is a single arched structure, flanked by two solid triangular
buttresses. There are no guard chambers. About fifteen feet from
the base a plinth projects, decreasing into a second, thinner band
a little higher up. Neither thickened band of masonry continues
across the gate, although the upper band connects with a thin string
course which may have marked the internal division into floors. A
pointed and segmented arch with two groined ribs supported the
superstructure. The interior face is now flush with the wall, but it
may not always have been so. The gate is built of large ashlar blocks,
and now stands about twenty-five feet (7.62 m.) high. Its plan is
unique amongst the town gates of Britain (plate 7).

KINGSTON UPON HULL   The first murage grant was received
in 1321 (*CPR*, 7), followed by others throughout the fourteenth
century. A chamberlain's account for 1321–3 shows that £110 was
spent on constructing a ditch and bank, £142 on timber and £40
on stone and brick (Corporation Records, M.479 [1]). A second
account of 1361–2 shows the receipts of murage (M.4).
   All traces of the walls and the four gates were destroyed by the
construction of the docks in the nineteenth century (J. Hirst, *Trans.
of East Riding Antiquarian Soc.* III, 1894, 24–39); a plan of the
town was drawn by Hollar *c.* 1640 (*VCH Yorks, E. Riding*, 412).

LANCASTER The town received its only grant of murage in 1316 (*CPR,* 512). There are no remains, and Speed's plan makes it doubtful whether any work, other than the repair of Roman fortifications, was done.

NEWCASTLE ON TYNE The first grant was received in 1265[1], and the series was nearly continuous until 1384;[2] from 1403[3] onwards money for the walls was supplied from other sources, possibly in addition to a regular levy of murage, from fines, ransoms, amercements and other profits from pleas or from the remission of subsidies granted in Parliament.

There are, however, a few indications of the progress of the work of enclosure. By 1246 there was already at least one gate, for in that year the sheriff of Northumberland was ordered to carry out its repairs.[4] It could well be that this refers to the Newgate, since this was on the road through the town to the castle and the bridge. It is not known whether there was an earlier circuit of earthen defences, and so it is impossible to say whether this gate was connected with defences or stood in isolation. The latter seems more probable since from later grants it is clear that the wall was being driven through land already built up, and was destroying property. Thus Hugh of Merchingleigh was paid compensation for the loss of property through the building of the wall. Merchingleigh lands lay on the west side of the town,[5] and indeed most of the documentary evidence concerning the walls refers to the sections between Newgate (Newgate Street) and the River Tyne at Riverside tower.

In 1280 the Friars Preachers, whose lands were in the north-west angle of the wall, were granted licence to make a narrow gate through the new wall to their garden.[6] Two openings in the wall now exist between the Heber and Morden towers, either of which could be the postern in question. The phrase 'new wall' in this context probably does not imply the existence of an older wall, but means one recently erected.

In 1290, ten years later, a licence was granted to the master and brethren of the hospital of St. Mary to 'make a postern in the wall now in making round the said town, the foundation of which has been commenced through the middle of the hospital'.[7] Their property lay under the site of the present Central Station.

This completes the documentary information for the building of the west walls, which bears out the observations of G. B. Richardson on the construction of the towers. He noted nine single-chambered towers (from Whitefriars tower to Morden tower) and six two-storied (Ever to Plummer towers).[8] The nine all lie within the area referred to in the documents and may therefore be of similar date, of the late thirteenth century.

Crossing to the east side of the town there is a grant of all lands in Pandon to the burgesses 'to be united with and included in the same town for the bettering and securing thereof', made in 1298.[9] The wall between the Corner tower and the Tyne is therefore to be dated after this. That the wall was built fairly soon is shown by a grant to the Prior and Carmelite friars 'of the place where the friars of the Sack used to dwell, in consideration of the new wall of the town passing through their close near the church'.[10] The fact that friaries are often to be found outside defences suggests that this grant refers to the angular extension of the wall on the east side, from the Corner tower to the Tyne.

An inquisition of 1300 makes reference to a tower near the Austin Friars;[11] presumably that which later came to be called the Austin tower so that one may assume the wall in this section to have been built by this date. It seems likely that by 1300 the circuit was nearly complete (the six two-storied towers may be slightly later than the single-storied); but it does not seem likely that the northern sector of the defences remained incomplete until the late fourteenth century as the names of the towers might suggest.[12] There is moreover an inquisition of 1314[13] into the destruction of property outside the north gate alleged by the bishop of Carlisle. The bishop was given compensation for the houses destroyed, for the building of the wall and the repair of the ditch.

The documentary evidence of the fourteenth century suggests that only repair work was being undertaken. In 1336 the keeper of the manor of Bywell was ordered to supply twenty oaks for the construction of the drawbridge, and for the repair of the West gate and the bridge.[14] In 1337 the mayor and bailiffs were ordered to spend up to forty pounds on the works.[15] The gate was said to be in the weakest part of the defences and in great part destroyed or broken. Although repair work continued no specific building work is known to have been undertaken until 1407, when a tax on coal was licensed for the construction of a high tower on the walls.[16] It

is tempting to relate this to the rebuilding of the watch-tower between the Heber and Morden towers noticed by Parker Brewis.
With this grant documentary information about the wall ceases.

The walls were surrounded by a ditch. In 1308 the Carmelites
were paid compensation of nineteen marks for the destruction of
property when the wall and ditch were taken through their buildings
which at that time lay close to the Wall Knoll tower on the east
side of the town.[17] A ditch also ran along the north walls and, as
appears in an inquisition taken in January 1317, had been cut in
1297–8.[18] The line of the ditch continued south to the river. The
Friars Preachers obtained a licence to construct a swing bridge over
it in 1312.[19] They already had a postern through the wall to their
garden and it is possible that the new licence indicates that the
ditch in this area had only recently been cut in 1312. In the preceding year 1311,[20] the community of Newcastle was ordered to
construct the ditch and wall by the mill of the hospital of St. Mary
Westgate, thus suggesting that the date of the ditch is slightly
earlier than the date of 1312–16 recently suggested.[21]

The walls are two miles in circumference, and they enclosed an
area of 150 acres. There were originally nineteen towers and seven
main gates (plate 8). Eight towers remain, but the gates have all
been destroyed. The character of the remaining masonry is remarkably uniform, consisting of large ashlar blocks, well coursed, with a
chamfered plinth at the base.

On the east side of the town the first remaining part of the defences is Wall Knoll tower. Any original work was obscured by
Dobson's superstructure and the surrounding buildings. The line of
the wall appears to have come up very steeply from the river, and
from this tower to have run across Pandon Dene though no trace
remains.[22] The wall re-appears at the Corner tower. The wall walk
passes through this tower, and the word tower is something of a
mis-nomer. It is no more than a covered passage for the walk as it
turns through a right angle. This suggests that the wall was at least
planned on a different line from that which it finally took, and was
probably intended to run straight down the hill. It can only have
been after the grant of Pandon in 1298 that this change of plan
occurred. On the inside of the wall the walk rests on corbels, and
there are traces of steps leading up to the walk. From this point the
wall has been obliterated by railway building; beyond Manors

Station it followed the line of Carliol Square to the Plummer tower. This has been much altered, and the internal arrangements have been lost. The back wall of the tower is flush with the wall on the inside, and the tower is semi-circular. The wall-walk passed through at first-floor level. The external appearance is even more difficult to reconstruct. Windows have been pushed through, but originally there may have been three slits at first-floor level, visible now as blocked up windows. There is a double chamfered plinth at the base of both the tower and the wall.[23]

From this point until St. Andrew's church yard is reached the alignment of Blackett Street destroyed the Carliol, Ficket and Monboucher towers, and the Pilgrim and New gates. There is thus no evidence for the appearance of the north walls except that provided in the drawings of the gates by Brand and Richardson.[24] In St. Andrew's churchyard the back wall of the Andrew tower can be seen in section in the wall, which runs on the north side of the church. The external face was destroyed in 1827–30. At the west side of the church yard the remains of a watch tower similar to the work at the Corner tower can be seen, as well as the corbels which carried the wall walk.

The wall continues on the west side of Newgate Street along Back Stowell Street to Bath Lane. The Ever, Morden, Heber, and Durham Towers lie on this section, presenting a semi-circular front to the field and having a slight rectangular projection within the line of the wall. The Ever tower was excavated in 1938, and its plan laid out in concrete by the side of the Bus Station.[25] It is thought that the Ever tower might have been built earlier than the others since it fits awkwardly in to relationship with the wall at a change in its direction. This might, however, be accounted for by the same explanation offered for a feature noticed at the Durham and Heber towers by Parker Brewis.[26] At the junction of the curtain wall with the north sides of these towers the ashlar of the towers is not coursed with, nor bonded with, that of the walls. It was suggested that this might either have been intentional, to allow of settlement of the towers without tearing them from the walls, or that it was the result of building the towers before the curtain wall.

The towers had similar, though not identical, arrangements. All were built of ashlar in well coursed blocks. The Durham tower has a single plinth at its base (plate 9), the Heber tower a double one.

The chambers were rectangular, and the towers were built in three storeys. At the Durham tower the ground floor room is seen to have had a vaulted roof, carried on three ribbed arches. Three embrasures with arrow slits provided the means of defence. The wall walk and the second floor chamber were reached by a flight of stone steps in the north angle of the room. The walk passed through this chamber, and was thus completely covered over. Nothing remains above this level at this tower, but at the Heber tower the stone steps lead up to a third floor. Otherwise the arrangements are the same, but with the interesting addition of a latrine built into the external face of the tower. There are at both these towers corbel stones built into the wall, some of two stones (Heber tower), others of three (Durham and the now demolished Pink towers). These were presumably intended to carry wooden bretasches. Of the Morden tower little can be seen; the upper storey was rebuilt in the seventeenth century. The most interesting feature of this section of the wall, however, is the watch turrets, of which there is one approximately halfway between each tower. Traces of one, largely destroyed when Stowell Street was driven through the wall, can be seen on the south side of the road. The most impressive turret is the one between the Heber and Morden towers (plate 11). It has at some date been rebuilt, since slight settlement is visible both inside and out, but the upper courses of the curtain are now level.[27] This may therefore be the tower which was specified in the grant of 1407. The wall walk passed through the turrets, ascending by a few steps which were protected by stepped merlons. The walk formed a chamber inside the turret, with a single loop facing outwards. The chamber was thirteen feet (3.96 m.) in length and two feet eleven inches (0.889 m.) wide. This was insufficient for drawing the bow; so behind the loop there is a rectangular recess in the wall to provide elbow space. On the outside there was a stone stair for access to the roof. The inside wall of the turrets starts with a corbel table at the level of the wall walk, the spaces between the corbels being bridged by a flagged course, and surmounted by squarish ashlar. Externally the turrets are flush with the walls but they had machicolations to defend the base of the curtain. Their tops were ornamented with carved stone demi-figures, similar to those found at Alnwick Castle.[28]

These turrets are a feature unparalleled in any other English town though they are to be found at Alnwick Castle, on the curtain wall, where again they are a unique feature in English castle architecture. The only parallel found for them so far is at Visby. It is not, however, very exact, since the Visby examples do not rise from the wall itself, but are placed saddle-wise across it.[29]

From the site of the West gate to the river almost nothing of the wall remains. Under the Gunner tower, which can be seen in Pink Lane, coins of Edward I were found in 1821.[30] The tower was similar to Durham tower. As far as can be judged from prints all the towers on this section were like those just described, except for the Whitefriar tower which seems to have had an octangular lower storey with a circular superstructure. They were destroyed to make way for the railway. The section of wall which has been incorporated in the Newcastle United Breweries is very similar to the Bath Lane stretch, though it stands here to its original height, complete with parapet, of about twenty feet (6·10 m.).[31] The wall ran along the Quayside,[32] with a gate at the bridge, to the gate at the bottom of Pandon Dene, Sandgate.[33]

The details of the towers are sufficiently similar to suggest that they were all built within a relatively short space of time, and the documentary evidence points to the later years of the thirteenth and the early years of the fourteenth century. The years 1265–1318 define the period of greatest activity.

PENRITH   The first murage grant was received in 1346 (*CPR*, 66), a second in 1391 (*CPR*, 499). There are no remains and it is not certain how much work may have been done.

RICHMOND   The first murage grant was received in 1313 (*CPR*, 555), and a second in 1337 (*CPR*, 414). There is no obvious line for defences, but a small tower to the west of the castle, and a bar across the western exit from Finkle Square are shown on OS 6 in., NZ 10 SE.

SCARBOROUGH   First murage grant was received in 1225 (*CPR*, 508), and others were intermittent throughout the thirteenth and fourteenth centuries. Other documentary evidence suggests, however, that the wall was in poor condition; in 1304 John Pychford was permitted to repair 200 feet (60.96 m.) of wall already in a state of collapse and then to build houses on it (*CPR*, 220). In 1312 it was found that Robert Uttred had a house which had destroyed 100 feet (30.48 m.) of wall (*Cal Inq. Misc.*, II, no. 144). Possibly, however, these buildings had only encroached on the part of the wall already rendered useless, since the street names 'Awburgh' and 'Newburgh' suggest an extension of the defences to include new settlement (M. Andrews, *The Story of Old Scarborough*, 1947, 34–7). There are no traces of defences. The remains of two towers on either side of Awburgh gate were found in 1812. Leland noted that the town was walled 'a little with stone, but mostly with ditches and walls of earth' (*Itinerary*, I, 59).

WARKWORTH   There is no documentary evidence, and it must remain an open question whether the town was ever completely walled. It is enclosed by a loop of the River Coquet, and is dominated by the castle; the remains of the town defences consist only of a single gate defending the bridgehead. There are, however, signs of a wall standing about twelve feet (3.66 m.) high which butted onto the eastern wall of the gate, which suggests the possibility of a complete circuit.

The gate is built of squared ashlar blocks and is rectangular in plan, measuring twenty-seven feet three inches (8.31 m.) by eighteen feet (5.49 m.) (S. Toy, *The Castles of Great Britain*, 1954, 262). The single archway was flanked on its western side by a guard-house, lit by narrow slits in the north and south walls. The vault of the arch is unribbed, and there is no sign that there was ever a portcullis, although there was a heavy door at the outer end of the gateway. Access to the upper floor was by a stair entered through a door opposite the guard chamber, and lit by three slits in the eastern wall. The original arrangements of the upper storey cannot be accurately restored; one large window, perhaps a modern insertion, faces north, and two smaller windows face into the town (plate 10).

YORK   The interest at York lies less in the fabric of the walls, which have been much re-built, than in the attempt to trace the extensions of the wall within the Middle Ages. The line of the medieval walls does not coincide exactly with that of the Roman defences, which were used in the later work only at the Multangular tower, although they dictated the course of the medieval wall in the south-west angle and on the western and northern sides.

The Roman Multangular tower, which marks the south-west corner, was incorporated in the medieval circuit; the medieval wall ran east on Roman foundations to St. Leonard's Hospital gate, and north to Bootham Bar, built on the site of the Roman west gate. From this point to the site of the north-east tower of the Roman fort the medieval wall is built on a high-bank which completely covers the Roman wall (plate 13). The bank was deliberately constructed and was not the result of the accidental accumulation of earth. Excavations conducted between 1925 and 1927 showed that the mound consisted of two thick strata of beaten occupation earth.[34] The lower stratum related to the Roman fortress wall. The upper covered the remains of the Roman wall, but neither appears beyond the eastern Roman tower where the wall continues to Layerthorpe. The excavators' conclusion was that the Normans had covered the Roman walls and extended the defences as far as the Ouse and the Foss at either end. More recent excavation has shown that there was a Danish, then a Norman and finally a thirteenth century bank.[35]

It seems possible also that one can date closely the section of wall running south to the river, where there is no bank underneath the stone walls. In 1260 the abbot and convent of St. Mary were given permission to build a stone wall below their abbey, and as far as the infirmary of the Hospital.[36] A detailed map shows that the medieval city wall joined the south wall of the Roman fort at exactly this point.[37]

The earth rampart existed at least to the point at which the Roman fortress wall turned south at the north-east angle tower, but it did not always cover the Roman work. Thus from Monk Bar to the angle, the medieval wall can be seen about twenty feet in front of the line of the Roman work, and the later wall was built on arcades perhaps to relieve some of the downward pressure on the bank. The medieval wall continued on an embankment until it reached Layerthorp. Beyond the angle tower the wall turns slightly to the south-east and then at an acute angle to the north-east to reach the postern at Layerthorp. The Custody of the Walls dated to 1315–16 mentions the section from Layerthorp to Monk Bar as one unit,[38] but the later Custody of 1380 divides the section into four parts.[39] The first was from Monk Gate to St. Helen's; the second from there to the tower on Herlothill by Peterhall; the third from there to the new tower over the corner by Jubiry; and lastly from there to Layerthorp. By 1380 the tower may no longer have been very new, but the document does show that in this section the wall was still under construction in the fourteenth century. Exact dates for the present line of the northern defences cannot be obtained, but it seems probable that the embankment is of mid-twelfth, and the stone wall of early or mid-fourteenth century date.

We must turn now to consider the whole question of the eastern defences of the city. It is not possible to say for how long the post Roman settlement at York remained bounded by the walls of the fort. Beyond the south wall there is only the church of St. Martin, mentioned in Domesday Book,[40] to suggest expansion in this area, and the main development of the city seems to have been concentrated in an eastward spread. Whereas parish boundaries run more or less on the southern line of the fort they take no account of the east wall, and by the end of the eleventh century there were at least eight churches outside its line. Cooper suggested that there was a Saxon line of defence on the line of Coppergate, Pavement, Saviourgate and so to the bend in the wall in St. Maurice's Road.[41] But there is no archaeological proof of the existence of such a wall, and perhaps little need to postulate its existence. If the line of the northern defences was continued to the Foss as seems probable, there is no need to have an east wall; the river would have been sufficient protection.

If such an eastern line existed it was only temporary, and was replaced at some date by the line of the wall as it now stands from the Red tower to Fishergate tower. The dates of the first references to churches suggest a steady expansion eastwards.[42] The area is known as Walmgate, and it is possible that the bank here, as elsewhere round the city, was constructed in the mid-twelfth century, since there is a reference to Walmgatebarre between 1150 and 1161.[43] Cooper stated that the area had been walled in 1215, but later said that it was not walled until the later thirteenth century.[44] There is no proof of his statements. It is also possible that the gate existed in isolation before the rest of the defences, and that the murage grant of 1267, which stated that it was for the 'enclosing

1. The siege and fall of Troy.

a ſeconde deſtruction de troye fait miceulx a racote
que la premiere car dion a cele raiſon. Si quel quant
le roy priain qui fut fitz du roy laomedon ouyt ſel mo
a la deſtruction de ſon pere. la confuſion du pays e le
et des barons e cheualiers e le rauiſſement de ſa ſuer. Si ke
a troye le plus toſt quil peut. Laquelle trouua deſtruite
unme luy deſſus dit. Si fiſt merueilleux dueil e plora ſa feme
enfas e ſa cheualerie qui auec luy eſtoyent Le premier fiz de
Le roy priain auoit belle femme e noble e roy vaillant
De grant linaige qui ecuba auoit nom Pa roy me auoit

2. *The pilgrims leave Canterbury.*

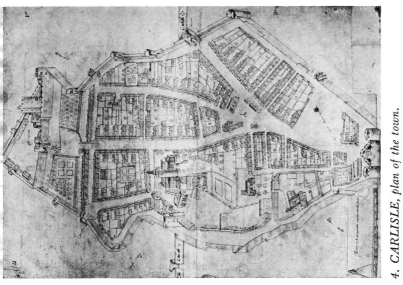

4. CARLISLE, plan of the town.

3. CARLISLE, the siege of 1315 as portrayed in the charter ot 1316.

5. *ALNWICK, Bondgate, exterior face.*

6. *BEVERLEY, North Bar, exterior face.*

of the street called Walmgate',[45] means that the bank was to be begun in this area; it could also mean that a stone wall was to be built (plate 12).

There is, however, evidence to show that if this was so the construction was carried out over a long period of time. Raine found a reference of 1326 to the defences as a boundary to property between Little Bretgate[46] and the line of the defences, in which they were described as consisting of a ditch and a mound. In 1389 the same boundary was described as 'the wall of the commonalty of the city of York'.[47] At the other end of the section a contract was made between master Thomas Staunton and the mayor and commonalty of the city only in 1345.[48] Staunton was asked to build twenty perches of wall 'beginning in the gate of Fishergate and extending towards the water of Foss above the castle of York, each perch to be six ells in length and six in height'. Fishergate tower was certainly in existence by 1428,[49] and was mentioned again in the chamberlain's accounts of 1442,[50] and the walls near Fishergate Bar were repaired over a stretch of sixty yards in 1487.[51] The Red tower, the only part of the defences built in brick, may have been built in 1490, but the earliest reference to it is not until 1511.[52] The wall between the tower and Walmgate Bar was rebuilt over a stretch one hundred feet in length in 1502,[53] and this may be represented by the section of the wall which is built on arcades.

York castle, sited on the peninsula between the confluence of the Foss and the Ouse, defended the city at this point. The city wall ran from a point on the moat to terminate on the river bank in a gate and a postern tower, called Davy tower. A chain was suspended from this tower across the river to Hyngbrig postern at the end of Skeldergate.

The last section of the defences are those on the south bank, from Skeldergate postern to Lendal tower. There is considerable evidence for Roman settlement, even defences, in this area.[54] Cooper divided the area into two parts, and to tie in with his hypothetical eastern line of defence on the north bank he suggested a continuation of the line along Carr Lane and Victor Street, to the line of the present walls near the semi-circular bastion, to the west of that street.[55] His hypothesis included a stone wall, later buried under the present bank just as the Roman wall on the north side was buried, and an extension of the walls from Victor Street to the river after

H

the construction of the Old Baile.[56] There is no evidence for this suggestion, but equally, little to condemn it. Victor Street was once called Lounlithgate. The name first appears between 1180 and 1190, and its meaning appears to be 'a street leading to a hidden, obscure gateway'.[57] The remains of a small gate were found when Victoria Bar was built in 1838.[58] The reference to this gate, coming at the same time as references to many of the other gates, suggests that there was some amount of activity on the defences in the mid-twelfth century, but would not prevent it being earlier.

The first documentary references to the fortifications come in the later years of the twelfth century. The Pipe Roll of 1196 records a rent of 6d was received for a room above the gate.[59] The first documentary evidence for the existence of ditches is an entry on the Pipe Roll for 1210 when the sheriff accounted for 6d 'for a place on the ditch of York by Micklegatebar within the wall the same as the land of Gilbert, nephew of Osmund, extends to the south'.[60] The defences are again referred to in 1228 when land in the south-west corner was granted to the Friars Preachers, one of the boundaries being the bank of the city ditch.[61] The word employed, *duna*, suggests that no more than a bank and ditch was in existence. The bank almost certainly by this date extended from Lendal tower to the Ouse at Hyngbrig. An inquisition conducted by the sheriff of York to inquire into the damage caused to the good men of York by the purprestures for the enlargement of the ditch and fortifications of the town in time of war (i.e. between John and the Barons) discovered that Herbert of Holderness had had seven houses on the edge of the ditch of Ploxwangate (Blossom Street) pulled down, and that fourteen others had suffered losses.[62] Cooper estimated that this would fill up the line of the ditch as far as the Old Baile.[63] Compensation was still being paid in 1246.[64]

By the time that documentary references become frequent, it is probable that the line of the earth banks on which the later stone walls stand had been established. Two, and perhaps four, gates were in existence and in two of these twelfth-century masonry can be seen.[65] The fact that the first reference to these fall in the second half of the century suggests that it was at this time that the defences were under construction.

The first grants of timber, supplemented by irregular grants of money, suggest the repair and strengthening of the defences.[66] Permission to levy murage was first received in 1226,[67] for a period of one year, but it seems unlikely that any sustained attempt to replace timber defences by a stone wall was made until the murage grants become an almost regular series, and even in the early fourteenth century the walls were still under construction. From 1251 until 1267 the citizens had permission to levy murage in every year.[68] There was then a break until 1284 when a further grant was received,[69] initiating a series which continued almost unbroken until the right to levy the toll was granted in perpetuity in 1449.[70]

NOTES

1   *Cal. Pat. Rolls, 1258–66*, 415.
2   *Cal. Pat. Rolls, 1381–5*, 485.
3   *Cal. Pat. Rolls, 1401–1405*, 255, 372, 465; *Ibid., 1405–1408*, 411; *Ibid., 1413–16*, 273, 381; *Ibid., 1416–22*, 343; *Ibid., 1461–7*, 341; *Ibid., 1476–85*, 509.
4   *Cal. Lib. Rolls, 1240–45*, 85.
5   Parker Brewis, *Arch. Aeliana*, fourth series, XI, 1934, 18.
6   *Cal. Pat. Rolls, 1272–81*, 397.
7   *Cal. Pat. Rolls, 1281–92*, 388.
8   Quoted by Sheriton Holmes, *Arch. Aeliana*, second series, XVIII, 1896, 9.
9   *Cal. Ch. Rolls*, II, 474.
10 *Cal. Pat. Rolls, 1301–1307*, 533.
11 *Cal. Inq. Misc.*, I, no. 2376, 632.
12 Nicholas Carliol was mayor in 1328; John Denton is mentioned in grants of the 1330s; Monboucher was sheriff in 1375–6 and 1377–80; Ralph Eure is mentioned in grants of 1390.
13 *Cal. Close Rolls 1318–23*, 54.
14 *Cal. Close Rolls, 1333–7*, 571.
15 *Cal. Close Rolls, 1337—9*, 39.
16 *Cal. Pat. Rolls, 1305–1308*, 380.
17 *Cal. Close Rolls, 1307–1313*, 40-41.
18 *Cal. Inq. Misc.*, II, no. 374, 93.
19 *Cal. Pat. Rolls, 1307–1313*, 461.
20 *Cal. Close Rolls, 1307–1313*, 369.
21 Constance M. Fraser, *Arch. Aeliana*, fourth series, XXXIX, 1961, 381–3.
22 R. E. Hoopell, *Arch. Aeliana*, N.S., X, 1886, 236-9.
23 *Procs. of Soc. of Antiqs. of Newcastle upon Tyne*, new series, 14, 1931, 61–3.
24 In J. Brand, *History of Newcastle*, 1789; C. H. Hunter-Blair, *Arch. Aeliana*, fourth series, XIV, 1937, 123–8.
25 H. L. Honeyman, *Procs. of Soc. of Antiqs. of Newcastle upon Tyne*, fourth series, IX, 1939, 37–8.

26 *Arch. Aeliana,* fourth series, XI, 1934, 20.
27 *Ibid.,* 7.
28 *Ibid.,* 8.
29 Otto Janse, *Visby Stadsmur,* 1962, 33, 49, 67.
30 *Arch. Aeliana,* second series, XVIII, 13; *Medieval Archaeology,* IX, 1965, 196.
31 J. E. Hutchison, *Procs. of Soc. of Antiqs. of Newcastle upon Tyne,* fifth series, I, 1951, 105–107.
32 *Procs. of Soc. Antiqs. of Newcastle upon Tyne,* N.S., VIII 1897–8, 123–4.
33 W. H. Knowles, *Ibid.,* second series, II, 1905–1906, 63.
34 *Journal of Roman Studies,* XVIII, 1928, 61n.
35 *Current Archaeology,* no. 17, November 1969, 167.
36 *Cal. Close Rolls, 1259–61,* 315.
37 *V.C.H. City of York,* 359.
38 Freeman's Register, I, ff.353–4.
39 *York Memorandum Book,* I, 151 (*Surtees Society,* 120).
40 *V.C.H. City of York,* 387.
41 T. P. Cooper, *York, The Story of its Walls, Bars and Castles,* 1904, 31. Cited as Cooper.
42 *V.C.H. City of York,* 365–404.
43 *Early Yorkshire Charters,* I, 251, ed. W. Farrer, 1914.
44 Cooper, 30, 106; cf. 83.
45 *Cal. Pat. Rolls, 1266–72,* 58.
46 Raine's identification of Little Bretgate with the modern Navigation Street is not certain, although it seems likely.
47 Angelo Raine, *Medieval York,* 1955, 12; cited as Raine.
48 Freeman's Register, ff. 351–2. Raine gives two different translations of the sentence specifying the work required (pp. 14, 20). Cooper thought it referred to the whole section.
49 Raine, 20.
50 Deposited in the city archives.
51 Raine, 18.
52 I am grateful to Dr. D. M. Palliser for this information.
53 *York Civic Records,* II, 171, ed. A. Raine (*Yorkshire Archaeological Society,* 1941).
54 R.C.H.M. *Inventory, City of York, Eburacum,* I, 48–51.
55 Cooper, 31.
56 H. Lindkvist, *Middle English Place-Names of Scandinavian Origin,* quoted in *Place Names of East Riding of Yorkshire, English Place Name Society,* XIV, 293.
57 Raine, 236.
58 The Old Baile was constructed in 1068 or 1069, Ordericus Vitalis, *Historia Ecclesiastica,* ed. A. LeProvost, II, 188.
59 *Pipe Roll, 8 Richard I,* 175.
60 *Pipe Roll, 12 John,* 218.
61 *Cal. Close Rolls, 1227–31,* 11.
62 *Cal. Inq. Misc.,* I, no. 10, 3.
63 Cooper, 109–110.
64 *Cal. Lib. Rolls, 1245–51,* 22–3.
65 D. M. Waterman, 'Late Saxon, Viking and Early Medieval Finds from York', *Archaeologia,* 97, 1959, 59–105.

66 *Rot. Litt. Claus.*, I, 195; the citizens were pardoned £100 in 1221, *Ibid.*, I, 456, and received £50 and £39 10s 7d in 1225, *Ibid.*, II, 34.
67 *Cal. Pat. Rolls, 1225–32*, 32–3.
68 *Cal. Pat. Rolls, 1247–58*, 88.
69 *Cal. Pat. Rolls, 1281–92*, 119.
70 *Cal. Pat. Rolls, 1446–52*, 221.

PART II

The Midlands

The Midlands was an area which was much contested in the tenth century, and in which there are towns fortified both by the Danes and by the English. Some towns failed to maintain their importance after the Conquest, although when fortifications came to be built in the early thirteenth century, towns which received murage grants early were usually those which had possessed pre-Conquest defences. Amongst the towns where decline had set in by the time of Henry I are Wallingford, Buckingham, Towcester, Derby and Tamworth. It is noticeable that the towns of later importance are situated on, or close to, the Fosse Way or the Watling Street. The area is characterised by the paucity of evidence, both architectural and documentary.

BOSTON   There are no murage grants; that claimed as support for the statement that walls were begun in 1285 (P. Thompson, *Collections for an account of Boston*, 1820, 32) is in fact a pavage grant (*CPR*, 165). There is no certainty that the ditch marked on Hall's map of 1741 was ever defensive in character (*Med. Arch.*, II. 200; *ibid.*, V, 323).

BUCKINGHAM   There is now no trace of either of the *burhs* said to have been built on each side of the river in 914 (*Anglo-Saxon Chronicle*).

CASTLETON   Traces of a ditch on the south and east sides of the town may be connected with the foundation of the borough in 1196. There is no documentary evidence (M. Beresford, *New Towns*, 417).

COVENTRY   The first murage grant was received in 1328 (*CPR*, 343), and references to the building and maintenance of the walls are frequently recorded in the fifteenth century Leet Book (ed. M. D. Harris, *E.E.T.S.* 134-5 [Orig. Series]). It is clear, however, that construction was spread over a long period of time. Excavation at Well Street revealed a ditch which was cut after 1250, possibly during the period of the Barons' Wars; it was later filled in, but the stone wall and ditch followed a similar line when they were built in the mid-fifteenth century (*Med. Arch.*, V, 325; E. Gooder, C. Woodfield and R. Chaplin, *Trans. and Procs. of Birmingham Arch. Soc.*, 81, 88-138).

Little remains of the original circuit of two and one-eighth miles; towers can be seen in King Street and north-east of Well Street, and two of the original twelve gates, Cook Street gate and Priory gate, survive. The very irregular plan of the walls is best seen on Speed's map of the town of 1610.

DERBY   The fortification of the town by 917 is implied by the Mercian Register (*English Historical Documents,* 196). There is no later evidence.

GRIMSBY   Two grants of murage were received, in 1261 (*CPR,* 144) and 1268 (*CPR,* 226). The Bailiff's account rolls of the time of Henry V show small expenditure on the defences (*Hist. Mss. Comm.* 37, 14th Rep. VIII, 263, 285). There are no remains.

LEICESTER   Fortifications of Roman origin are said to have been raised in 1174 (M. Paris, *Chronica Majora Rolls Series,* II, 289). Medieval defences followed the same line, along Soar Lane, Sanvey Lane, Church Gate, Gallowtree Gate, Horsefair Street and Millstone Lane to merge with the Newarke and the castle defences in the south-west of the town. (C. J. Billson, *History of Leicester,* 1920.)

Three murage grants were received, in 1286 (*CPR,* 221), 1293 (*CPR,* 424) and 1316 (*CPR,* 512). Detailed accounts, as well as leases of gates and towers, suggest that building work was far more extensive than the murage grants suggest (M. Bateson, *Records of the Borough of Leicester,* 1899-1901, I, II).

LINCOLN   The first grant of murage was received in 1225 (*CPR,* 518), and others were frequent throughout the thirteenth and early fourteenth century. Work was probably in progress in the early 1270s, since in 1274–5 the jurors reported that the collectors of murage had sold the stone bought for the walls for their own profit (*Rot. Hund.* I, 345-6).

Traces of the walls remain; the medieval line followed that of the expanded Roman city; traces of Newport gate in the north wall of the city remain; the east and west walls extended to the south wall running along Newland, Guildhall Street and Saltergate.

NEWARK   There are no murage grants. A pre-Conquest date is suggested for the original defences, whose ditch was filled in at least on one section in the early fourteenth century, and surmounted by a slight stone wall (*Trans. of Thoroton Soc.*, 26, 106-109; *Ibid.*, 65, 10-18).

NORTHAMPTON   The original Danish fortifications on the line of Scarletwell Street, Bath Street, Silver Street, College Street, Kingswell Street and thence to the river was later expanded; the later line was on Mill Road, St. George's Street, Upper and Lower Mounts, Cheyne Walk and along St. Peter's Way to the river which in both periods formed the fourth side. Nothing remains, either of the walls or of the four gates.

The first murage grant was received in 1224 (*CPR,* 499), but the expansion may have taken place before that date (F. Lee, *Arch. Jnl.* CX, 164–74).

NOTTINGHAM   The town was already fortified by 921 when it was captured by Edward, who repaired the defences, and further strengthened the town by providing a second *burh* on the south side of the river. Nothing remains of this. On the north side the defences ran between Water Lane and Carter Gate, between Hockley and Woolpack Lane and turned south between Bridlesmith Gate and Fletcher Gate. The southern line of the defences was probably the cliff above the river. The later fortifications, enclosing almost four times the acreage, used the eastern and southern line, but formed a new western line, departing from the castle and running on the inside of Park Row, along Parliament Street to Plat Street. Nothing remains of either the walls or the four gates (R. H. Wildgoose, *Trans. of Thoroton Soc.*, 65, 19–26; A. Stapleton, *Ibid.*, XVI, 135–49).

The first murage grant was received in 1267 (*CPR,* 57), and others were received until the fifteenth century. The town records contain only casual references (W. H. Stevenson, *Recs. of Borough of Nottingham*, 1882–3).

OXFORD The fortifications are first mentioned in the Burghal Hidage, where a figure of fifteen hundred hides is quoted; this length is not that of the later defences. The line of the pre-Conquest wall, keeping Carfax as the centre of the town, may be on the line of Bulwarks Lane to Catte Street, south through the garden of the President of Corpus, and west to the end of the former Church Street. This would account for the otherwise anomalous wall found running north-south in the Clarendon Quadrangle (F. H. Penny and W. M. Merry, *Buried Oxford Unearthed*, 1899), and for the kink in the wall at the top of Catte Street where the extension meets the earlier alignment. The date of this extension has not been established, but the early tenth century is a possibility: at this time Oxford suffered several attacks, and was a prosperous town, neither of which was the case by the time of Domesday. Moreover, mural mansions, houses charged specifically with the maintenance of the defences, are found within the line of the extension, a situation unlikely if the inhabitants received none of the benefits of the protection to which they contributed.

The course of the wall was altered again after the construction of the castle at the end of the eleventh century, and the late medieval wall ran from the eastern edge of the moat inside the line of George Street and the Broad, inside the line of Holywell, outside and then parallel with Merton Street, and then joined the earlier line at Corpus Christi College; the later line ran below the edge of the gravel scarp, parallel to Church Street, to meet the western edge of the castle moat.

There were originally at least twenty-one bastions, five gates and one postern; of the two latter, nothing has survived. Remains of the crenellated curtain wall, standing to a height of about twenty-five feet (7·62 m.), and five half-round towers, are preserved in New College garden, the north-east corner of the town. The towers are open-backed, and the wall walk passes round the top of each. Some have three, others four, loops set in deep embrasures at the level of the lower storey; the upper storeys each have three. The wall is in two builds with a slightly battered base; the upper is probably late fourteenth century and later. There are two blocked posterns in this section. (R. C. H. M. *Oxford City*, 1939; A. G. Hunter and E. M. Jope, *Oxoniensia* XVI, 28–41.)

Murage was first received in 1227 (*CPR*, 138), and grants were received until the end of the fourteenth century. The chamberlains' accounts indicate only small expenditure on the walls (*Munimenta Civitatis Oxonie*, ed. H. E. Salter, *Oxf. Hist. Soc.*, LXXI). Plate 14.

STAMFORD The town may have been fortified in the early tenth century; there was certainly a *burh* on the south side of the river, although no trace of this now remains (*Anglo-Saxon Chronicle* 918).

A grant of timber was received in 1218 (*Rot. Litt. Claus.*, I, 370), but much of the effort to wall the town came in the later years of the century after the receipt of the first murage grant in 1261, (*CPR*, 155). Others were received through the first half of the fourteenth century. The north-west corner tower remains, and the walls ran from the river up Austin Friars Street, West Street, North Street and East Street. None of the seven gates remains.

TAMWORTH The town was first fortified in the tenth century; excavation at Brewery Lane has shown the existence of a palisaded bank and ditch (J. Gould, *Lichfield and South Staffs. Arch. & Hist. Soc. Trans., IX*, 17–29).

TOWCESTER The tenth-century *burh* is said to have been provided with a stone wall (*Anglo-Saxon Chronicle*, 917). The town was not of later importance.

WALLINGFORD Remains of the tenth-century fortifications are considerable; except on the north-east side of the town, where they were destroyed by the castle, it is possible to trace the whole circuit. The bank stands about twenty-five feet (7·62 m.) above a ditch twenty feet (6·10 m.) wide (N. Brooks, *Berks. Arch. Jnl.*, 62, 17–21). The fourth side was protected by the River Thames. The defences were repaired in the early thirteenth century (*Rot. Litt. Claus.*, I, 199), but there was never a grant of murage (plate 15).

WARWICK The town was first fortified in 914, but no trace of the defences has come to light. Murage grants were received in 1305 and 1317 (*CPR*, 318, 301). Nothing remains of the wall; of the three gates the North gate has been destroyed. The East gate is used as a school, the West gate houses Lord Leycester's Hospital.

PART III

East Anglia

In East Anglia there was considerable change in the towns' fortified before and after the Conquest. The military needs of the Danish wars dictated the siting of several towns, which inevitably declined after the conflict ceased. The increasing economic prosperity of the eastern coastal region in the late eleventh and twelfth century affected the importance of towns. Colchester, the largest Roman town of the region, always retained its importance. Bedford, Tempsford, Witham, Hertford and Maldon, whose importance is stressed in the *Anglo-Saxon Chronicle,* began to decline in the middle of the twelfth century, although specific reasons for loss of prestige are not easy to suggest. Thetford, never mentioned in documentary sources, has been shown to have been a flourishing town in the late eleventh century, but it was unable to maintain its ascendancy. On the other hand, Bury St. Edmunds, where the monks are recorded as building defences in the early fourteenth century, may have had defences before the Conquest. The fortifications of Norwich, King's Lynn and Yarmouth, built in the fourteenth century, bear close resemblances to each other: whether this is because they were subject to the same trading influences, or whether the same men built, or were connected with the building of, the walls is not known. The defences of these towns compare favourably with the poverty and paucity of the remains in the rest of the region. The notable reliance on ditches suggests difficulty in obtaining stone.

ACRE   A square village enclosure lies west of the castle. There is no documentation (D. Renn, *Norman Castles,* 1967, 86).

BEDFORD   In 915 King Edward ordered the *burh* on the south side of the river to be fortified (*Anglo-Saxon Chronicle*); the name, King's Ditch, preserves its memory.

BURY St. EDMUNDS. A charter of 1121/38 laid on knights as well as on burgesses an obligation to share in the maintenance of defences, which suggests that they were already in existence. The town is laid out on a grid plan, and may have been deliberately founded.

Two murage grants were received, in 1304 (*CPR*, 267) and 1330 (*CPR*, 526).

CAMBRIDGE   Limited archaeological investigation has suggested that an early system of gates and ditches remained in use throughout the medieval period (P. V. Addyman and M. Biddle, *Procs. Camb. Antiq. Soc.* LVIII, 74–137). There is no documentary evidence.

COLCHESTER   The Roman lay-out of the defences was retained throughout the Middle Ages, and most of the circuit, which enclosed 108 acres, can still be seen. Roman, rather than medieval, masonry has survived. The external semi-circular bastions, of which three remain, are medieval additions. They can be seen from Priory Street.

A grant of timber was received in 1215 (*Rot. Litt. Claus.*, I, 193). Later, money for building was provided by the unique means of exemption from the duty of sending a member to parliament, so that his allowance could be spent on defence (1382, 1388, 1394, 1404, 1410, *CPR*, *sub annis*). Town records indicate the common presentments for the theft of stone in the early fourteenth century, suggesting that the defences were not highly regarded (quoted H. Harrod, *Report on the Records of the borough of Colchester*, 1865, 8).

DUNWICH   A single grant of murage was received in 1253 (*Close Rolls*, 312). There are no remains, and it is possible that the money might have been for a sea-dyke rather than for defence against land enemies.

FRAMLINGHAM   A ditch to the north and east of the castle may be the remains of defences which enclosed the town, not now traceable for the whole of its course. It may be of twelfth century date.

HARWICH   Murage was granted twice; in 1338 (*CPR*, 88) (although this may have been revoked), and again in 1378 (*CPR*, 162). The re-fortification of the town at the time of the Armada probably destroyed the medieval defences, and has in its turn been destroyed.

HERTFORD   Nothing is known of the pre-Conquest defences, constructed in 912, on either side of the River Lea (*Anglo-Saxon Chronicle*).

IPSWICH   Archaeological evidence suggests that the town was protected only by a ditch and an earth bank, first cut in the eleventh century beneath the line of the later Rampart, which was constructed in the early thirteenth century. This ditch was re-cut in the later thirteenth century, and before the end of its life had had inserted on its line a trench with vertical sides, perhaps a foundation trench for a stone wall, never completed. If this is indeed the case it might be linked with the licence to crenellate issued in 1352 (*CPR*, 314) and revoked in 1354 (*CPR*, 144). Plans for a stone wall, however, may have had an earlier origin, since a murage grant was received in 1299 (*CPR*, 421) and an entry on the Great Plea Rolls for 1302–1304 made a grant of land conditionally, 'unless it shall happen that a stone wall shall be erected to enclose the town'. (S. E. West and D. Charman, *Procs. Suffolk Institute of Archaeology*, XXIX, 233–303.)

KING'S LYNN   The remains of the wall at King's Lynn are fragmentary, and its line is not certain, especially in the northern part of the town where indications of its course were obliterated by the construction of the railway line to Alexandra Dock. Only a small section at the end of St. Ann's Street remains. From there the wall ran east, including St. Nicholas' Chapel in its bounds, and turned south on the line of Kettlewell Lane.

The section of wall remaining here resembles the walls of Norwich and Yarmouth in constructional detail. The wall was built in flint rubble, but much of the facing has been robbed. The arrow slits, twenty inches (0·813 m.) long and two inches (0·051 m.) wide, were faced on the outside not with brick as at Norwich and Yarmouth but with blocks of ashlar thirty-three inches (0·838 m.) high and twenty-three inches (0·584 m.) broad. There was one slit to every arcade. Viewed from the outside the wall stands to a height of eight to ten feet (2·44 m.–3·05 m.); the inside level has been raised considerably. The wall appears to have had footings, but not the additional strengthening of a bank. Protection in part was gained from the slope of the ground to the River Gaywood.

The wall continued south, and can be seen on the east side of Wyatt Street (Littleport Terrace). It has, however, been much patched and only the outlines of the arcades can be traced. South of the Railway Station the course of the defences can be seen roughly on the line of the walk across the park. Hillen doubted whether a stone wall was ever built in this sector;[1] the Buck engravings do not suggest a wall. The East Gate, and probably also a length of curtain wall on either side must, therefore, have stood in isolation on the banks. The present structure is an eighteenth-century rebuilding of the medieval gate, which now appears as a single-arched structure with two foot passages. The authenticity of these pedestrian entrances can be challenged. They lead down a steep slope into the ditch. From an engraving of 1809 the gate appears to have been a single pointed arched erection, two storeys high. The arch was flanked by four polygonal towers.[2]

The line of the defences continues south, turning slightly south-west on Guanock Terrace. At the end of this stretch and straddling the London road stands the South gate (plate 16). There are frequent references to its repair in the chamberlains' accounts of the fourteenth century,[3] but in or shortly after 1416 Robert Hertanger, a London mason, contracted to rebuild the gate which was found to be in a dangerous condition. Before half the work was completed, however, he had spent all the money voted for its repair. He was excused payment of the deficit 'because of his poverty', and another mason finished the work.[4] In 1520 an indenture was sealed between the mayor and burgesses of Lynn and Nicholas and Thomas Hermer of Burwell for making the South gate.[5] In its present form, therefore, the details of the gate belong to the sixteenth century. There is a central arch about twenty feet (6·10 m.) high, flanked by two foot passages. Above the arch is a chamber lit by two three-light windows in both south and north faces. Access to this seems to have been by a stairway in the north-east angle of the gate, lit by small square openings. A string course separates the floors. The grooves of a portcullis can be seen protecting the wooden doors, and there are six circular gunports measuring ten inches (0·254 m.) in diameter. Four of these are positioned above the foot passages, the other two are at first-floor level in the towers. The gate was further protected by a dyke.

The wall may not have continued from the gate to the River Great Ouse since the town was protected naturally first by the dyke and then by the River Nar. Whether there was a continuous line of defence along the Ouse is not clear. It seems unlikely, although there were defended watergates.

Before the stone wall was built the town was defended by four 'wooden bretasches', which probably represent some form of timber defences on the site of the later gates.[6] The east and southern bretasches were certainly in such positions, and, by analogy, the northern bretasch, referred to in a deed of 1270 as 'the bretasch of the bishop', may have been in the vicinity of St. Ann's gate. The western one must have guarded the water-front and was possibly near the site of the late Purfleet gates. In the Leet Roll of 1330 Thomas Valour and fifty-five citizens were each fined threepence for stopping the common watergate near the western bretasch. The community seems also to have relied on portable wooden towers. In 1298 the tallage which Benedict of Weasenham owed the community was remitted in lieu of the rent he sacrificed in storing a timber bretasch for eighteen months.

In is unfortunate that more of the wall does not remain, since the chamberlains' accounts form an almost continuous series from 1327, and frequently name the stretch of wall under repair. It seems clear, however, that the greater part of the work had been completed before the accounts begin, and this view is supported by the pattern of the murage grants. The first licence to levy murage was received in 1266,[7] perhaps as a result of the attack on the town by the Disinherited in Easter week.[8] That some work followed this is suggested by a commission of oyer and terminer issued to settle the problem of how to punish 'certain persons who having houses and other buildings adjoining the wall

7. *HARTLEPOOL, Sandwell Gate, exterior face.*

8. *NEWCASTLE, plan of the town.*

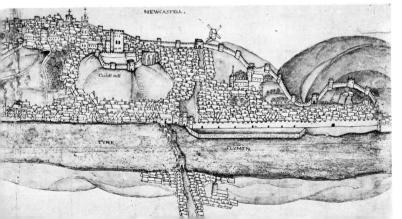

9. NEWCASTLE, *Durham Tower from the south-west.*

10. WARKWORTH.

11. *NEWCASTLE, garrite in Back Stowell Street.*

12. *YORK, Walmegate bar, exterior.*

13. YORK, the wall and ditch in the north-east.

14. OXFORD, north wall.

pierce it and pull it down'.[9] Murage was again received in 1294 for six years,[10] and in 1298 there were complaints by the mayor and burgesses 'touching the discords which have arisen between them and Ralph Bishop of Norwich, about their enlarging the ditch on one side of the town . . . and their making sluices for keeping water in the ditches round the town which had been broken down by the bishop and his men'.[11]

A third murage grant was received in 1300 for seven years.[12] After its expiry there was a commission to audit the accounts of the collectors, since in 1311 the commonalty of the town had levied amounts in excess of the assessments and had applied the money to their own use.[13] The enquiry was to investigate the accounts until 1 October, 1310, which suggests that murage may have been levied without a licence. The next grant was not issued until 1339.[14] In the previous year the mayor and burgesses were empowered to levy a subsidy on those dwelling within their town, to preserve it against attacks of enemies. This was confirmed in 1376.[15] In 1385 the commonalty voted a tax of £200 for the defences, to be levied on rents and chattels.[16] In the next year they voted a further £100 for 'guns, springalds and other armaments'.[17] In 1403 everyone in the town had to contribute to the cleaning of the moats and to the repair of the fortifications.[18]

The evidence is slight but suggests that much of the work was done on the proceeds of murage raised between 1294 and 1307. There are hints also in the chamberlains' accounts that this was so. The total amounts spent in the period covered by the accounts are considerable only in the years 1338–9 (£80 6s 9½d) and 1376–7 (£37 9s 1½d). In 1331–2 twenty-nine shillings was spent on the mending of the East Gate. A key was bought for the South gates in 1335–6 and there is no reference to the North gate until 1373–4, and then only to minor repairs. It seems likely, therefore, that the shape of the defences had been determined by the 1330s. The North gate was moreover relatively unimportant, except perhaps as a defence against attacks from the sea. Very little was spent on the maintenance of the defences in the fifteenth century.

NORWICH   There were two and a quarter miles of wall enclosing nearly a square mile.[19] Twelve of the original twenty-four towers remain,[20] but none of the ten gates. The wall is built of flint rubble strongly bonded with mortar. It is sometimes faced with knapped stone. Arcades carrying the wall walk, and recessed to cover the embrasures of arrow slits, were built throughout the length of the wall except on the section which ascends Carrow Hill. The similarity of details throughout suggests either a fairly short period of construction, or a uniform plan behind the whole programme.

The East Boom tower is a free-standing circular tower on the bank of the River Wensum. It is now in a fairly ruinous condition, much of the walling having slipped away, making it impossible to reconstruct the original internal and defensive arrangements. The base is very slightly battered, but the highest part of the wall is now not more than twenty-five feet (7·62 m.) on the eastern side. The tower is about sixty-five feet (19·81 m.) in circumference with an internal diameter of about twenty-one feet (6·40 m.). It is particularly unfortunate that so much detail has been lost, since this is one of the towers for which there is specific documentary evidence in the record of Richard Spynke's works in the fourteenth century.

On the opposite bank stands the second boom tower, and between the two an iron chain was suspended, presumably both as a means of defence and to facilitate the collection of tolls from passing boats. A similar feature was adopted at York, also bisected by a river. This tower also has a battered base and rises to a height of about twenty feet (6·10 m.) except on the north (interior) side. The inside, with an internal diameter of sixteen feet (4·88 m.), has been gutted, and entrance to the ground floor exists in the adjoining garden, though this is unlikely to be original. At first floor level there remain three arrow slits of the usual type, brick-faced in the flint wall, and they covered the river approach and provided flanking fire along the wall.

The wall walk can be seen clearly entering the tower at first floor level, but is not carried on arcading until after the Black tower at the top of Carrow Hill. There appear to be no arrow slits in the stretch of wall from the boom tower to the site of Conisford Gates in King Street. West of this point, at the foot of the ascent of the hill, regularly spaced slits appear, apparently unconnected with arcades. How such slits would be used poses a problem, since they are now well above the present ground level. A slight bank remains from this point until the Black tower. On the outside the wall was built with a slight batter, but this is now being undermined.

The Wilderness tower stands at the angle of the wall where it turns north up the hill. It is a relatively small circular tower with an internal diameter of ten feet nine inches (3·28 m.), and walls five to six feet (1·52–1·83 m.) thick. It stands now to a height of about thirty feet (9·14 m.) on the south-east side, and afforded covering fire as far as the river. The tower was heavily fortified. It was entered through a pointed archway with brick quoins and moulded lintel, and at this level were four arrow slits, one of which covered the city, the others attack from outside. The first floor had four slits, all of which were directed outwards. Access to these must have been by a ladder through a trap door in the wooden floor whose joist holes are still visible. There is no sign of a stone stairway in the internal walls which are built of a mixture of knapped and unknapped flints and stand to a height of about fifteen feet (4·57 m.) from the internal ground level.

The stretch of wall 160 feet (48·76 m.) in length running up the hill to the Black tower presents some interesting features. It is built of rough flints on both inside and out, and on the exterior there is a slight batter to the footings. The width of the wall as it traverses the steep ascent appears to be less than at other points, and the top of the wall goes up in steps at intervals of eight to ten feet (2·44–3·05 m.). This may be modern; certainly the cement capping is not old. The wall stands to a height of twelve to fifteen feet (3·66–4·57 m.). On the inside face arrow slits are sheltered by embrasures. There are six of these spaced approximately twenty to thirty feet (6·11–9·14 m.) apart. Only two could be used from ground level, and four are well above ground level. If they were ever to be used, wooden scaffolding would have had to have been erected, possibly on poles dug into the ground. It seems possible that the square brick-lined holes in two rows, one about six feet (1·83 m.) above ground level, the second five feet (1·52 m.) higher, were intended to support such scaffolding. Collins' suggestion[21] that they were used as spyholes does not seem to be very plausible. It is scarcely possible that the upper row could be used in this way, and it leaves unanswered the problem of how the wall was to be defended.

The Black tower is the most impressive of the remaining towers at Norwich. At the base it is about thirty feet (9·14 m.) in diameter, with an internal diameter of twenty-two feet (6·7 m.), and stands to a height of nearly forty feet (12·19 m.). It was very heavily fortified, though the modern windows have made it difficult to reconstruct exactly the numbers of slits on the upper floors (plate 17). The ground floor is entered through a door which has a brick lintel and quoins. The eight arrow slits (each in an embrasure) command all directions. Those which look inwards were presumably intended to enable fire to be brought to bear on invaders penetrating the booms or the Conisford gate, which are both within bowshot. The 1964 report describes the first floor windows as 'large double lancet windows with brick dressings, probably fourteenth century'. Not only are such windows unlikely in a defensive structure but their bricks differ in size from those in the door quoins of the stairs. These windows are probably eighteenth-century insertions, perhaps made when the tower was used as a snuff-mill.[22] It is almost certain that the original fenestration of the first floor corresponded to that of the ground floor: five arrow slits survive beside the windows just mentioned and each directly above the slit on the ground floor.[23] Nothing can be learned of the original construction above the first floor.

Access to the first floor, the roof and the wall walk was by a stair accommodated in the wall of the tower to the north of the ground floor entrance. This retains its original brick steps and brick lining, though the tower itself is built in knapped flints. The walk left the tower at first floor level and is four feet (1·22 m.) wide. The wall is eleven and a half feet (3·51 m.) high, probably nearly the original height, and stands on a slightly battered base. It is built of large flints throughout, although the arcades, which start from this point, are turned in brick. The bays are of very much the same size, eight feet eight inches (2·64 m.) high at the apex of the arch, four feet seven inches (1·40 m.) wide and recessed two feet nine inches (0·838 m.). The average width of the piers is six feet (1·83 m.). In the arcade the embrasure of the arrow slit is twenty-two inches (0·559 m.) deep, and seventeen and a half inches

(0·229 m.) wide. The base of the arcade was built in flint, but brick was used at a height of four feet (1·22 m.) for the embrasure and apparently for the piers.

There are twenty-five of these arcades to the north of the Black tower, and, after a slight gap at the entrance to Wilderness House, another six.

The course of the wall then runs to the base of a tower in the garden of 11 Bracondale; from that point until the Ber Street re-entrant angle it has been destroyed. The remaining piece of Ber Street shows where the wall turned south from the line of Ber Street, which may be connected with an earlier line of defence. The section is unique in retaining what appears to be the original, or at least a medieval, capping to the parapet, the only piece of evidence to support the documentary evidence printed in Blomefield and dating from *c.* 1377 which enumerates the number of battlements in the wall. The wall here is of unknapped flint.[24]

From this point until the tower near St. Stephen's in Queen's Road is reached the wall has been destroyed, and houses built across the line. This tower appears to be very similar in plan to that excavated in Barn Road in 1948. It is semi-circular, projecting about fifteen feet (4·57 m.) beyond the line of the wall. Its back wall is flush with the city wall. A nineteenth-century door has been cut into the exterior face, but the entrance from the tower side is original. The ground floor chamber was vaulted in brick, about ten feet (3·05 m.) high, and nine feet nine inches (2·97 m.) in diameter. The tower stands now to a height of about twenty-five feet (7·62 m.), and the wall walk can be seen clearly passing through the first-floor chamber. There was no access to this room from below. On either side of this tower stands an arcaded section of wall, standing to the level of the wall walk.

Six arcades remain in Caley's forecourt, off Chapel Road, but the arrow slits have been blocked. Houses have been built around the wall and towers on this stretch; one tower is incorporated into 80 Chapel Field Road.

The wall can be seen on the inside from the Corporation Car Park in Chapel Field East where it stands to eighteen feet (5·49 m.). At the western end blocked embrasures can be seen. It is built of unknapped flints, like the tower in the Public Park, now unfortunately obscured from the inside by public lavatories. The tower stands to a height of about eighteen feet (5·49 m.) and is semi-circular in plan, projecting about twelve feet (3·66 m.) beyond the line of the wall. No further details can be reconstructed, though the tower was built without any batter at the base, and seems to stand on a slight bank.

From this tower to the site of Heigham gates the wall is in a ruinous condition. No remains of the old Drill Hall tower are visible now. From the site of St. Giles' gate arcading, standing to a height of eight to ten feet (2·44–3·05 m.) can be seen from Welling-ton Lane, where there are remains also of a small square tower. It has been suggested that this is possibly part of Tudor repair work. The wall continues down the hill, and can be seen from Lower Wellington Lane. Arcading is just visible, but the wall has been much robbed, and no original facing remains.[25]

The wall north of St. Benedict's gates is in an equally ruinous condition alongside Barn Road, though it has been cleared of buildings. A tower was excavated, and can still be examined. The original facing was of knapped flints. Beyond this point to the site of Heigham gates the line of the wall is largely conjectural; beyond the cross roads of Barn Road with Heigham Street and Westwick Street to the river entirely so.

The line of the wall on the north bank of the river is continued from a point about half a mile upstream. There seems to be no trace of a wall along the bank, and perhaps the marshy ground was considered sufficient defence. St. Martin's tower is circular and stands now to a height of about ten feet (3·05 m.); the original facing has disappeared and trees are growing in the inside. The course of the wall is much interrupted here, but a section standing about fourteen feet (4·27 m.) high and sixty feet (18·28 m.) long can be seen from the electricity sub-station in St. Martin's-at-Wall Lane. This lane, like Wellington Lane, must represent the *pomerium*. Arcades are again visible, and the exterior is faced in a mixture of knapped and unknapped flints.

Another section, to the east of St. Augustine's gates is visible from the road outside 75 St. Augustine Street. It clearly has been much repaired though traces of the arcades and arrow slits can still be seen. The wall stands about sixteen feet (4·88 m.) high, and ends in a semi-circular tower in the back of 2 Magpie Road. At the end of this section, remains of more arcades can be seen immediately to the west of Magdalen Street where the wall stands to the original height of the wall walk, about twelve feet (3·66 m.). In April 1965 the demolition of the Swan Inn made it possible to view the scarred exterior face of the wall, but because of the whitewash still covering the facing no detailed observations can be made. It is unfortunate that so much of this closely dated section should have been destroyed.

Houses along Bull Close Road have destroyed a closely dated section, that referred to in the settlement in 1331 of the dispute between the Prior and Convent of Holy Trinity and the citizens of Norwich.[26] The parties agreed that 'a plot that the said citizens lately encroached upon the land of the said prior and convent as they say, without the walls of the said city between Barrgates and Fibridge Gate in enlarging of the dykes of the same city abide to the said citizens, their heirs and successors for ever'. The road probably marks fairly accurately the line of the ditch, and until within about fifty feet (15·24 m.) of the corner tower nothing remains of the defences. The arcades and wall walk then become visible. The tower has been restored and now has an octagonal external face with brick quoins at the angles. Whether or not this was the original plan is not clear. The tower is twenty-seven feet (8·23 m.) high, and is the only one to retain its top storey vaulting.

About 170 feet (51·81 m.) of wall still remains south of Barracks Road to the now destroyed tower which completed the circuit at the river's edge, but it is much obscured by sheds.

The Cow tower stands in isolation on the city side of the southward turn of the river. It is brick-built, standing on a stone plinth above which stand four courses of galleted flints. The tower is about fifty feet (15·24 m.) high and is now only a shell though originally there were three storeys. Access to these was by a brick stepped staircase accommodated in the wall of the tower. The internal diameter of the tower is twenty-four feet (7·32 m.), with walls six feet (1·83 m.) thick at the base. Quartrefoil slits are visible in the south walls.

The traditional date for the beginning of the enclosure of the city is 1253,[27] and the present line of the walls certainly dates from this time. This does not, however, rule out the possibility of earlier fortifications enclosing a more circumscribed area, although the case for such an inner line, advanced by several writers, is not strong.[28] It rests almost entirely on a confirmation to the abbot of Holme that he would not lose his land, enclosed within the new ditch that the burgesses of Norwich had made without the town after the death of Henry I.[29] There is as yet no confirmation from archaeological sources, and the line must have excluded much of the new settlement to the west of the castle without being a good defensive line. The alternative, that the present line of the walls had already come into existence, is also open to objections, since there is considerable evidence to suggest that 1253 is indeed the date at which a ditch and bank were first constructed. Although it is known only from the cartulary of Binham Priory, there is no reason to doubt the licence of 1253 to enclose the town. In the same year, a petition from the citizens asked that they should be pardoned the fine imposed on them at the sheriff's tourn before which they had been presented by the country people, who could no longer enter the town where they wished because of the new fortifications.[30] The record of the licence is followed by a document recording the grievances of the monks of the Cathedral Priory. They claimed that the enclosure had deprived them of the jurisdiction of certain areas which were enclosed by the wall although these had not, up till then, belonged to the city.[31] These documents together suggest that a new line was being established, and upsetting former rights. When in 1288 certain persons were presented because they had undermined the ditches and had made a purpresture under the *murus* in the neighbourhood of Chapel Fields, it may be assumed that work had progressed thus far.[32] It is also significant that references to six out of the nine gates should appear first between 1253 and 1297, whereas only Conesford gate can definitely be said to have existed before this.[33] Excavation at St. Benedict's gates showed that the stone gate had been built slightly earlier than the wall. It is possible that the references to the gates mean that they were under construction, and that they all preceded the construction of the wall, which almost certainly followed the murage grant of 1297.

Blomefield stated that a grant of murage was received in 1294, but this cannot be substantiated.[34] The first grant recorded on the Patent Rolls is that of 1297, for a term of seven years.[35] It was renewed in 1305 for five years.[36] In 1308, the bailiffs, apparently having had trouble over the matter, were empowered to levy contributions towards murage on everyone having property in the city, whether they resided there or not.[37] A third murage grant was received in 1317 for three years,[38] and a fourth in 1337 for five years.[39] It was renewed in 1343 for seven years specifically 'to make a dyke for the fortification of the wall which they (the citizens) have built with the said murage, as there is at present an open access to the same wall'.[40] In 1378 the bailiffs were ordered to cleanse the river and the dry ditches which were said to be choked with mud and filth, and to repair the walls and turrets.[41] They were also commanded to rebuild the paling on the river bank. There is very little evidence from the city archives to show that anything was done. In 1392 the commonalty received land in mortmain to the value of one hundred pounds towards the cost of the walls,[42] and in 1410 they were granted the proceeds of the ulnage for seven years for the same purpose.[43] Very little was spent on the walls in the fifteenth century, even by way of maintenance. The only significant amounts occur in 1420–21, when the sum of £10 7s 1d was spent on Coslany gates. In 1452 and 1458 the mayor was commissioned to repair the walls and turrets, and to cleanse the ditches.[44]

The murage grants thus suggest that building was spread over a period of fifty years between 1297 and 1350. The features of the wall are similar throughout its length although sections may be separated by wide intervals of time; it is possible to draw further conclusions from other documents. Part of the circuit can be dated closely from the record of the work of Richard Spynko, who laid out his own resources both on the provision of weapons and on building the walls in 1343–4.[45] Much was done on the northern defences from St. Martin's tower to Magdalen gates. The detailed account of his work omits any mention of the section between Magdalen and Pockthorpe gates, which is that referred to in the dispute of 1331, and which may therefore have been completed by that date. It also omits to mention the wall from Pockthorpe gates to the river bank at tower 24. This section is also omitted in the enumeration of the battlements entered in the last folio of the Book of Customs, and dated to *c.* 1377.[46] It may be that the wall was not completed in this section until after the 1378 grant. But the murage grants of 1337 and 1343 coincide with Spynk's generosity, and suggest that an effort to finish the walls was being made. They were complete by the time that the series of treasurer's accounts becomes continuous in 1378, since these reveal only small repair jobs to the gates, with the exception of a detailed account for miscellaneous repairs in 1394–5, a detailed account for the building of the Cow tower in 1397–8, and extensive repairs to Coslany gates in 1420–21.

PLESHEY   A ditch surrounds the town, and was probably planned as a whole with the construction of the castle to include both a church and a deliberately founded town. Excavation suggests a twelfth-century date. There is no documentary evidence. (P. A. Rahtz, *Pleshey Castle; first interim report*, 1960.)

SOUTHWOLD   A grant of murage coupled with licence to crenellate was received in 1250 (*CPR*, 108). There are no traces of this or of the sixteenth-century fortifications, where the plan was to isolate the town by a wall on the landward side (S. P. Dom. 219. f. 62).

TEMPSFORD   The fort is usually said to be Cannock's Castle, an oblong central platform 120 feet (36·58 m.) by eighty feet (24·38 m.), surrounded by a strong inner rampart and a moat twenty feet (6·10 m.) wide, lying south-west of the village.

THETFORD   The original settlement on the south side of the river was defended by the eleventh century by a ditch on the landward side. It ran from St. Margaret's cemetery on the London Road to Red Castle on the Brandon Road : at one point it was found to be eleven feet (3·35 m.) deep and forty feet wide (12·19 m.), (*Med. Arch.*, IV, 136; XI, 189–208).

TILBURY   The townsmen received orders to impress workmen to dig fortifications in 1402 (*CPR*, 113), but the town was re-fortified in the sixteenth century, since when all traces of the defences have been obliterated (J. Burrows, *B.A.A.J.*, 38 [NS] 83–125).

WITHAM   King Edward is said to have constructed a *burh* in 912, but nothing is known of it now. (*Anglo-Saxon Chronicle.*)

YARMOUTH   The documentation for Yarmouth is very good. There is the usual series of murage grants and also accounts of the chamberlains for the years between 1336 and 1345, containing both expenses and receipts, and a further set of receipts for three consecutive years, 1447–50.

Although Swinden suggests that there may be an earlier murage grant, of which there is now no trace, the enrolled series of grants begins in 1261. The first was for six years only, and was granted on condition that the town should remain loyal to the king.[47] It is not clear whether any use was made of this grant; on the Fine Rolls for 1262 an entry records the payment of the issues of murage to Robert de Ludham, a yeoman in the king's service, after a dispute about their levy.[48] In 1279 a commission was ordered to audit the accounts of the collectors of murage, and the suspicion of peculation carries with it a suspicion that little had been done.[49] However, by 1285 the treasurer and barons of the Exchequer were ordered to discharge the burgesses of forty marks said to have been spent on the defences.[50]

A second murage grant was received in 1285,[51] to last for seven years, and there does not seem to have been another until 1321.[25] From this date the series is almost continuous until 1448. In 1457[53] the townsmen received £20 from the fee farm of the town, and in 1458 and 1462[54] two further murage grants. Much of the 1457 grant seems to have been spent on the harbour defences.[55]

The accounts of the collectors of murage for 1336–7, 1337–8, 1342–3, 1343–4 and 1344–5, printed by Swinden,[56] suggest that much had still to be done, and that most of the fortifications probably date from the middle and later years of the fourteenth century. The accounts throw much light on the construction of the walls. The soil from the foundation trench must have been carted away since there is no sign that the walls stood on a bank. The wall was then built in vertical sections of different height, some to a height of sixteen feet (4·88 m.) straight away, some to heights of eight feet (2·44 m.) with bretasching, some to eight feet (2·44 m.) without bretasching, and others from the foundations to eleven feet (3·35 m.). Thus in 1342–3 four masons were paid £12 'for raising the wall from the middle to the top for a length of 23½ rods with the round tower', so that the wall was being brought up to full height in part of its length. Theoretically it should be possible to identify the two stages of the work, but they are now obscured, perhaps because of later repairs. It is possible that the building of the wall in sections has some connection with the brick arches which supported the wall walk. These, although their exact height cannot be measured, must have approached eight feet (2·44 m.).

As one might expect, it is difficult to fit the accounts to the extant remains. Swinden, and following him, all subsequent historians of Yarmouth, have written that the building started at the north end of the town and moved southwards. This scarcely fits with the evidence of his own transcriptions, from which no clear picture emerges. It seems more probable that building took place all round the town, with the wall standing to different heights at different places. In the years covered by the accounts a total of 664¾ (607·846 m.) yards of wall was built from the foundations, and 129¼ (118·179 m.) yards were heightened. It is never clear where these sections were, and it is not easy to identify them in the remaining fabric.

In 1337–8 there is mention of men 'digging at the gate', and also of lime bought for the great gate. Swinden took this to mean the south gate, a perfectly possible description of the gate. The gate is clearly of mid-fourteenth century date,[57] and it is possible that its construction, and that of three rods (15·974 m.) of wall attached to it, perhaps the length of wall between the gate and the river, may be referred to in this account of 1337–8. Work was still in progress in 1344–5 when £2 15s 10d was paid to John Almigamen for raising the foundations.

Further work was done on the south walls of the town in 1342–3 when a tower was completed. One hundred planks at ten shillings, and lead for the roof was bought. Twenty-three and a half rods (118·18 m.) of wall were increased in height at the same time. This almost certainly refers to the section of the wall between the Blackfriars tower and the South-east tower where the join between the two layers of wall can be seen, and where the Caen stone, bought in the same year, can be seen on the arrow-slits.

In the next year, 1343–4, tools were taken from the south to the north of the town, and foundations were being dug for the wall and one of the towers at this end of the town. Men were paid for filling in the foundation trench, '*post recuperationem fundi muri et turriculi*'. In the same year John Almigamen and William

Weston and their mates were paid for making the foundations and a turret over the gate. This passage may refer to the completion of the north wall, since there is an entry of sevenpence paid for a board 'for the top of the door next the north tower'.

It seems clear that work was in progress at both ends of the town simultaneously, and a detailed examination of the extant remains suggests that the walls were built over a relatively short space of time, since the plans and details of the towers are very similar. Whatever the accounts may show about the direction in which the walls were built, they provide fairly clear dating evidence for one of the towers at the south of the town, and the differences between this and those at the north are slight, if any. Despite the writ to the treasurer in 1285, a sustained building programme is not likely to have been undertaken until the series of murage grants began in 1321. But the defences make no provision for the use of cannon, and can therefore be dated to the first half of the fourteenth century, although building may not have been complete by the 1380's, when two wills gave money for the completion of the defences.[58]

The total length of the walls is 2,238 yards (2,046·43 m.) enclosing an area of 133 acres. The circuit contained thirteen towers, eleven of which remain, and ten gates, none of which is now extant. The walls were built of rubble, composed chiefly of Norfolk flints interspersed with flat, hard bricks finely united by mortar. The external facing is generally of squared cut flints with the Caen stone used for the loop-holes, noticeable especially in the South-east tower, and for some of the ornamental work. The walls ran from the edge of the River Bure to the bank of the River Yare. All trace of the boom tower which stood on the edge of the river at the south end of the town has disappeared; the wall from there to the site of the South gate is buried under heaps of scrap metal. The first tower now visible is that known as the Palmers tower. It stands now to a height of twenty-five feet (7·62 m.), and had two chambers, one at the level of the wall walk, the other above this. There are three arrow-slits now visible in the upper storey and from the way these are arranged (three on the east side) it seems probable that there were originally six providing flanking fire from all possible angles. There seem to have been no slits in the lower chamber, but at this level the original squared flint facing of the tower has been much obscured by later buildings. There is no ground floor chamber. Like all the other towers in the walls it was bonded into the wall, and has neither batter nor plinth at the base.

The wall between this tower and the Blackfriars tower is still hidden by houses on its outer face, and on the inside is obscured for a great part of its height by the accumulation of soil. But, as at Norwich and King's Lynn, the wall walk is carried over arches, each containing an embrasure and arrow-slit. The arrangement can also be seen by the Alma Road playground, where the Corporation has restored the wall to its full height, and in St. Mary's School playground and the adjoining cemetery.

The wall adjoining the Blackfriars tower is still standing to a height of about fifteen feet (4·57 m.), and the tower rises approximately another fifteen feet (4·57 m.) above this. Probably the wall walk provided the means of access to the first chamber, though Palmer writing in 1864 said that 'the guard-chamber was approached by an external staircase from the rampart, the greater part of which still remains'.[59] This is no longer the case. The tower is D-shaped, presenting the flat face to the inside; this has been much repaired, and possibly the only original feature remaining is the decorative flint arches which fill the wall space of the upper chamber. The outer face is semi-circular, and the squared flint facing is in much better condition. Three arrow slits are now visible in the lower chamber; possibly a fourth is concealed by the roof of J. W. Ball's shop. Corresponding with the decorative flint work of the inside face, the exterior was adorned with three courses of brick squares filled alternately with squared flints and brick and pebbles, the latter being whitewashed. The passage way underneath the tower is modern.

The stretch of wall to the south of the South-east tower is unlike any other part (plate 18). It is no longer in good condition and has been much damaged in the course of demolishing the buildings which once stood against it, though it must stand almost to its original height of twenty-five feet (7·62 m.). It shows a double row of slits, a feature paralleled at Tenby. They represent the slits at the level of the wall walk, and in the embrasures. The lower set are of the usual vertical slit type but those in the upper layer are more like those found in the South-east tower, which may be later insertions. It is difficult to decide whether this upper row has been inserted into the crenellations or whether these have not survived and would have added a few more feet to the total height. It is possible that this is one section of wall referred to in 1342–3 as being raised in height.

The South-east tower stands to a height of about thirty feet (9·14 m.) (plate 19). The wall walk almost certainly by-passed the tower at the level of the first floor chamber, but the original arrangements have been obscured by the improvements of later occupants. As on the projecting face of the Blackfriars tower the square panel decoration appears, but this has been pierced with arrow slits of a unique type. The slit measures fifteen and a half inches (0·381 m.) and is two and a half inches (0·051 m.) wide, broadening to three and a half inches (0·076 m.) at its widest point. They are carved from a rectangular block of Caen stone, twenty-one inches (0·533 m.) by fifteen inches (0·381 m.). In each of the two top storeys there is a row of five slits, positioned under each other, and there are two slits outside this pattern, the position from which they were used not being clear.

Beyond Alma Road (where the wall has been cleared of buildings) it has been destroyed by St. Peter's church, built across its line. Beyond that it is obscured by houses. A tower standing to the north of Lancaster Road survives as the basement to 15 Deneside. The walling stands to a height of about twelve feet (3·66 m.), and the tower was D-shaped, projecting twenty-six feet (7·92 m.) beyond the wall. The wall is visible in short stretches to the north, standing to a height of twenty-five to thirty feet (7·62–9·14 m.), but it is not in good condition. A double row of slits is again visible, though the openings have been bricked up.

The details of the tower north of St. George's Road have been completely obscured by the Nurses' Home built against it. In shape it appears to be similar to the others.

The Pinnacle tower is visible from Alexandra Road. It has been much altered, and the original arrangements cannot be restored. The upper storey has been given square windows, and a doorway has been inserted at ground level in the exterior face. At the base of the tower the walls are three feet ten inches (1·17 m.) thick; the internal length is eleven feet (3·35 m.), and the internal width fifteen feet three inches (4·65 m.). The facing is of the usual

144 · Town defences in England and Wales

squared flint, in good condition. One interesting feature demands notice, namely the attaching of the tower to the wall at the top by a primitive type of diminished squinch.

This feature is to be found at the next tower by the Eastern Electricity Board's yard in Jubilee Place, to the north of Middle Market Road, and again at St. Mary's tower. Its purpose is not clear; it did not carry the wall walk, since at St. Mary's tower this is clearly seen passing through the tower in the usual manner. It might be that it carried a parapet walk for a second row of arrow slits such as existed south of the South-east tower. The wall is again visible north of St. Nicholas Road as part of the back wall of gardens on one side of a vennel. One medieval tower, St. Nicholas', was destroyed in 1642 and the medieval wall can again be seen at King Harry's tower, at the corner of St. Nicholas' churchyard. It is octagonal in plan, and stands to a height of about twelve feet (3·66 m.). Nothing of the superstructure remains, though according to Palmer[60] the lower chamber had a vaulted roof.

From this point the wall runs west and then north to a corner tower which now has no sign of defensive provisions and the facing of which may be modern.

In local legend the North gate is supposed to have been built from money collected by those who buried the plague victims. Whatever the factual basis of the legend, it is a surprisingly accurate reflection of its date. An indication of its appearance is given in the drawing by J. P. Neale,[61] and its plan was drawn by Desmaretz in 1734.[62] This suggests a parallel with Rye and a mid-fourteenth century date.

The next tower, the Ramp tower, has been destroyed, and the circuit is completed by the North-west angle tower. This stands to a height of about thirty feet (9·14 m.), but original details cannot be reconstructed except that the wall walk seems to have passed through the lower chamber. There is no sign that this tower ever had the chess board decoration of the other towers.

NOTES

1 Henry J. Hillen, *History of the Borough of King's Lynn, 1907*, 757.
2 The print, engraved by J. Sillet and published by W. Whittingham, can be seen in Norwich City Library, Local History Section, Prints.

3   For example in 1335–6, 1357–8 and 1373–4.
4   Hillen, *History*, 760–61.
5   Hillen, *History*, 760–61.
6   Hillen, *History*, 759.
7   *Cal. Pat. Rolls, 1258–66*, 596.
8   *Chronicle of Bury St. Edmunds*, ed. A. Grandison, Nelson's Medieval Texts 1965, 34.
9   *Cal. Pat. Rolls, 1272–81*, 238.
10 *Cal. Pat. Rolls, 1292–1301*, 74.
11 *Cal. Pat. Rolls, 1292–1301*, 458.
12 *Cal. Pat. Rolls, 1292–1301*, 491.
13 *Cal. Pat. Rolls, 1307–1313*, 317.
14 *Cal. Pat. Rolls, 1338–40*, 240.
15 *Cal. Pat. Rolls, 1374–7*, 459.
16 *Red Register*, ed. H. Ingleby, 1919, II, 20-21.
17 *Red Register*, 11, 27.
18 *Cal. Pat. Rolls, 1401–1405*, 359.
19 A. E. Collins, *Report of the City Committee as to the City Walls*, 1910; Cited as Collins; *Report on the City Walls of Norwich by the Norfolk and Norwich Archaeological Society*, 1964.
20 The Cow tower is an isolated tower at the north-east corner of the town, on the bend of the River Wensum.
21 Collins, 63.
22 Hochsteller and Neele's map, 1710.
23 One slit can be seen on either side of the north window, one on the north side of the west window, one on either side of the south window and one on the north side of the east window.
24 F. Blomefield, *History of County of Norfolk*, 1806, IV, Part I, 97. Cited as Blomefield.
25 Plans of the arcades to the north and south of St. Benedict's gates were drawn in connection with the excavations of 1951 and 1953 and 1954. J. G. Hurst and J. Golson, *Norfolk Archaeology*, XXXI, 1955, 4–112; J. G. Hurst, *Ibid.*, XXXIII, 1963, 131–79. Cited as *Norfolk Archaeology*, XXXI, and XXXIII.
26 W. Hudson and J. C. Tingey, *Records of the City of Norwich*, 1906–1910, II, 366–8. Cited as Hudson and Tingey, *Records*.
27 W. Dugdale, *Monasticon Anglicanum*, 1823, IV, 14.
28 R. Fitch, *The Gates of Norwich*, 1861, 8; J. Kirkpatrick, *The Streets and Lanes of Norwich*, ed. W. Hudson, 1889, 104; B. Green and R. Young, *How the City of Norwich Grew into Shape*, 1964, 10.
29 *Register of the Abbey of St. Benet of Holme*, ed. J. R. West, Norfolk Rec. Soc., II, 1932, 14.
30 PRO SC 8/179/8942; quoted in Hudson and Tingey, *Records*, I, 59.
31 W. Hudson, *Norfolk Archaeology*, XII, 1892, 38–41.
32 *Leet Jurisdiction in the City of Norwich*, ed. W. Hudson, *Selden Soc.* 1892, V, 11. *Murus* here almost certainly means bank.
33 Quoted from Collins, 32, 39, 44, 47, 49, 54; *Norfolk Archaeology*, XXXI, 7.
34 Blomefield, 67.
35 *Cal. Pat. Rolls, 1292–1301*, 327.
36 *Cal. Pat. Rolls, 1301–1307*, 317.
37 Hudson and Tingey, *Records*, II, 325–7.

K

38   *Cal. Pat. Rolls, 1317–21,* 50.
39   *Cal. Pat. Rolls, 1334–8,* 529.
40   *Cal. Pat. Rolls, 1343–5,* 149.
41   *Cal. Pat. Rolls, 1377–81,* 121.
42   *Cal. Pat. Rolls, 1391–6,* 121.
43   *Rot. Parl.,* III, 637–8.
44   Hudson and Tingey, *Records,* II, 318–19; *Cal. Pat. Rolls,* 1452–61, 441.
45   Blomefield, 86–7.
46   Blomefield, 97–8.
47   *Cal. Pat. Rolls, 1258–66,* 177.
48   P.R.O. C 60/59 m. 5.
49   *Cal. Pat. Rolls, 1272–81,* 315.
50   *Cal. Close Rolls, 1279–88, 328.*
51   *Cal. Pat. Rolls, 1281–92,* 177.
52   *Cal. Pat. Rolls, 1321–4,* 35.
53   *Cal. Pat. Rolls, 1452–61,* 387.
54   *Cal. Pat. Rolls, 1452–61,* 468; *Cal. Pat. Rolls, 1461–7,* 200.
55   P.R.O. E 364/98.
56   H. Swinden, *The History and Antiquities of Great Yarmouth,* 1772, 79–92.
57   *The Builder,* 4 September, 1886, 358.
58   Swinden, *History,* 76–8. One of these, of 1382, bequeathed two weys of salt, the other, of 1386, twenty shillings.
59   C. J. Palmer, *Norfolk Archaeology,* VI, 113.
60   *Ibid.,* 121.
61   Drawing in Norfolk City Library, Local History Section, Prints.
62   P.R.O. WO 55/1548/15.

PART IV

The South East

This was always a vulnerable area, since it offered three possible means of entry into England, up the Thames, from a base on the coast, or north from Southampton. It has, therefore, been continuously and heavily defended, and the continuity of fortification is demonstrated in many towns. Five of the towns were Roman foundations: Rochester, London, Winchester, Chichester and Canterbury. The defences of Chichester and Winchester are mentioned in the Burghal Hidage and are thus known to have been re-used in the tenth century. The same document also lists Porchester, Burpham, Eashing, Southwark, Hastings and Lewes: of these, only the two last retained their importance into the later Middle Ages. The *burh* of Eorpeburnan, as yet unidentified, is assigned to the area. In this region, more noticeably than elsewhere, the late twelfth and early thirteenth centuries saw considerable interest in the repair of Roman fortifications, and work was undertaken at Rochester, Canterbury and Winchester, as well as at Lewes and Southampton. Most building, however, was undertaken in the later years of the fourteenth century, whether in towns with earlier defences, or on new sites such as Rye, Winchelsea, Dover and, later, Sandwich. This activity can be ascribed to fear engendered by the war with France, and this fear explains why many towns received substantial royal subsidies at this time. It explains also why money was spent on maintaining the walls throughout the fifteenth century. Perhaps because of the constant threat of attack and consequent need for defences, the documentary evidence is abundant and the remains amongst the most splendid in the country.

ARUNDEL   A single grant of murage was received in 1295 (*CPR*, 147). The course of the remains was traced in 1834 as a line running from the edge of the moat surrounding the 'Castle

Gardens' to the now destroyed Marygate; it then swept south to descend Mount Pleasant and Park Place to the river, which completed the circuit. Marygate was a square flint structure with a single entrance flanked on either side by a chamber. In the west tower a stair ascended to the upper storey which was used as a chapel. The gate was protected by a double portcullis (M. A. Tierney, *History of Arundel*, 1834, II, 711–12).

BURPHAM Nothing is known about the site, mentioned in the Burghal Hidage.

CANTERBURY The line of the medieval walls at Canterbury follows that of the Roman defences. In 1011 Roger of Hoveden tells of besieging Danes thrown from the walls of Canterbury, which suggests that in the twelfth century the walls were in sufficiently good condition to inspire his imagination.[1] The Domesday Survey noted that there were eleven houses in the ditch, which implies that perhaps the defences were in a less good state of repair.[2] The Pipe Roll for 1166–7 contains the entry that Hugh of Dover accounted for £5 19s 6d '*in operatione civitatis Cantuar' claudende per visum Prioris de Sancte Augustino*'.[3]

But from this time until the second half of the fourteenth century there is a complete gap in the documentary evidence, except for a grant of timber from Hubert de Burgh,[4] and there is no architectural evidence to show that any work had been done in the intervening two centuries. In 1363 a commission of inquiry was ordered; reciting that 'the walls of Canterbury are for the most part fallen because of age, and the stones thereof carried away, and the ditches under the walls are obstructed', it went on to say that the citizens then proposed to repair the walls and cleanse the ditches.[5] By 1378 work had begun. The bailiffs of Canterbury were issued with a writ of aid to help them find stonemasons in Kent for work at Canterbury.[6] In the same year, as a result of a petition to Parliament,[7] the bailiffs and citizens were permitted to levy murage for five years on certain goods coming into the city for sale, and in addition to levy a rate on the inhabitants, both native and foreign. In June 1379[8] they received a second grant of murage, this time for ten years. In 1380 there is a reference on the Patent Rolls to the 'new gate at Westgate',[9] and in the next year protection was given to William Louveneys, mason, 'working with the archbishop of Canterbury on the new city wall of Canterbury'.[10]

In 1385 a grant of £100 from the issues of Kent was made to the archbishop, bailiffs and commonalty of Canterbury for two years, to be expended under the supervision and testimony of Sir John Cobham, William Topclif, John Roper and Master Henry Yevele.[11] A grant of murage was also made for five years.[12] On the Close Roll of 1386 there is a memorandum noting that the bailiffs and commonalty had spent £419 11s 10d over and above the £200 granted in 1385.[13] The bailiffs were also ordered to cease levying contributions on the lands and rents of the convent of Christchurch, since the monks had undertaken to spend the appropriate amount on the walls and ditches towards their own manse and close under the same general direction of Sir John Cobham and Master Henry Yevele.[14]

In 1387 the king ordered the good men and commonalty of the town to re-elect as their bailiffs Henry Lincoln and John Proude since the king had heard 'by report of certain nobles whom he trusts that they have spent great sums and worked diligently in furtherance of the said work' (i.e. the building of the walls).[15]

That the grants of murage obtained in 1379 and 1385 were not concurrent with that resulting from the petition of 1378, but were intended to run consecutively, is suggested by the fact that another grant was not made until 1399, the end of the sum total of the periods of these grants. In 1399 a grant was made for five years,[16] followed in 1402 by a grant for three years.[17] The next year, however, the bailiffs received 'strict order to put away excuse, negligence and delay, and with all speed to proceed to execute the king's commission concerning the walls, towers, gates and ditches'. The defences were said to be so broken down and ruinous that the city would be in grave peril if the king were to make war with his enemies.[18] This sharp reprimand must, however, be seen in its context. Building had already been in progress since 1378 so that the walls cannot still have been in total ruin. Moreover, a survey made in 1402, known as Ickham's *Mensuration*,[19] shows that the city was completely walled except for a short stretch by the River Stour between the West gate and the North gate. It was perhaps to close this gap that the bailiffs' power to assess the inhabitants was renewed for a limited period of three years, at the end of which another murage grant, for three years, was received.[20] In 1409 the bailiffs and citizens were given licence[21] to acquire in mortmain lands to the yearly value of £20 to offset the costs of fortifications, and presumably to provide for their maintenance, since after this date the Chancery documents provide no further evidence of building activity.

There is much in the documents to suggest that the building of the walls was a well-planned operation, designed to provide the city with defences in as short a time as possible. The murage grants run without a break for thirty-one years. The fact that permission to levy murage was obtained in advance in 1379 and 1385 again suggests that the project was planned. It is noticeable also that both inhabitants and those passing through were compelled to contribute to the work, a feature which is not universally true. Moreover, both the cathedral convent and the town were involved, as the writ of *supersedeas* of 1386 reveals, and this is probably one of the few occasions on which the two bodies did co-operate. That both were under the supervision of the same people, notably that of Master Henry Yevele, is also significant. Not only does it stress the unusual degree of co-operation between the lay and clerical organisations (Yevele was at the time working in the cathedral) but it again suggests that there was a definite plan behind the building operations. Yevele was to supervise both the monks' building and that of the commonalty. It has been suggested that he was responsible for the design, and even for some of the work in the West gate.[22] Architectural evidence makes it possible to suggest that the thirty years 1378–1409 saw the construction of the West gate, of the wall to the south as far as Worth gate, and of the wall to the north as far as North gate. The wall between North gate and Quening gate was built between 1390 and 1394 by Prior Chillenden.[23] But these thirty years did not see the completion of the walls. In the fifteenth century not only was repair work carried out, but one large section of the walls was completed. The obituary of Prior Selling (1472–94) states that he built the wall between the church of St. Michael and the old wall enclosing the garden of the monks.[24] Within the same period Burgate was rebuilt, in 1475, and this probably marked the end of the section under construction.[25] In 1485–6 there is a letter referring to the enclosing of 'le Dungeon'.

This was a field, now the War Memorial gardens.[26] The medieval wall in this section is built on Roman foundations, but it is doubtful to what extent these could have been used to repel attack.

Thus the documentary evidence shows two periods of wall construction. Against this must be balanced the evidence obtained from archaeological investigation. A trench has been cut against the wall at three different points on the defences. The first, dug in 1944 by Mrs. Audrey Williams, in Burgate Lane against the interior face of the wall showed a bank of bright yellow clay, which probably represented the Roman bank. This was followed by a pit, containing late thirteenth century pottery and the foundations of the late medieval wall oversailed the bottom five feet (1·52 m.) of pit filling. At this point the wall was four feet (1·22 m.) thick, and stood to a height of four feet (1·22 m.) on foundations eighteen inches (0·457 m.) deep. It was built of roughly coursed Kentish ragstone with foundations chiefly of flint and clay. The excavator's conclusion was that the pit had been filled in and the wall built about 1300.[27] Another trench was dug close to this by Professor S. S. Frere in 1954; his conclusions are similar, though more reserved with regard to date. He found the Roman wall still standing to a height of eight feet (2·44 m.), though by the time of the medieval rebuilding its upper part had become so ruinous that its line had to be trenched down to solid Roman masonry through over a foot of soil. Professor Frere also sectioned tower 15 but lack of finds prevented any attempt to date the wall.[28] An excavation of the base of a bastion was conducted by Mr. F. Jenkins in the Old Cattle Market.[29] It was built of flint rubble and encased with well-coursed blocks of Kentish rag. Stratified deposits within the structure produced pottery which suggests that it could not have been built until *c.* 1390. It was also clear that the wall had been refaced, and the bastion was not bonded into it.

The results of archaeological investigations therefore suggest different conclusions from those of the documents. By the twelfth century the Roman wall was largely in ruins, and probably of little value for defensive purposes. The Pipe Roll entry for 1166–7 is perhaps not so out of context as it seems, but it clearly does not refer to large scale repair work. A twelfth or thirteenth century rebuilding may only have concerned the wall, leaving the bastions to be fitted in with the documentary evidence of the late fourteenth century, except for those sections of wall we know to have been built by Prior Chillenden and Prior Selling.

The defences enclosed an area of one hundred acres. There was once a ditch, now filled in, and Hasted says that there were twenty-one turrets.[30] Seventeen of these remain. The West gate is perhaps the finest part of the defences. It stands almost unrestored to its original height (plates 20 and 21). It is closely dated to 1380, when a grant of land to the south of the gate was made to the prior and convent of St. Gregory on which to rebuild the church of St. Cross demolished by Archbishop Sudbury to make way for his new gate.[31] Two drum towers flank a high central arch. Slightly battered at the base they are built in three storeys, divided by string courses. Each floor is lit only by gunports of the keyhole type. They are not arranged symmetrically; both towers have three at ground floor level and two on the second floor, but on the first floor the southern tower has four while the northern tower has only three. It has been suggested that this is an early example of the planning of artillery fire, to provide a wide field of fire from a very restricted front.[32] Above the arch is a chamber which probably housed the winding gear for both the drawbridge and the portcullis. The holes through which the ropes passed can be seen on either side of the arch. Above this a battlemented parapet is carried on five corbels.

The interior face is less defensive in character, although the square room which was built onto the towers was lit only by one two-light window. The room measures about twenty feet square. A stair in the northern tower gave access to the roof.

There are three towers on the section between the West gate and the North gate. The first is a square tower, three storeys high. It is flint faced with stone quoins. The windows appear to be modern, and the original height has been lost. The wall walk passed through at first floor level. The second and third towers are half round. Much of the original detail has been lost, but the second tower preserves one gunport at first floor level. The chambers of two of these towers may be those referred to in the account of 1392 as having been completed.[33] The wall, however, was still under construction in 1401–1402. The city accounts record payment to two men for bringing earth and putting it under the wall of the city at 'Longewalle', and again in 1402–1403 various items were purchased for the towers near Westgate.[34] Extensive repairs were carried out on the tower opposite the mill of the abbot of St. Augustine in 1467–8, which must be one of those on this section.[35]

Neither Northgate or Burgate has been preserved. Both had been destroyed before Hasted wrote in 1779, though he noted that Burgate had been rebuilt in brick with stone quoins in 1475.[36] Repairs were carried out to the East gate in 1469–70.[37] The towers on this section are of two types. The first four towers are all square in plan, and were built in flint with ashlar quoins. All were built in three stages, although there is now no access to the lowest room since the accumulation of a low earth bank. The two lower chambers were furnished with three gunports, one in each face. The wall walk passed through at first floor level, from which there was an external stone stair to an open watch-tower which formed the third storey. The original height of all but the fourth has been lost. This tower, however, would appear to stand to almost its original height, since it preserves the string course which presumably marks the roof level, and provided the open watching platform. The gunports at first floor level have been replaced by modern single-light pointed windows, two in each face. They had been built by 1418, and are shown on the seal of the Prior and Convent which depicts the cathedral seen over the city wall.[38] Finally, at the end of the fifteenth century, as part of a general settlement of points of contention the citizens surrendered the military road known as Queningate Lane, which lay between St. Michael's (or Bur-) gate and Northgate, for which the king's licence was obtained. The Chapter were exempted from contributing to the repair of any part of the wall except that just acquired by them.[39]

The next two towers are both half-round in plan, flint-faced, and battered at the base. The first is built in three stages, divided by two string courses. There are three gunports at the bottom level, and two single-light windows at first floor level. Access to the roof is by an external stone stair. The second is the model for all the remaining towers. It is built in only two stages without dividing courses. It appears to have been provided with only two gunports at the level of the wall walk, both of a quatrefoil design. The wall from the postern between the towers to Burgate is battered to a height of about ten feet (3.05 m.), and here rests on Roman foundations.

A tower between Burgate and Newingate (St. George's gate) stands now only a few feet above its battered base. It is now used as a chapel.

Newingate is said by Hasted to have been built about 1470, possibly in imitation of the West gate since it had two circular towers of squared stones. It was probably built slightly earlier than 1470 since Roger Ridley, mayor, gave five marks towards its building in 1452, and William Bigg, mayor, £10 in 1460[40]. The fact that it was the city water reservoir saved it from demolition until 1801.

Two towers have recently been completely rebuilt from the foundations. They have been reconstructed on a half-round plan without the battered base which is a feature of the other towers of this type.

Between Riding gate and Wincheap gate there are four towers, half-round and open-gorged (plate 22). They were battered at the base, being built against an earth revetment. They had two stages. There were three gunports at the cardinal points of the compass, and above this open-backed platform was the timber floor of the upper firing platform. The second probably stands to near original height and is still crenellated. It may also provide an indication of the original height of the wall above the wall-walk, which one might take to be the height of the buttress. The wall itself is here about three feet (0·914 m.) thick and has a core of chalk and rubble, revetted on the inside by a substantial earth bank.

Between Wincheap gate and West gate the wall has completely disappeared. A tower is now part of a private house. It appears to have been square in plan, but apart from three gunports on the ground floor level none of the original details can be reconstructed. The wall to the West gate may be the eighteen perches (90·52 m.) the completion of which, together with the tower, was recorded on the account for 1392.[41]

CHICHESTER The first murage grant was received in 1261 (*CPR*, 189), although repairs to the Roman defences had been ordered in 1204 (*Rot. Litt. Pat.* 45–6). Most work, however, was concentrated in the later years of the fourteenth century (see *VCH Sussex*, III, 72).

The walls were laid out on a decagonal plan; none of the four gates, set at the cardinal points, survives, but the walls stand about twenty feet (6·10 m.) high except on the western side of the city where they have been destroyed. The bastions are of Roman origin, but neither they nor the walls show much evidence of Roman work, having been continuously repaired. A ditch surrounded most of the town; excavation showed that one or two ditches contained fourteenth-century pottery, and could be the ditch referred to in the grant of 1377 (*CPR,* 72; A. E. Wilson, *The Archæology of Chichester City Walls,* Chichester Papers no. 6, 1957).

DOVER   The first murage grant was received in 1324 (*CPR,* 51), and thereafter the series was almost unbroken until 1483. Chamberlains' accounts are extant from 1365 onwards and show continuous heavy expenditure on the defences (B.M. Add. Mss. 29615, 29616, 29617, 29618, 29810; Egerton 2090, 2091, 2092; P.R.O. E 101/462, m. 45).

Nothing now remains of the defences, whose extent is known from plans only (B.M. Cotton Augustus I (i) 45, I (i) 46 and I (i) 19). The southern line appears to have run from a point east of Eastbrook gate (across the former Woolcomber Street) along Town Wall Street and Snargate Street, turning north to cross Adrian Street; there were three gates in the western wall, which curved east over the Folkestone road to cross Cannon Street and then turned south through Pencester Gardens to return to the southern wall. Nothing remains above ground today, but even Leland seems to have been uncertain whether the town was completely walled (*Itinerary,* IV, 49-50).

HASTINGS   There is no documentary evidence for the defences after the time of the Burghal Hidage, although a short section of stone wall is preserved behind the flats, Hastings Walls, off Winding Street.

LEWES   Only two murage grants were received, in 1266 (*CPR,* 590) and in 1334 (*CPR,* 517).

A section cut through the defences on the west side of the town produced middle Saxon pottery from the lowest layer of a turf bank (*Med. Arch.* XII, 163). Traces of the pre-Conquest defences may survive in earthworks on the west side of the town, which elsewhere may have relied on the natural slope of the ground and on the river for protection. The later fortifications ran north-east from the castle along Abinger Place to the Church of St. John sub Castro and then to Green Wall and along Eastgate Street, Friars Road, Lansdowne Place and Southover Road. This is the only place where the wall can be seen. It turned north towards the West gate east of the line of Keere Street. None of the three gates survives, although the two drum towers of the West gate were still standing twelve feet high in 1799.

LONDON   Murage, first received in 1233 (*CPR*, 22), was received until the early fourteenth century; it was preceded by gifts of money (Close Roll for 1215, *Pipe Roll Soc.* 31, no. 15), and of stone from the Jews' houses (R. Coggeshall, *Chronicon Anglicanum, Rolls Series,* 171). The Letter Books provide details of the maintenance of the walls and ditches, of the collection of murage and the regulations concerning the safeguarding of the city (ed. R. R. Sharpe, 1901–1907).

The medieval wall, a little over two miles long, followed the line of its Roman predecessor as far as Ludgate, after which the medieval wall ran further to the west, to accommodate the Blackfriars' monastery. It contained at least twenty-five bastions, some of which were of Roman origin, others, hollow, not solid, medieval. It is unlikely that any belong to the reconstruction of the defences in 886. Much of the medieval work was limited to rebuilding the Roman wall and has now been destroyed : visible parts of the wall are therefore largely Roman. Its course is easily traced, but much is preserved in basements and is not easily accessible. The eastern end of the circuit lies within the Tower of London, where the towers of the outer ward are built above Roman bastions. A section of Roman wall about ten and a half feet (3·26 m.) long can be seen east of the White tower. Another piece is visible in the sunken garden on the north side of Tower Hill. One of the best sections is that preserved close to Midland House, 8-10 Cooper's Row, where the wall stands about thirty-five feet (10·67 m.) high, from the Roman base plinth to the medieval parapet. Only thirteen feet (3·96 m.) of this is Roman work; some of the surviving facing has been removed to show the rubble core. In the medieval work there is a window and four loop holes for archers. There are also traces of a stair leading to the wall walk. The arch is modern.

The wall runs parallel to Coopers' Row, along Crutched Friars, where there are remains in the basement of Roman Wall House, and the line is marked by the frontages of the east side of Jewry Street. This street and Moorgate may preserve the line of the road behind the wall. The wall itself continues under the middle of Duke's Place and on the north side of Bevis Marks and Camomile Street to Wormwood Street and London Wall. On the north side of the church yard west of All Hallow's Church, whose vestry is built over a bastion, a much restored section of medieval wall is visible. The new street, London Wall, has a misleading name, since it intersects the line of the wall at its eastern end. Part of the Roman wall is preserved in the underground car park. Beyond this, the north wall of St. Alphege's church yard preserves two walls, the outer of which is the northern wall of the fort which preceded the Roman city wall, the inner a thickening of this wall when it was incorporated into the city defences. It was later rebuilt in the Middle Ages, and this section, standing to the medieval battlements, shows three separate building styles : a Roman base, ashlar facing mixed with courses of knapped flints and tiles, and brickwork crenellations, the work of a Lord Mayor, Sir Ralph Jocelyn, in 1476.

Beyond St. Giles' church yard, whose southern wall marks the line of the wall, the wall turns through a right-angle to the south. A medieval bastion in the angle marks the north-west angle of the Roman fort, and two others can be seen before the line of London Wall is crossed. On the west of Noble Street the Roman wall is surmounted by a wall largely nineteenth century. The south wall of Alder House, itself built above Aldersgate, marks the line of the defences, which cross Postman's Park as the southern boundary of the church yard. The wall turns south again east of Giltspur Street and runs parallel to the Old Bailey to the east side of Ye Olde London pub. South of Ludgate the wall ran on the north side of the modern Pilgrim Street on the east side of the Fleet river, to the Thames.

Documentary evidence suggests that although there was probably no established line of defences along the river front there were defended watergates, and that in time of war provision was made for bretasching along the wharves (*Liber Custumarum*, ed. H. T. Riley, II, 367; *Letter Book* H, p. 64).

Nothing remains of the seven gates, all of which, except Moorgate, enlarged from a postern in 1415, had Roman predecessors. The names alone survive in street names. (W. G. Bell, F. Cottrill and C. Spon, *London Wall Through Eighteen Centuries*, 1937; R.C.H.M. [England] *London*, III, 68–106; R. Merrifield, *The Roman City of London*, 1965.)

PORTSMOUTH   The first murage grant was received in 1342 following an attack on the town (*CPR*, 562–3). Two years later the townsmen petitioned for its cancellation, saying that because of the tax, from which they had made no more than 40s, trade was being lost to the town (*CPR*, 322). In 1378–9 a more serious attempt was made to wall the town when the payment of the fee farm to the king was suspended for ten years (T. Madox, *Firma Burgi*, 1726, 290). The successful progress of the work may be doubted since in 1386 a commission was appointed to take measures for the defence of the town (*CPR*, 214).

The extent of the medieval defences is difficult to determine because the town was re-fortified in the sixteenth century; the earlier defences may have been no more than a line along the harbour, to include the Round tower and the Square tower; the first is known to have been built in 1415, the second in 1494 (P.R.O. E. 101/479/25; A. Corney, *Fortifications in Old Portsmouth*, 1965). Leland described the defences as 'a mud wall armed with timber, having a ditch without it' (*Itinerary*, I, 238).

ROCHESTER   Repairs to the Roman defences were carried out in 1193 at a cost of £9 10s 3d (*Pipe Roll 5 Richard I*, 166). Permission to levy murage was never granted, but substantial grants were received in 1225 (*Rot. Litt. Claus.*, II, 56) and in 1262, on this occasion for work on the gates and for making breastworks round the town (*Cal. Lib. Rolls*, 104). The prior and convent received permission to build a wall in 1345 (*CPR*, 1343–5, 262, 539). Other work was done at the end of the fourteenth century (*CPR*, 1396–9, 137; 1399–1401, 379).

The course of the walls on the north side can be traced. A section of wall stands under the railway bridge, about ten feet (3·05 m.) high, of rubble masonry coursed in herring-bone fashion in the lower levels. Glimpses of the wall, now a property boundary above the line of the buried Roman wall, can be seen from Corporation Street. A semi-circular bastion stands in the school playground, about twenty-five feet (7·62 m.) high. There were probably three stages above the base plinth; three arrow slits can be seen at ground floor level, but other original arrangements cannot be reconstructed. Between the bastion and the site of the East gate the wall stands about twenty-five feet (7·62 m.) high; some crenellations exist. Beyond the gate both wall and ditch survive. A bastion masked by ivy marks the southern angle, after which the wall turns west to merge with the cathedral precinct. The castle, in the south-west corner, and the river on the west probably closed the circuit; the possibility that the river was used as additional defence on the northern side is suggested by a map of 1638 in Alnwick Castle. Recent excavation has made untenable theories of Norman extensions to the defences advanced in the nineteenth century (G. M. Livett, *Arch. Cant.*, XXI, 38–72). The ditch cut in 1225 was found one hundred feet (30·48 m.) south of the Roman wall, filled in when a new ditch was cut beyond it, together with a new line of walling lying between the two ditches. This in its turn was abandoned in favour of a further extension, late in the fourteenth century (A. C. Harrison and C. Flight, *Arch. Cant.*, LXXXIII, 55–104).

RYE   The remains of the town wall are scanty, with the exception of the magnificent Landgate. The town occupies a site commanding both land and sea, and the line probably taken by the walls is fairly clear. It was surveyed and measured in the middle of the nineteenth century, and this is the only guide to its line we possess (W. Holloway, *The History and Antiquities of the Ancient Port of Rye*, 1847, 585–90).

No trace now remains of the wall on the eastern and southern sides of the town where the cliff falls away steeply, but Holloway's measurements give a length of 1,228½ feet (374·45 m.) from the Landgate to the south-east angle where a postern, called Baddingsgate can still be seen. From that point it was 1,644 feet (507·18 m.) to the first remains in the south-west quarter, above the street now known as the Strand. This is only a short stretch of fifty feet (15·24 m.), and it abutted on the Strand gate which was partially destroyed in 1766, and finally pulled down in 1820.[42] A shield from the gate, bearing the arms of the Cinque Ports, has been re-set in the wall of a house at the corner of Mermaid Street.

A section of the wall is still standing to a height of about fifteen feet (4·57 m.) on the further side of Strand gate, and can be seen from both The Mint or from Wish Ward between which the wall runs. The masonry is of irregularly coursed rubble. There is no trace of the wall until it forms the boundary of the car park in Cinque Ports Street, between Market Road and Conduit Hill. Here again it is of irregularly coursed rubble, and the projection with a wooden superstructure must represent the bastion recorded by Holloway at a point 481 feet (146·605 m.) from the Strand gate. A section of the wall visible on the west side of Conduit Hill shows the wall to have been about fifteen feet (4·57 m.) thick. A postern, destroyed in 1736, stood at this point. The line of the wall from here to Landgate has been lost, but from the way in which it abuts onto the gate it may be supposed to have taken a line between the present Tower Street and Tower Lane.

The more gentle slope of the ground on this side of the town makes it natural that there should have been a ditch for additional protection. It is marked by the line of Wish Ward, Cinque Ports Street and Tower Street, and was traced by Holloway for a distance of 1,337 feet (407·48 m.). It is said to have been fifty feet (30·48 m.) wide and five feet (1·52 m.) deep.[43]

The Landgate is an imposing structure (plate 23). Two round towers flank a single entrance, twelve feet (3·66 m.) wide. The towers stand to a height of forty-seven feet (14·32 m.). The external diameter is fifteen feet (4·57 m.). Though they are similar in appearance they are not identical; the western tower appears to have had a cellar, perhaps built merely to take advantage of the slope of the ground, whereas this is lacking, and was less necessary, in the eastern tower. Above the base plinth, common to both towers, the towers are built in three stages, each floor being lit on the north side by three slits. A fourth lit the eastern tower on its southern side at ground level. There was an entrance up a flight of stairs into each tower, but access to the upper storeys seems to have been only from a spiral stairway in the western tower. The chamber to which this led was twenty feet (6·10 m.) long and nine feet (2·74 m.) wide, and was lit by two small trefoiled windows in both the north

15. *WALLINGFORD, aerial view.*

16. *KING'S LYNN, South Gate, exterior face.*

17. NORWICH, *Black Tower and arcades.*

18. *YARMOUTH, the wall adjoining the South-east Tower, exterior.*

19. *YARMOUTH, the South-east Tower, from the south.*

20. *CANTERBURY, West Gate, exterior.*

21. *CANTERBURY, West Gate, interior.*

and south side. The stairway continues in the western tower to the third floor room, lit by a single-light window, and from there to the flat roof. Above the western tower a small octagonal watch tower stands eight and a half feet (2·59 m.) above the roof level. This is a unique feature amongst English gates. In the eastern tower a garderobe was put in the south-east buttress.

The north face presents a defensible front to the main approach to the town along the London Road. The gate was defended by a portcullis and wooden gates. Above the arch two small circular holes can be seen, presumably the holes through which pulley ropes for a drawbridge passed. At roof level the machicolated parapet provided additional defence. It was built in a different stone,[44] and may have been added in the middle of the fifteenth century. A building account for 1448-9 suggests that much repair work was carried out.

The southern, or interior, face is little less defensible in character than the north front. The second floor chamber is lit by two small windows, the third by a single ogee arched window, of which there may originally have been a second. The back wall of the archway is almost flush with the line of the towers, and there is no projection of the chambers above into the town as at the West gate at Canterbury or Bargate, Southampton. This suggests that the gate may be earlier in date than these structures, though possibly by only a few decades.

The documentary evidence for Rye is considerable, the references of the Close and Patent Rolls being supplemented by the Memoranda Rolls and the city chamberlains' accounts. The first grant of murage was received in 1329,[45] and was renewed at three yearly intervals until 1336.[46] Another grant was received in 1343,[47] renewed for a further period of five years in 1348 after the townsmen's petition that the total destruction of the town was feared.[48] That much had been achieved by that date is therefore doubtful.

In 1369 another request for permission to levy murage was made, because 'for lack of enclosure the town had been lately burned in time of war, . . . and in view of the perils which may ensue if the town remains unenclosed the mayor and commonalty had ordained that 1½d of every twenty shillings worth of rent, and ½d of every twenty shillings worth of goods and money weekly was to be applied to the enclosure of the town until it was complete'. The king

L

granted them licence to crenellate the town, and empowered the mayor and bailiffs to distrain any who were unwilling to pay their portion of such assessment.[49] This again suggests that little had been done with earlier grants but the burning of the town in time of war must be that of 1339.[50]

But that a more determined effort was made to wall the town in the 1370s is suggested by a grant of £8 per year from the rents of the manor of Iden for three years, 'in aid of making certain walls, dykes, gates and palings in and around the town'.[51] In 1377, after the burning of the town a second time by the French in the previous year, the townsmen again received murage 'in consideration of the fact that they had so speedily taken order for its defence'. This grant was to run for five years, and might then be renewed if peace had not been made with France.[52] It did not, however, provide sufficient revenue, and in 1379 the townsmen sent a petition to parliament asking that the fines levied in Sussex should be given to the town for the building and repair of the walls.[53] No answer is recorded to this petition on the Parliament Rolls, although on the Patent Roll for February 1380 it is recorded that £18 yearly for two years from the farm of the bailiwick of that town had been granted with the consent of the prelates and magnates of the realm.[54] It was accounted for only in 1415–16 when it is recorded that £27 was received, although £43 16s was spent. In 1382 the mayor and commonalty were granted the profits of the bailiwick of Rye towards the fortification of the town, and it was laid down that the town was to be walled within three years, on pain of a fine of £100.[55] Later, this fine had to be remitted, even though the wall had not been finished.[56] In 1385 five men, amongst them Sir Simon Burley, John Cobham and Sir Edward Dalyngrig, were appointed to supervise the fortification of the town, and were permitted to fell two hundred trees in Crowhurst park for the 'fencing and fortification of the town'.[57] In the same year dues paid on fish landed at ports between Hastings and Whitstable were to be given to Rye for walling the town.[58] The money raised was collected under the supervision of John Melton, who received 12d per day wages, totalling £8 9s. The total amount received was £312 14s 1d between 13 February, 1385 and 31 July, 1386 : the total expenditure was £427 5s 8d.[59] The next account records the receipt of £22 13s 4d and one hundred oaks; £336 7s 9½d was spent, some of it on a drawbridge.[60] The last account in the series records the receipt of £27 received as a result of the petition of 1379, and the expenditure of £43 16s.[61]

SANDWICH   The remains of the earth defences which protected the town can be traced with very little difficulty except along the riverside. The most impressive section is the south-east corner, where the bank rises steeply above the ditch to a height of about twenty-five feet (7·62 m.). There were five gates in the circuit, of which only two now remain. That known as the Barbican is probably a mid-fourteenth-century structure, and consists of two circular towers flanking a single archway. Only the base of the towers remains, standing to a height of about ten feet (3·05 m.); a modern superstructure has been erected. Part of the wall remains on the west side. Fishergate, a three-storied building, has been dated to 1571, but this may refer only to the upper storey which is built in brick whereas the lower two are of flint. The rectangular plan makes it possible that the gate was originally erected in the fifteenth century.

Canterbury gate stood at the north-west corner of the town; it was demolished about 1792, and consisted of two circular towers flanking a plain pointed archway.[62] Excavations in 1929 uncovered half the plinth of the northern tower of the gates.[63] It measured thirteen and a half feet (4·11 m.) in diameter, and three courses of masonry remained to a height of three and a half feet (1·07 m.). The outer face had a slight batter. Pottery was found, which was vaguely dated to the fourteenth and fifteenth centuries. There was also evidence of a destructive fire in the same period. The town, attacked in 1400 and in 1438, was certainly burnt in 1457, and the gate might have been destroyed then.

Engravings show Woodborough gate was a rectangular structure, of two square towers flanking a single pointed archway.[64] Sandown gate is pictured as a square structure with two half-round towers of only slight projection flanking a single entrance.[65]

It is not clear at what date Sandwich was first defended. The town played a part in the Barons' Wars, although there are no specific references to fortifications until 1274–5 when the townsmen rebelled against unpopular civic arrangements.[66] Their case was investigated, and judgement went against them. At the same time it was ordered that the trenches constructed during the late disturbance in the realm should be filled in and levelled with earth, and that the barbican and the rest of the fortifications constructed to oppose the king should be taken down, and removed to Dover Castle at the expense of the commonalty.[67] The ring leaders suffered a short spell of imprisonment,[68] but whether any steps were taken to fill in the defences is not known. The barbican was presumably a wooden structure, possibly very similar to the wooden wall which Walsingham describes as having been brought to the town in 1386.[69]

The townsmen received permission to levy murage for a period of seven years in 1321,[70] but although the town was an important base during the Hundred Years War, by comparison with the issue of murage grants to other towns in the area little seems to have been done towards fortifying it against attack. In 1339 all those who had left the town to avoid paying for its fortification were ordered to return, but there is no other indication that defence was seriously contemplated.[71]

In 1385 Sir Simon Burley, as constable of Dover Castle, was ordered to summon before him all who held soil not built on in perilous places in Sandwich, and to instruct them to fortify the town.[72] The rents and profits of the lands concerned were to be used to pay for the work, but the commonalty also received a grant from the customs for two years,[73] and a further grant of murage for two years in 1387.[74] It was said that the town had been weakened by plagues and other grievous calamities and it had not been possible to finish the fortifications they had begun. Burley was also empowered to impress masons, carpenters and other labourers for the work.[75]

Sandwich is peculiar amongst the towns of England in that considerable effort was expended on the fortification of the town in the fifteenth century. There seems to have been an effort to wall the town in stone, though no trace of stonework remains, as well as the building of the gates. Thus in 1405 the mayor and commonalty received a grant of murage for seven years,[76] which was renewed in 1412 for the same term.[77] The Hornblow in 1436 ordered that the ditches were to be scoured and cleansed. Earth walls were to be raised on the west side of the town, perhaps implying that hitherto it had been undefended, and a month later it was decided to dig up the road to Worth and all other roads, and also to continue the wall of the town to the Delf. Planks were to be placed over the town doors neighbouring the Haven, and within the walls so that men could cross from house to house for the defence of the town. Those dwelling on the sea-front were to collect 'bolestones', and to put them on their quays to be ready for attack. The cost of these preparations was met by a tax on properties in the town.[78] In 1451 the south-east corner of the town was fortified with a two storey erection, armed with guns and known as the 'Bulwark'.[79] In 1456 the Council decided to press ahead with the Newgate, apparently already begun in the south walls, and ordered also that strict watch should be kept every night.[80] These preparations were made under growing threat of attack from France, a fear which materialised in August 1457. John de Waurin's account of the attack shows that the 'Bulwark' provided a considerable obstacle to attackers,[81] although the town was eventually sacked.

In the years following, efforts to improve the fortifications continued. In 1458 the Council began to collect up old debts, and a new rate of taxation on properties in the town was imposed. Timber and nails were obtained through the purchase of two hulks, at a total cost of £3 6s 8d. Repair work was carried out at the Great Bulwark, and it was decided to erect a second, of brick, near Fishergate.[82] In 1461 a grant of £100 annually was made to the mayor and barons, to which they were to add £20 for the repairs.[83] The accounts for some of this money are enrolled on the Memoranda Rolls.[84] This grant was replaced in 1465 by exemption from the payment of various customs duties,[85] a privilege which was renewed in 1477.[86] Accounts for work done between 1464 and 1474 survive amongst Exchequer accounts.[87] They suggest that much of the work was concerned with the erection of stone walls, since a considerable quantity of stone was bought. There is mention also of the purchase of '15 crenells' in 1471–2, surely an indication that it was the wall itself, as well as Dorlby gate, mentioned in the account for 1466–7, that was under construction.[88]

Finally, in 1483, the mayor and barons received a grant of £100 from the customs.[89]

SOUTHAMPTON The remains of the medieval walls of Southampton are considerable, about half the original total circumference of 1 mile 221 yards having survived. Of an original total of twenty-

166 · Town defences in England and Wales

nine towers and seven gates, thirteen towers and four gates remain. Forming a rectangle, the walls are nearly complete on the north and west sides of the town, but the south and east walls are only fragmentary. The defences were described by Leland,[90] and were portrayed in Philip Brannon's picture of the arrival of Philip of Spain (1554), (plate 24). Three descriptions of the walls already exist.[91] The conclusions presented here, based on a close re-examination of the documentary evidence, differ from those of earlier writers, although I am indebted to them for certain descriptive material.

At the south-east corner of the defences stands God's House gate, which is a plain oblong structure, two storeys high, twenty-three feet (7·01 m.) deep and thirty feet (9·14 m.) broad. The southern end projects beyond the line of the town wall, and presumably gave some protection to the quay which was reached through the gate. God's House tower, which abuts onto the gate, projects for about eighty-five feet (25·90 m.) outside the angle made by the defences. Built in three stages, it stands to a height of about fifty-five feet (16·76 m.) and is thirty feet (9·14 m.) broad. On the middle floor there is a gunport of the inverted keyhole type on each side of the tower. The building is clearly later than the other parts of the wall in this area, and may have been built in the early years of the fifteenth century, and later than the wall to the north.

One hundred and sixty feet (48·76 m.) to the north is a half-round tower twenty-three feet (7·01 m.) in diameter. It is built of fairly small blocks of rubble masonry, not very well coursed. The tower is open-gorged and it is probably safe to guess that the wall walk was continued across the tower in much the same way as at Conway or Caernarvon, namely by a plank which could be removed easily in case of assault.[92] This would enable the defenders to isolate an attacking party, so that the latter could be contained within one section of the wall. Ninety feet (27·43 m.) to the north lies a small rectangular tower, twenty-two feet (6·71 m.) broad, and a further ninety feet (28·95 m.) north is a second, thirty feet (9·14 m.) broad. These stand to a height of only about ten to twelve feet (3·05-3·66 m.), and the masonry is of a different character, being smaller and neater than that of the half-round tower; it is O'Neil's style II, dated to the late twelfth or early thirteenth century, but this does not fit very intelligently into the general plan of the fortifications.[93]

To the north of the larger rectangular tower the curtain is built against it with a straight joint, the new masonry belonging to O'Neil's style III—more medium sized stones with occasional evidence of coursing. It is found also in the original work in the north walls, at the base of the Polymond tower for example. This fits in with the archaeological evidence brought to light by the excavations of John Wacher.[94]

The line of the walls has been preserved in the lane 'Back of the Walls', where a short stretch of masonry still stands immediately south of the site of the East gate. It is built of large stones with no evidence of coursing, probably therefore of the earliest building period. The East gate is shown in prints to have been a large heavy structure with two circular side towers, and a front thrown well forward. Above the gate was a chapel dedicated to St. Mary to which Agnes le Horder left a bequest in 1384.[95]

One hundred and forty-five feet (44·19 m.) north lay a small tower, now no longer extant. Beyond that, at the north-east corner of the walls, lies the Polymond tower (or St. Denys tower, from the priory responsible for its maintenance). It is a drum tower, twenty-eight feet (8·53 m.) in diameter, built of medium sized stones, roughly coursed. There is a string course which runs from the tower to the Bargate. The original date of the tower, and indeed of the two towers 160 feet (48·76 m.) and 280 feet (85·34 m.) further west and of the curtain walling, can probably be ascribed to the late years of the thirteenth century. Much of the work in the towers underwent restoration or rebuilding in the later years of the fourteenth century, as the inserted gunports show, and as the name suggests.[96]

Bargate is of three periods of construction.[97] The original gate had a plain semi-circular arch which was about ten feet (3·05 m.) wide. There was probably an upper storey above the arch, though there were no flanking towers. In the early fourteenth century the two drum towers with narrow arrow slits were added to the north face on either side of the arch (plate 27). At much the same time the south front was added (plate 28). It was carried further to east and west than the line of the old gate to give a larger room above, which was used as the Gildhall. The south front is not of defensive character, having a flat face divided into two storeys. In the upper storey are four two-light windows of fourteenth-century date. On the

ground stage are three archways, the central one being of fourteenth-century date. The two outer archways belong to the eighteenth century. Originally the entrance to the hall above was on
the eastern side; the western opening is now blocked, though it
formerly led to the prison. Under the arch on either side are the
loop-holes which once commanded the ditch.

The north front is the last addition to the gate, and probably
belongs to the early years of the fifteenth century. The stone of this
work is different from that used in the rest of the building, and is
said to have come from the Isle of Wight. It was probably obtained
after the receipt of a grant of 1400, which gave permission to quarry
as much stone as was necessary for the walls in the island.[98] The
front is a projecting forebuilding, with its east and west angles
canted off. The central gateway was placed between a pair of boldly
designed buttresses. Above the arch is a band of panels with heraldic
shields. Above this a battlemented parapet is carried on three tiers
of corbels overhanging about two feet (0·610 m.) beyond the wall.
The parapet has five embrasures, the third of which is out of centre
with the gateway, just as the middle of the three oillets has not been
spaced to come over the apex of the archway. In the corbel table
there are two small arches outside the eastern buttress, but only
one, of wider span, outside the western. The four differ in width.
There is now no apparent means of access to the roof, but it may
have been by an external stair since destroyed from the level of
the wall walk which passed through at first floor level. This is suggested by Brannon's picture. This northern projection may have
been designed to house the portcullis and its winding gear, which
up till now must have been located in the middle of the Gildhall.

One hundred feet (30·48 m.) west of the gate was a half-round
tower. This is no longer in existence. This stretch of wall is similar
in character to that east of Bargate. A change is discernible only
near the Arundel tower where both a short length of wall and the
tower itself are built in smaller stones, uncoursed, with a few larger
stones at the top. O'Neil dated the tower to *c.* 1260. It seems unlikely, however, that an isolated drum tower twenty-two feet (6·71 m.)
in diameter and some fifty to sixty feet (15·24-18·29 m.) high would
have been built at such an early date. The style of the masonry is
very similar to that of the two round towers of Bargate, and can
probably be dated therefore to the early fourteenth century, possibly

to the period of the renewed murage grants (1321 onwards). Before this tower was built one may assume that the wall ran to the edge of the cliff, possibly ending in a bank of earth, as O'Neil suggested.

About 130 feet (39·62 m.) south of the north-west angle stands Catchcold tower,[99] (plate 29). Clearly a later insertion into the original wall, it is built of large roughly-dressed sandstone blocks, fairly well coursed. It is about twenty feet (6·10 m.) in diameter, and stands now to a height of about thirty feet (9·14 m.). At the level of the wall walk there is a vaulted chamber, below a widely corbelled parapet. The chamber was clearly intended for use with guns since it contains three keyhole gunports. Their circular openings are eleven inches (0·279 m.) in diameter; the vertical slits are eleven inches long.

South of this the town wall merged with the wall of the castle bailey, and the two were common almost to the sharp re-entrant angle which covered Biddlesgate. Below the gate the walls are about four feet (1·22 m.) thick and stand to a height of thirty feet (9·14 m.). In a stretch of 260 feet (79·25 m.) the walls of domestic buildings have been incorporated and strengthened by an arcade of nineteen arches, of sufficient depth to provide a rampart walk defended by a battlemented wall along their entire length (plate 25). An early gun loop[100] is to be found in this section. The arches seem to have been strengthened by three towers; one by Biddlesgate, the second in front of the fourth arch and the third beyond the ninth arch.

South of this stands the West gate, a plain rectangular structure flush with the outer face of the walls (plate 26). It is twenty-three feet (7·01 m.) broad and thirty feet (9·14 m.) deep. The roadway, ten feet (3·05 m.) wide, pierces the lowest of the three storeys and is covered by a low pointed vault. The entrance was defended by a heavy door and two portcullises. The wall walk entered the gate at first floor level, and access to the top floor must have been by an internal stairway only. There seems to have been no means of access from the guard chambers to the upper floors. The windows on the west side, recessed into the wall, have remained unaltered. There is one on the first floor and three above. The gate was crenellated and was built of fairly large roughly-dressed stones, well coursed, with dressed quoins.

This style continues south for the length of the fifteenth-century timber guardhouse built against the inside face of the wall. The wall then projects west for about nine feet (2·74 m.), and then continues south for about fifty feet (15·4 m.), where there is a bastion some forty feet (12·19 m.) broad. Behind this bastion are masonry remains which show that the rampart walk was carried on arches, a point well illustrated in Brannon's picture. A much rebuilt section continues from this bastion for seventy feet (36·58 m.) to Bugle tower; it too was arcaded, and two of the original five arches remain.

The south-west and southern stretches of the wall are very fragmentary. From Bugle tower to the Square or Corner tower there is a section of 300 feet (91·44 m.) in which are embedded some stone cannon balls, possibly lost at the time of Henry V's expedition to France in 1415.[101] From the Square tower to the Water gate a stretch of 600 feet (182·88 m.) was destroyed in 1803, and it included the two towers of St. Barbara's and Woolbridge. Water gate, which crossed High Street, was a deep wide structure with a low pointed central arch. Above there was a boldly projecting parapet with seven machicolations. All the windows on the second stage faced into the town. On its western side the gate was recessed and protected by the rounded curtain. On the east the approach was entirely covered by the town wall which at this point made a projection to the south-east for about 110 feet (33·53 m.) until it reached the Watch tower on the sea front. From here the wall ran south for about 250 feet (76·20 m.) until reaching God's House gate.

It is possible to detect in the masonry evidence of several building periods, but it is less easy to date them with any exactness. The most that can be done is to attempt to put them into a coherent sequence and to relate them to the documentary evidence. In 1202 and again in 1203 an allowance of £100 was made to the men of Southampton to help them in the enclosing of the town.[102] It seems unlikely that at this date the money was applied to walling the town in stone, and it seems more probable that the town was enclosed by the earth banks on which the wall was later built. A deed of 1217 implies the existence of an East gate, when a tenement was described as being 'intra burgum Hampton iuxta portam orientalem versus austrum'.[103] The existence of an earth bank into which stone gates were later inserted was shown by an excavation conducted by Mr. John Wacher in which a section across the wall and bank between the Polymond tower and the East gate revealed a bank earlier than the walls, much eroded and scarcely more than three feet (0·914 m.) high.[104]

It may be presumed therefore that the defences were of earth until the first murage grant was received in 1260.[105] It was for a term of ten years, and was renewed for a further five in 1270.[106] In 1282 murage for three years was granted,[107] and in 1286, after an interval of a year, the period was extended for a further five years.[108] Assuming that the money was not diverted to other ends (though some of the proceeds of both the last grants was set aside to be used on the castle) there was a period of at least fifteen, and possibly of thirty years in which there must have been considerable building activity. By the end of this time it seems plausible to suggest that some parts of both the north and the east walls had been completed. Bargate stood in its early thirteenth-century form with the wall to the west ending in an earth bank, and to the east complete to the further side of Polymond tower. The evidence to support this conclusion, which differs from that reached by O'Neil, is firstly the change in the masonry just before the Arundel tower, where a join in the work can be seen and where the new work overlaps the old. Secondly, the masonry of this tower closely resembles the flanking towers added to Bargate in the fourteenth century, and is closer to this style than to the work in the wall to the east of the gate. Thirdly, excavation at the base of the Polymond tower at its junction with the east walls showed a straight joint and a considerable difference in the depth of the footings. This perhaps goes some way towards explaining the two styles of masonry noticed by O'Neil in the east walls. The walls were clearly not contemporary, and taken with the words of the 1353 inquisition,[109] that 'none of the timber of the parapets or the engines has been removed; the parapet on the eastern wall was made with poplar boards and earthen walls for a length of two quarentaines, and has been destroyed by wind and rain to the danger of the town', the suggestion that even by the mid-fourteenth century the east walls were not complete is strong. The line of the north walls would certainly seem to be the earlier, and it is unfortunate that the eastern defences have been destroyed for the most part, and that what survives is in ruinous condition, making it impossible to be more definite about their date.

The series of murage grants which continued throughout the fourteenth century began in 1321 with a grant for three years.[110] It is tempting, though a matter of pure conjecture, to suggest that this paid for the construction of the Arundel tower and for the two round towers flanking Bargate. Some of the later grants were clearly intended to be spent on the western and southern walls, since in 1327 the burgesses were granted quayage 'to complete the quay and enclosure which they are making by the king's order'. [111] The grant was renewed in 1336 so that they could replace the wooden barbican by one of stone, and it was renewed in 1341 for a further period of five years.[112] These grants may refer to the quay under construction at God's House gate, started in 1299.[113] It may even have been at this time that the work on the walls of the southern front was continued from God's House tower (a structure which can almost certainly be dated to the fourteenth century) to St. Barbara's tower at the foot of Bugle Street. This conclusion is put forward largely on the ground of the architectural similarity of the tower plans of this section and those of the east and north walls. All the half-round towers on the walls fall in this section, with the exception of towers 3 and 4 which may very well belong to rebuilding in the 1370s by the Friars Minor, revealed by a straight joint to the north of tower 4.[114] This explanation links better with the rest of the documentary evidence than do other theories.

The French raid on the town in 1338 provides many indications of the state of the defences in addition to the obvious fact that what did exist did not prove effective. It is unfortunate that the results of the inquisition by which Richard, earl of Arundel, was to discover through whose fault the town was taken are not extant. But it is surely significant that such an enquiry was made, and that following this, in March, 1339, the sheriff of Southampton was ordered to impress carpenters, smiths, masons, plasterers and other workmen for the work of enclosing the town, and to provide them with materials.[115] The chronicle evidence suggests that the western shore was not completely walled,[116] since the town was captured from the sea, and this impression is borne out by the more detailed statements of the 1363 inquisition. An earlier one, of 1353, suggests that there had been a certain laxity amongst the officials responsible for the murage, and it may have been this which enabled the French so thoroughly to plunder the town. Further light is thrown on this matter by a memorandum on the Close Roll for July 1339.[117] Here it was noted that 'Nicholas Mundelard, late one of the collectors of custom in the said port of Southampton was pardoned imprisonment having made a fine, and undertaken to restore to the king what pertained to him'. This was followed in 1341 by a commission of oyer and terminer touching the accounts of the money collected as 'barbicanage' under the grant of 1327.[118]

The right to levy murage for six years was renewed in 1345, and granted again in 1347 for four years.[119] These grants seem to have run consecutively, for at the end of their sum total, in 1355, murage was granted for a period of ten years.[120] Following the disaster of 1338 it is natural that building activities should have increased, but it seems probable that better planned results followed on the recommendations of a three-jury inquisition, taken in 1363.[121] It is indeed possible that most of the west walls were built as a result of it.

The inquisition was to enquire as to the obstruction of the defence of the town by porches and gardens adjoining the wall, the defects in the wall itself, and the engines and other appliances there for defence. They reported that 'it would be well to have the gate at Pilgrimesputte walled up and the wall beyond it raised. The little postern in the cellar of John Wytegod should be closed with a wall as thick as the wall of the cellar. All the doors and windows of the houses towards the sea should be walled up three feet [0·914 m.] thick or more at the cost of the lords. All the great gates and posterns of the town should be thickly walled up except Northgate, Southgate, Westgate, Eastgate and the gate of Neweton. A common way should be made within the walls and enclosures around the town of the width of twelve royal feet [3·66 m.], and every man having gardens within the town should take away all the dung lying in the way, each against his own plot. All the gardens outside the town should be destroyed from the town ditch to the ditch of Saltemarch. All the houses in the suburb which might be hurtfull to the town in time of war should be removed by view of the Keeper. A double ditch should be made towards the sea from Pylgrimsputte to the gate of Bolestrete. A cutting should be made from Houndwell to the town ditch so that the running water may have its way to the ditch. One sentry box or more should be made round about the town between every two towers. A wall of earth or stone should be made on one side of the town for the length of five hundred paces.'

Some elucidation of this survey is necessary to understand its full significance. The 'gate at Pilgrimsputte' refers to a gate somewhere on the west side near the site of Biddlesgate.[122] The walling up of the doors and windows must have resulted in the arcade, and seems to rule out the possibility that a wall which could need raising already existed to the south of Biddlesgate. The wall beyond Pilgrimsputte probably refers therefore to the castle wall lying to the north. The fact that houses stood in this part of the town in such a way that by merely walling them up a suitable defence could be made also suggests that until now there had been no protection. The sentence recommending that a ditch should be made from Pilgrimsputte to Bolestrete makes is possible to suggest that the inquisition resulted in the walling of the town from a point near Biddlesgate to the southern end of Bugle Street (derived from Bolestrete), especially when one considers also the definite recommendation that a wall of earth or stone should be made on one side of the town for the length of five hundred paces, a measurement which is approximately correct. The topographical reconstruction would imply that Westgate had been standing in isolation until this date, and this does not seem impossible. Southgate is the gate now called Watergate, but originally known as Newgate. It is referred to in this way in the Patent Rolls of 1378, and in 1396 in a quit-claim in the town archives as *'portam novam vocatur Watergate'*.[123] This carries with it the suggestion that a great deal of building followed the inquest. Traces of the common way remain in the lane 'Back of the Walls' and more especially in Cuckoo Lane, all of which lies behind the section of wall which it is suggested was built at this time. On the western side it could not have existed further to the north because of the houses.

Much of the western wall was therefore built after 1363, and the bulk of the murage grants postdate the inquisition. In 1369 the mayor and bailiffs were empowered to compel all who dwelt in the town or who had rents there to contribute to the repairs.[124] In 1374 they were to find twenty hewers of stone to work on the walls.[125] But this was not enough, and in 1376 the commons and tenants of Southampton sent a petition to parliament asking both to be pardoned payment of the fee farm because many of the inhabitants had departed, and for grant of the farm towards the cost of fortifications, since both the farm, and £500 more, had already been spent.[126] Their petition was granted, their arrears pardoned and remission for two years granted.[127] A week later the mayor and bailiffs were enjoined to compel all inhabitants to pay their share of the costs.[128] In 1379 the fee farm was again remitted, this time for three years,[129] a favour renewed for a further three years in 1382.[130] In 1386 two of the inhabitants, Sir John Sondes and John Polymond, were appointed to survey the condition of the town and to put it into a state of defence against the threatened invasion.[131] It was probably at this time that the Polymond and Arundel towers received their names, Polymond being a prominent burgess, Sir John Arundel the governor of the castle. Both men were associated with the building operations.

In 1400 the king granted the burgesses £200 from the customs duties on wool and a further £100 from the fee farm to be taken annually for as long as it should please the king.[132] The extant accounts, though there are no particulars, show an annual expenditure exceeding revenue by a considerable amount.[133] Some of the money may have been spent on the northern extension of Bargate, since in 1400 the mayor received a licence to take as much stone as before from the Isle of Wight.[134]

The last account in the series relates to the building of God's House tower, when £100 is recorded as having been spent.[135] In 1417, £100 had been allocated from the customs duties for the same purpose though it may already have been spent.[136]

The construction of the Catchcold tower seems to have been the last undertaking of the town. The first mention of the tower is found in April 1439 when the Stewards Book records the payment of 20d. to Jacob Johnson and Laurence Strode for carrying piles to 'Le Cachecold', and payments to a total of eighteen men who worked for three days are recorded in May.[137] This is clearly no more than repair work, but it does at least provide a *terminus post quem* for the date of the tower. Its purpose was probably to accommodate new weapons and to provide opportunities for the use of new weapons.

The expenditure on the walls throughout the fifteenth century was constant if inconsiderable.[138] In 1460 the mayor, aldermen and sheriff of Southampton received a commission of array to enable them to resist Richard, duke of York, Richard, earl of Warwick, and Richard, earl of Salisbury and the king's enemies who purposed to enter the said town; and to fortify the walls, and make defences called *'loupes'* thereon, and to appoint watches, scouts and keepers of the gates day and night.[139] In 1478 the mayor and commonalty were granted £40 yearly for seven years from customs duties, which was to be expended 'from time to time on the repair and fortification of the walls'. It looks as though the money was supplied by two merchants of Southampton who in the same year were pardoned payment of a debt of £250 due to the king in return for providing £40 for seven years.[140] That the walls were regarded as still being important is shown by the fact that in a general act of Resumption passed in 1482[141] it was specifically stated that it should not be prejudicial to any letters patent or grants made to the mayor, burgesses and inhabitants of Southampton for the repair of the walls.

SOUTHWARK   Nothing is known of the Saxon *burh* listed in the Burghal Hidage.

TONBRIDGE   A single grant of murage was received in 1318 (*CPR*, 133). There is nothing now to indicate defences, although there is a plan in S. Toy, *The Castles of Great Britain*, 1954, 59. The town might have been walled largely through the efforts of its lord because of its importance as the *caput* of the honour of Clare rather than as a strategic centre.

WINCHELSEA   The town enclosed a triangular area of approximately 150 acres on top of a hill. It seems doubtful from both the archaeological and documentary evidence whether the circuit was ever enclosed by a stone wall, although Ditchfield mentions that foundations and footings had been discovered.[142] Except for a short stretch of about one hundred yards (91·44 m.) north-west of Pipewell gate where the wall is two feet two inches (0·660 m.) thick and stands to a height of seven feet (2·13 m.) on the inside, there are traces of only a bank and ditch. The small amount of documentary evidence available bears out the hypothesis that the banks were the most important part of the defences.

The first murage grant to the new town of Winchelsea was made

22. *CANTERBURY, towers in the south-east corner.*

23. *RYE, Landgate, exterior.*

24. SOUTHAMPTON, *view of the town in 1554.*

26. SOUTHAMPTON, West Gate, interior.

27. *SOUTHAMPTON, Bargate, exterior.*

28. *SOUTHAMPTON, Bargate, interior face.*

in 1295, for a term of five years.[143] In 1321–2 the abbot of Iham, through the abbot of Fécamp, sent a petition to parliament asking for compensation for the losses he sustained when the men of Winchelsea had driven the ditch across his property.[144] The immediate reply was that his petition would be considered in the Council. In the same year the townsmen received murage for seven years.[145]

During the middle decades of the century there is no indication from documentary sources that any work was done on the defences, but in 1380 three men were appointed 'to certify in what ways and at whose cost the town may best be fortified'.[146] From the French attacks of 1359, when the town had been burnt, and of 1380 when it is said to have been captured,[147] one must suppose that the defences had not been completed. We do not know whether the commission made any recommendations. The next documentary references are not until 1414 when another commission was instructed to inquire into the proposals of the mayor and commonalty 'to enclose the town with a wall of lesser circuit than the former site of the town, to enclose the whole of which would be a considerable burden'.[148] On this occasion arrangements were to be made to satisfy the owners of the land over which the wall would extend. The new line was to run across the king's waste land,[149] and to assist with this work the corporation received a grant of 200 marks annually for three years from the customs duties in adjacent ports.[150] It seems possible that much of this was never received, although the explanation may lie in the defects of the Memoranda Rolls. The total amount received seems only to have been £136 13s 3d in the course of 1414–15,[151] and there is no evidence for later years. Between 20 April and 12 May 1415, masons were working on a tower 'near the canons of the town', and possibly therefore at the north-west corner, in the field called Friars Orchard, and between 24 May and 13 October 1414 work was being done on the ditches. An agreement was made with one David Hammer to dig eight virgates of the ditch at 37s 6d per virgate.[152] In 1417 men were employed for a total of 2,801 working days on the ditches, and a further contract with one Thomas Baron specified that he should make six virgates at 33s 4d per virgate.[153] Part of the work done can still be seen between the north-west angle of the town to the corner of the site of St. Giles' church yard.[154]

The documentary evidence is therefore concentrated on the

M

earth defences, and there is nothing to indicate at what date the three stone gates were erected.[155] Strand gate is probably the earliest, and can probably be dated to the middle years of the fourteenth century (plate 30). Four round towers flank a central archway, each tower linked by short stretches of curtain wall. The entrance was protected by a double portcullis, the grooves for which can still be seen in both the north and south faces. Covering the archway was a vaulted ceiling, but only the springers and the wall ribs are still in position. The vault must have supported a chamber to house the portcullis machinery. The room was reached by a door and stairway in the north-east tower, which presumably also provided access to the top of the towers. The original height of the gate has been lost; the towers at present stand to a height of about twenty-five feet (7·62 m.). Their defensive provisions are difficult to re-construct especially since the towers are little more than five feet (1·52 m.) in diameter, and do not appear to have had any timber staging. There was in any case scarcely room for a man to fire, whether cannon or bow and arrow. Any attacks must have been repelled from the top of the towers, now missing. A section of curtain walling abutted on to the south face of the south-east tower at an approximate height of twelve feet (3·66 m.), and continued its northward line from the north-west tower. All the masonry is made up of irregularly coursed rubble work.

In the line of the north wall, and guarding the second approach to the town, stood Pipewell gate (also called the Land or Ferry gate). An earlier structure is said to have been destroyed in 1380, and the existing gate was almost certainly built in the early years of the fifteenth century. The shield in the west face of the gate, now much weathered, is said to contain a squirrel over which is inscribed 'I. HELDE', presumably standing for John Helde, mayor in 1404–1405. The gate is a plain rectangular structure, with internal measurements of sixteen and a half feet by thirteen feet (5·03 m. x 3·96 m.), which now presents no defensive features; it is not even certain whether there was an upper storey. The arch was roofed over with a flattish barrel vault, of which only the springers remain. The town wall, three feet (0·914 m.) thick, joined the gate at the north-east corner; it continued its line westwards from the south-west angle.

The New gate, on the original southern boundary of the town

on the Hastings road, stands at the junction of the southern stretch of the town wall with the western wall. The bank and ditch can be seen very clearly at this point, and the line of the defences, here below the brow of the hill, was clearly intended to defend the harbour. This may have been the reason for the enclosure of such a large area, and it suggests that the construction of the gate was started before 1414. The gate is a single-arched structure, with two three-sided towers on either side. It is flanked by a short stretch of walling to each side, which may have been constructed only to help with the defence of the gate, since there is no sign of the wall above the ditch for any length. The width of the entrance is ten feet four inches (3·15 m.) and the structure is eleven feet (3·35 m.) in depth.

WINCHESTER   The defences enclose an area of 138 acres. There were five gates, two of which remain, a postern and two turrets, none of which now exists. Archaeological and documentary evidence is plentiful.

The West gate is the finest remaining part of the defences (plate 31). It was cleared of the houses which abutted onto its northern side in 1940 and underwent extensive restoration.[156] The windows in the east wall suggest that the original rectangular structure is probably of thirteenth-century date. Much of the original work was in flint, with ashlar quoins, but much of the present ashlar is modern re-facing. The details of the west face suggest that it was added in the late fourteenth century, although there is no documentary contemporary record of its construction.[157]

The gate had a machicolated top, and was divided into three stages by string courses. Beneath the upper of these is a pair of quatre-foiled panels, which enclose shields charged with the royal and city arms. They are flanked by sculptured heads through which the chains of a drawbridge passed. Below are two gunports. The lower string course is said to be carved with the white hart couchant, the badge of Richard II. The condition of the carvings has deteriorated since this was first pointed out, but if it is correct, it means that the west face cannot be earlier than 1390, the date at which Richard II adopted the badge for his livery. O'Neil suggested that the style of the two gunports might fix the date more closely. They can be paralleled in a tower in Canterbury dated to the years

1390–94, and O'Neil ascribed the examples at Winchester to the years 1392–4, when negotiations for the truce finally signed in 1394 were at a standstill, and the threat of invasion was still hanging over people's heads.[158] This hypothesis is further strengthened by the fact that it was at this time that the town was in receipt of substantial grants from the ulnage subsidy, a point which O'Neil overlooked.

Of the internal arrangements of the gates as they relate to the defence of the town, little evidence remains. The recess for the portcullis remains in the western wall. It is seventeen feet six inches (5·33 m.) high and twelve feet (3·66 m.) wide. Above are two iron staples, from which the portcullis was lowered on ropes. The two gunports were between these ropes. The battlements, and presumably also the wall walk, are reached from a further flight of stairs. The point at which the wall abutted onto the north face of the gate was marked in flints by the restorers of 1940. It was commanded by a small arrow slit.

From the gate the wall ran south for roughly one thousand feet (304·8 m.), and was interrupted by the castle wall.[159] It then turned east. The South gate, destroyed in 1771, stood to the south of the meeting of South Gate Street and St. Swithun's Street.[160] Little survives of the wall from this point to King's gate although its line is clearly that of the garden walls of houses on the south side of St. Swithun's Street. The two small sections which can be seen both show a core of flint and sandstone set in bright yellow mortar standing to a height of ten feet (3·05 m.). Another section, under Wykeham's Motors showrooms, was seen in 1965.[161]

King's gate is the only other gate to survive. It is of an entirely different character from the West gate, and gives little indication of ever having been a defensive work. It is first mentioned in 1148,[162] and is referred to again in 1264,[163] but the present structure is probably a fifteenth-century rebuilding. The gate is a low structure. supporting a chapel over three archways. The westernmost of these is modern, and the others have been much restored. The central arch may date from the fourteenth century; it is of two moulded orders and is set between small buttresses. There is no vaulting either over the road or the pavements. The windows of the chapel were repaired in 1484.

The best preserved section of the medieval wall stands between

King's gate and the site of the East gate, which was pulled down in 1768. The section which formed part of the enclosure of the bishop's palace of Wolvesey stands in places to a height of twenty feet (6·10 m.), and though much of the facing is modern, it is still possible to distinguish patchings in three different mortars; the bright yellow of the late fourteenth century, the cream of the thirteenth century, and the pinky buff of the Roman work. Crenellations still survive in parts. In the grounds of Wolvesey castle the wall is banked by an earth ramp twenty to thirty feet (6.10-9.14 m.) wide, and up to six feet (1·83 m.) in height. This has been shown to be of Roman construction. A section cut across the defences near the south-east corner revealed that the Roman wall remained to a height of seven feet (2·13 m.), and had been refaced for the top two feet (0·610 m.) with a cream mortar. The level contemporary with the refacing contained fragments of a thirteenth-century pitcher. The wall had been repointed a second time in hard bright yellow mortar with chalk flecks.[164] Mortar of this type was also found in the cuttings in Colebrook Street, nearer to the East gate, and can be seen in the fourteenth-century work in the West gate.[165] The date of the work at Wolvesey, however, receives independent confirmation from the Pipe Rolls of the bishopric of Winchester. In 1374, £34 11s 10d was spent on the repair of fifty-one perches (256·487 m.) of wall from Wymondshed towards the great gate.[166]

Excavations in Colebrook Street, nearer to the East gate,[167] showed that by the twelfth century the Roman wall was little more than a stump and that in the thirteenth century the wall was reconstructed on the line of the front of the Roman work, and was repaired in the fourteenth century. The gate is mentioned in 1148, and had a chapel over it.[168] The final stretch of the wall before the gate is reached has been incorporated in property boundaries.

The section of wall north of the gate has been destroyed, and its line awaits clarification. Speed's map shows that it was far from straight, and probably it made an angle to cross the mill-streams. Durngate, at the north-east corner of the defences, was probably never more than a postern; it was not mentioned in either of the twelfth century surveys, and was walled up in 1377.[169] Speed shows two entrances to the city in the section between the East and North gates, a feature not substantiated by other evidence.

North Walls are now largely only property boundaries, with modern re-facing. Sections showed that in the thirteenth century a new wall had been built partly on the stump of the Roman wall and partly south of that line. It was later re-faced, possibly in the late fourteenth century.[170] The North gate was destroyed in 1771, and from this point until the West gate the wall has been almost entirely destroyed. The Hermit's tower at the north-west corner is a modern erection on the site of an earlier drum tower; the two towers shown by Speed on the section of wall between the corner and the gate have also been destroyed, but one has recently been excavated. The fabric had been totally robbed, but the robber trenches of the north and south walls, each five feet (1·52 m.) thick and ten feet (3·05 m.) apart internally, were clearly defined. All traces of the front wall of the tower had been removed so that its form must remain uncertain, and there was no dating evidence.[171] Whether it can be linked with the grant of 1217 must remain uncertain.

Documentary and archaeological evidence converge to show that there were two building periods, the first in the earlier part of the thirteenth century, the second in the later years of the fourteenth century. There are earlier references to the walls. With the exception of Durngate and King's gate they were all mentioned in the Winton Domesday of 1110, and again in 1148, with the exception of Durngate. In 1217 the north gate was granted to Brito '*balistarius*'.[172] The town also received a gift of timber to help in the making of towers and alures, an exactness of phraseology not often found in grants of this kind.[173] In 1228 the king remitted payment of fifty marks of the last tallage to the men of the town, '*in auxilium ville claudende*'.[174]

The first in a series of murage grants was received in 1228,[175] but the grants fall into no very clear chronological pattern. Repairs were probably continuous throughout the Middle Ages. The grant of 1228 ran for two years, and was renewed only in 1233,[176] for a further two years. Apparently concurrent with this was another grant running from Michaelmas 1234 to 1236.[177] This was renewed until 1239,[178] and a further grant was received in 1241 for three years.[179]

The next building period was from 1256-78. An entry on the Liberate Roll orders the sheriff to 'crenellate well the buttress from the bottom of the tower ditch to the top of the tower, and to finish the town wall as far as the said tower'.[180] It provides no more than an indication that work was being done in the south-west section of the defences. In the same year a murage grant for seven years was received.[181] It was renewed for the same period in 1264, [182] and again in 1271.[183] The citizens of Winchester attacked and burnt the buildings of the prior and convent in 1264,[184] including King's gate, and it was perhaps this attack which caused the mayor and prior to re-affirm their responsibilities for the repair of the wall between King's gate and South gate, and to battlement the sections.[185]

The years 1285–96 were covered by three grants: 1285–8; 1291–2, and 1292–6.[186] A single grant for seven years was received in 1316 at the instance of John Sandale, king's clerk, and bishop-elect of Ely.[187]

From this date until 1369 there seems to have been a pause in building activities, although the murage grants show that murage was still collected,[188] perhaps under the writ issued in 1339,[189] which ordered the mayor and three others to hold a commission of investigation into the state of the walls, and the men in the city were commanded to contribute to the upkeep of the defences of their own city. Probably nothing was done after this, for in 1369 the mayor and bailiffs received another commission enjoining them to see to the repair of the walls, and empowering them to distrain the inhabitants to pay, each according to his means.[190] They were also given a grant of the ulnage subsidy for five years to be spent on the repair of the walls.[191] This was renewed in 1389 and again in 1393 and 1397,[192] although there was no answer to the petition to the parliament of 1376 which had asked for either the renewal of the ulnage or for a remission of the fee farm.[193]

In 1406 the mayor and bailiffs were again empowered to compel all having lands and rents to contribute according to their means for seven years,[194] and this was repeated in 1422.[195] Finally, in 1410 the mayor and citizens were permitted to acquire lands and rents so that they could sustain the charges of the walls and gates.[196] In 1441 and 1452 they were granted forty marks for fifty years from the ulnage subsidy.[197] Provision was thus made for the maintenance of the fortifications throughout the fifteenth century.

Although the town accounts are voluminous and show that much work was done on the walls, they provide few details. The heaviest expenditure on the defences was in the late fourteenth century, but the money was received from the ulnage subsidy, not from the ordinary levy of murage ward by ward. Thus between 1389 and 1394, £20 was received annually from the subsidy,[198] £52 between 1393 and 1395,[199] and £26 17s 4d between 1396–7.[200] The city archives record the expenditure of £40 12s 8½d in 1397–8,[201] but it must remain a matter of conjecture whether any of this was spent on the West gate, although it is probable.

Throughout the fifteenth century the walls were maintained, the most detailed account being that for the repair of a section between King's gate and South gate in 1473–4 when £15 11s 8d was spent.[202] The West gate received minor repairs in 1416–17,[203] and the East gate in the following year, 1417–18, when over a period of eight weeks £9 11s 9d was spent.[204] The wall at the North gate was repaired at the same time at a cost of £2 8s 4d. The east wall, near the Hospital of St. John, was repaired in 1397–8 and in 1407–1408.[205] Finally, minor repairs were carried out on Durngate in 1462-3.[206]

NOTES

1   *Chronica Rogeri de Hoveden (Rolls Series)*, 75.
2   D.B., I, f. 2.
3   *Pipe Roll, 13 Henry II*, 196.
4   Quoted from W. Somner, *Antiquities of Canterbury*, 1640, 10.
5   *Cal. Pat. Rolls, 1361–4*, 373.
6   *Cal. Pat. Rolls, 1377–81*, 274.
7   *Rot. Parl.*, III, 53.
8   *Cal. Pat. Rolls, 1377–81*, 370.
9   *Cal. Pat. Rolls, 1377–81*, 450.
10 *Cal. Pat. Rolls, 1381–5*, 8.
11 *Cal. Pat. Rolls, 1385–9*, 103.
12 *Cal. Pat. Rolls, 1381–5*, 555.
13 *Cal. Close Rolls, 1385–9*, 120–21.
14 *Cal. Close Rolls, 1385–9*, 207.
15 *Cal. Close Rolls, 1385–9*, 342.
16 *Cal. Pat. Rolls, 1396–9*, 592.
17 *Cal. Pat. Rolls, 1401–1405*, 118.
18 *Cal. Close Rolls, 1402–1405*, 194–5.
19 Quoted in Somner, *Antiquities of Canterbury*, 13.
20 *Cal. Pat. Rolls, 1405–1408*, 85.
21 *Cal. Pat. Rolls, 1408–1413*, 104.
22 John Harvey, *Henry Yevele*, 1946, 61.

23 Quoted from R. Willis, 'The Conventual Buildings of the Monastery of Christ Church in Canterbury', *Arch. Cant.*, VII, 1868, 189.
24 *Ibid.*, 9.
25 E. Hasted, *History of Kent*, IV, 413, 1797–1801.
26 *Hist. Mss. Comm.* 9th Rep. 145.
27 *Arch. Cant.*, LIX, 1946, 69–71.
28 I am indebted to Professor Frere for this information.
29 *Med. Arch.*, IV, 1960, 149. The statement here that Richard II gave 250 marks towards the building of the walls in 1390 is not accurate; it is to be attributed to Hasted, IV, 412, but without further substantiation.
30 Hasted, *History of Kent*, IV, 413.
31 *Cal. Pat. Rolls, 1377–81*, 450.
32 D. F. Renn, 'The Southampton Arcade', *Med. Arch.*, VIII, 1964, 226–8.
33 P.R.O. E 364/27.
34 Treasurer's Accounts F/A/3. The city archives are deposited in the Cathedral Library.
35 Treasurer's Accounts F/A/5.
36 Hasted, *History of Kent*, IV, 413.
37 Treasurer's Accounts F/A/5.
38 The seal is illustrated in *V.C.H. Kent*, II, opp. p. 114.
39 *Cal. Pat. Rolls, 1485–94*, 388.
40 Hasted, *History of Kent*, IV, 414.
41 P.R.O. E 364/27.
42 *V.C.H. Sussex*, IX, 41.
43 Holloway, *History*, 587.
44 *V.C.H. Sussex*, IX, 41, notices the difference in the stone and suggests a date *c.* 1380–85. There is no attempt to link it with the account, deposited in the East Sussex Record Office, Rye Ms 60/2.
45 *Cal. Pat. Rolls, 1327–30*, 403.
46 *Cal. Pat. Rolls, 1330–34*, 304; *Cal. Pat. Rolls, 1334–8*, 230.
47 *Cal. Pat. Rolls, 1343–5*, 43.
48 *Cal. Pat. Rolls, 1348–50*, 93.
49 *Cal. Pat. Rolls, 1367–70*, 224.
50 Knighton, *Chronicon*, II, 9 *(Rolls Series)*.
51 *Cal. Pat. Rolls, 1370–74*, 203.
52 *Cal. Pat. Rolls, 1377–81*, 74–5.
53 *Rot. Parl.*, III, 70.
54 *Cal. Pat. Rolls, 1377–81*, 434; *Cal. Close Rolls, 1377–81*, 288. The account is to be found in P.R.O. E 364/57.
55 *Hist. Mss. Comm.* 5th Rep., 497.
56 P.R.O. Anct. Petitions 4275.
57 *Cal. Pat. Rolls, 1381–5*, 525.
58 *Cal. Pat. Rolls, 1381–5*, 588.
59 P.R.O. E 364/31.
60 P.R.O. E 364/22.
61 P.R.O. E 364/57.
62 William Boys, *Collections for a History of Sandwich*, 1792, 335.
63 *Arch. Jnl.*, 86, 289–90. It should be noted that the repair work said to have been done on this gate in 1541 was in fact done on Newgate, and the reference to Boys' *History* is to this.

64 Boys, *History*, 312.
65 Boys, *History*, 284.
66 The details are given in Dorothy Gardiner, *History of Sandwich*, 1954, 34–35.
67 *Select Cases before King's Bench*, I, 13–14 *(Selden Society)*.
68 They were released in June 1275; *Cal. Close Rolls, 1272–9*, 194.
69 There is some confusion over the fate of this structure. Walsingham, *Historia Anglicana*, II, 147 *(Rolls Series)* says that it was brought to Sandwich; Knighton, *Chronicon*, II, 212 *(Rolls Series)* to Winchelsea.
70 *Cal. Pat. Rolls, 1321–4*, 14.
71 *Cal. Close Rolls, 1339–41*, 237.
72 *Cal. Close Rolls, 1381–5*, 520.
73 *Cal. Pat. Rolls, 1381–5*, 534.
74 *Cal. Pat. Rolls, 1385–9*, 268.
75 *Cal. Pat. Rolls, 1385–9*, 140.
76 *Cal. Pat. Rolls, 1401–1405*, 489.
77 *Cal. Pat. Rolls, 1408–1413*, 425.
78 Quoted from Gardiner, *History*, 135–6, from the Old Black Book, ff. 29–30.
79 Quoted from Gardiner, *History*, 136.
80 Quoted from Gardiner, *History*, 137.
81 John de Waurin, *Chronicles, 1447–71 (Rolls Series)*, 385–8.
82 Quoted Gardiner, *History*, 139–40, Old Black Book, f. 104d.
83 *Cal. Pat. Rolls, 1461–7*, 63.
84 P.R.O. E 364/112 m.B, 1462–3; E 364/112 m.A, 1463–4.
85 *Cal. Pat. Rolls, 1461–7*, 465.
86 *Cal. Close Rolls, 1476–85*, 47–8.
87 P.R.O. E 101/468/27, 28, 29.
88 P.R.O. E 101/468/28.
89 *Cal. Pat. Rolls, 1476–85*, 405.
90 *Itinerary*, I, 276–7.
91 J. S. Davies, *History of Southampton*, 1883; *V.C.H. Hampshire*, III, 496–503, (1908), to which I am especially indebted for many of the measurements quoted; B. H. St. J. O'Neil, 'Southampton Town Wall', in *Aspects of Archaeology*, ed. W. F. Grimes, 1951.
92 A. J. Taylor, *Conway Castle and Town Walls*, 32.
93 See p. 170.
94 See p. 171.
95 B. M. Cartulary of St. Denys, Add Mss. 15314, ff.85, 86.
96 See p. 175.
97 R. M. D. Lucas, *Hants. Field Club*, IV, 1898–1903, 131–6.
98 *Cal. Pat. Rolls, 1399–1401*, 239.
99 O'Neil, *Castle and Cannon*, 31.
100 The association of Henry Yevele with this work is not attested by documentary evidence as D. F. Renn suggests, *Med. Arch.*, VIII, 1964, 226–228.
101 A. H. Skelton, *Hants. Field Club*, II, 1890–93, 81–3.
102 *Pipe Roll 4 John*, 78–9; *Pipe Roll 5 John*, 145. The wording of the grant, 'ad villam claudendam' makes it unlikely that the inner arch of Bargate is connected with the grant as O'Neil suggested, 'Southampton Town Wall', 251.
103 B.M. Add. Mss. 15314, f. 35.

104 *Med. Arch.*, II, 1958, 198.
105 *Cal. Pat. Rolls, 1258–66*, 126.
106 *Cal. Pat. Rolls, 1266–72*, 492.
107 *Cal. Pat. Rolls, 1281–92*, 13.
108 *Cal. Pat. Rolls, 1281–92*, 229.
109 *Cal. Inq. Misc.*, III, no. 113, 38.
110 *Cal. Pat. Rolls, 1317–21*, 590.
111 *Cal. Pat. Rolls, 1327–30*, 64.
112 *Cal. Pat. Rolls, 1334–8*, 240–1; *Cal. Pat. Rolls, 1340–43*, 136.
113 Quoted from Davies, *History*, 455, but not found on either the Close or Patent Rolls.
114 O'Neil, 'Southampton Town Wall', 249; grant in *Hist. Mss. Comm.* 11th Rep., 69.
115 *Cal. Close Rolls, 1339–41*, 55.
116 Murimuth, *Chronicon (Rolls Series)*, 87.
117 *Cal. Close Rolls, 1339–41*, 241.
118 *Cal. Pat. Rolls, 1340–43*, 326.
119 *Cal. Pat. Rolls, 1343–5*, 467; *Cal. Pat. Rolls, 1345–8*, 279.
120 *Cal. Pat. Rolls, 1354–8*, 254.
121 *Cal. Inq. Misc.*, III, no. 425, 154.
122 Davies, *History*, 86.
123 *Cal. Pat. Rolls, 1377–81*, 230. The quit-claim is quoted from Davies, *History*, 97.
124 *Cal. Pat. Rolls, 1367–70*, 239–40.
125 *Cal. Pat. Rolls, 1370–74*, 405–406.
126 *Rot. Parl.*, II, 346.
127 *Cal. Pat. Rolls, 1377–81*, 76.
128 *Cal. Pat. Rolls, 1377–81*, 80 and P.R.O. E 364/12 m.E.
129 *Cal. Pat. Rolls, 1377–81*, 448.
130 *Cal. Pat. Rolls, 1381–5*, 184.
131 *Cal. Pat. Rolls, 1385–9*, 258.
132 *Originalia Roll* I Henry IV, pt. 2, Rot. 27, quoted from T. Madox, *Firma Burgi*, 1726, 290.
133

Year	Receipts			Expenses			P.R.O. Reference
1377–8	£202	10s					E 364/12 m.E.
1400	£300	0s		£300	7s	3d	E 364/37 m.B.
1400–1401	£300	0s		£336	18s	2d	E 364/36 m.G.
1400–1401	£300	0s		£303	17s	4d	E 364/36 m.G.
1402–1403	£300	0s		£417	0s	4d	E 364/36 m.H.
1403–1404	£300	0s		£345	2s	0d	E 364/39 m.D.
1421	£100	0s		£100	0s	0d	E 364/25 m.C.

134 *Cal. Pat. Rolls, 1399–1401*, 239.
135 P.R.O. E 364/55.
136 *Cal. Pat. Rolls, 1416–22*, 109. O'Neil is, therefore, incorrect when he states that the earliest reference to the tower is in 1424 in the *Black Book of Southampton*, ed. H. B. Wallis-Chapman (Southampton Record Society), I, 78n.
137 *Southampton Stewards' Book*, ed. H. W. Gidden (Southampton Record Society), II, 78, 82, 95–6.
138 *Stewards' Books, passim.*
139 *Cal. Pat. Rolls, 1452–61*, 602.
140 *Cal. Pat. Rolls, 1476–85*, 76; *Cal. Close Rolls, 1476–85*, 109.

141 *Rot. Parl.*, VI, 201.
142 P. H. Ditchfield, *B.A.A.J.*, N.S. 30, 1924, 120–31.
143 *Cal. Pat. Rolls, 1292–1301,* 147.
144 *Rot. Parl.*, I, 393a.
145 *Cal. Pat. Rolls, 1321–4,* 14.
146 *Cal. Pat. Rolls, 1377–81,* 566.
147 Walsingham, *Historia Anglicana (Rolls Series)*, I, 287, 439.
148 *Cal. Pat. Rolls, 1413–16,* 224.
149 *Cal. Pat. Rolls, 1413–16,* 368–9.
150 *Cal. Pat. Rolls, 1413–16,* 273.
151 P.R.O. E 364/57 records receipt of £56 13s 4d and an expenditure of £56 13s 8d; E 364/54 receipt of £79 19s 11d and expenditure of £80 1s 4d; E 101/491/12 is the particulars of E 364/57, but adds nothing.
152 P.R.O. E 364/54.
153 P.R.O. E 364/57.
154 G. E. Chambers, *Arch. Jnl.*, XCIV, 1937, 196.
155 More detailed architectural descriptions of the gates can be found in *V.C.H. Sussex*, IX, 63–4.
156 B. H. St. John O'Neil, *Procs. Hants. Field Club*, XV, 1943, 58–61.
157 The suggestion that William Wykeham designed the gate was made by W. H. Jacob, *Procs. Hants. Field Club*, IV, 1905, 51–9; see also O'Neil, *Castle and Cannon*, 17. There is no documentary evidence to substantiate the idea or to refute it.
158 B. H. St. John O'Neil, *Procs. Hants. Field Club*, XVI, 1947, 56–8.
159 Much of the following description is taken from the *V.C.H. Hants.*, V, 3–5, or B. Cunliffe, *Procs. Hants. Field Club*, XXII, 1962, 51–81, cited as Cunliffe. Martin Biddle, *Antiq. Jnl.*, XLIV, 1964, fig. 2 for the relation of the castle and the town defences in this area.
160 Foundations of the Roman gate were uncovered and briefly reported in *Journal Roman Studies*, XVIII, 1928, 207.
161 M. Biddle, *Antiq. Jnl.*, XLV, 1965, 237.
162 *Winton Domesday (Rec. Comm.* 1816), 559.
163 *Annales Monastici, De Wintonia et Waverleia,* 101 *(Rolls Series)*.
164 Cunliffe, 71.
165 Cunliffe, 69.
166 I am indebted to D. Keen and I. Fisher for this information; Pipe Rolls of the bishop of Winchester, Hants. Rec. Office, 159382, m.35d.
167 Cunliffe, 69.
168 *Winton Domesday (Rec. Comm.,* 1816), 555.
169 P.R.O. C/47/60.2.
170 Cunliffe, 63–4.
171 M. Biddle, *Antiq. Jnl.*, XLV, 1965, 238.
172 *Cal. Pat. Rolls, 1216–25,* 44.
173 *Rot. Litt. Claus.*, I, 240.
174 *Cal. Close Rolls, 1227–31,* 54–5.
175 *Cal. Pat. Rolls, 1225–32,* 189.
176 *Cal. Pat. Rolls, 1232–47,* 32.
177 *Cal. Pat. Rolls, 1232–47,* 64.
178 *Cal. Pat. Rolls, 1232–47,* 149.
179 *Cal. Pat. Rolls, 1232–47,* 250.
180 *Cal. Lib. Rolls, 1251–60,* 307–308.

181 *Cal. Pat. Rolls, 1247–58,* 533.
182 *Cal. Pat. Rolls, 1258–66,* 389.
183 *Cal. Pat. Rolls, 1266–72,* 613.
184 *Annales Monastici, De Wintonia et Waverleia (Rolls Series),* 101.
185 Quoted from W. H. Jacob, *Procs. Hants. Field Club,* IV; the original is in the Guildhall Archives.
186 *Cal. Pat. Rolls, 1281–92,* 196, 421, 472.
187 *Cal. Pat. Rolls, 1313–17,* 525.
188 See Appendix B.
189 *Cal. Pat. Rolls, 1338–40,* 281.
190 *Cal. Pat. Rolls, 1367–70,* 246.
191 *Cal. Pat. Rolls, 1367–70,* 250–51.
192 *Cal. Pat. Rolls, 1388–92,* 115; *Cal. Pat. Rolls, 1391–6,* 332; *Cal. Pat. Rolls, 1396–9,* 73.
193 *Rot. Parl.,* II, 346.
194 *Cal. Pat. Rolls, 1405–1408,* 276.
195 *Cal. Pat. Rolls, 1416–22,* 410.
196 *Cal. Pat. Rolls, 1436–41,* 400.
197 *Cal. Pat. Rolls, 1436–41,* 507, 531; *Cal. Pat. Rolls, 1446–52,* 512.
198 P.R.O. E 364/24, 25, 26, 27, 28.
199 P.R.O. E 364/33.
200 P.R.O. E 364/37.
201 City Archives 38/Bx/CR 1(9).
202 City Archives 38/Bx/CR 3(30).
203 City Archives 38/Bx/CR 2(14).
204 City Archives 38/Bx/CR 2(14).
205 City Archives 38/Bx/CR 2 (11).
206 City Archives 38/Bx/CR 3(23).

PART V

The South West

This area was of more importance before, rather than after, the Conquest: it illustrates clearly the decline of the Saxon fortified centres. It reveals, too, an apparent shift in the balance of military and economic predominance from the south-west to the eastern half of England, so that many of the pre-Conquest fortified towns lost their previous importance and were not re-fortified. Thus Lydford, Bridport, Wareham, Twyneham, Axbridge, Langport, Lyng, Watchet and Cricklade had all declined in importance by the time of the Domesday Survey, and their positions were not filled by other towns; only three of the pre-Conquest fortified towns were replaced, Halwell by Totnes, Pilton by Ilfracombe and Wilton by Salisbury. Exeter, and to a lesser extent, Bath, retained their importance; both were Roman foundations. Malmesbury, amongst the towns listed in the Burghal Hidage, may have maintained its fortifications, however. Taunton was fortified in the early thirteenth century, but it is not known whether the fortifications were maintained.

BARNSTAPLE   Leland mentioned the existence of defences (*Itinerary*, I, 169), but there is no documentary or material evidence to support his statement.

BATH   The first murage grant was received in 1369 (*CPR*, 277), although some repairs had been carried out in the early thirteenth century (*Rot. Litt. Claus.*, I, 454, 456). By the 1270s, however, there were accusations that stone was being robbed from the walls (*Rot. Hund.*, II, 123, 132). The walls enclosed an area of twenty-three acres in a pentagonal shape; of the original five gates only the East gate at Boatstall Lane still stands. The course of the wall can be traced along Upper Borough Walls, east to Bridge Street where the south-east angle is largely covered by Woolworth's and then along Lower Borough Walls. There is little to suggest that medieval work was more than localised re-facing of the Roman wall which has been examined in several places (W. J. Wedlake, *Somerset Arch. and N. H. Soc. Procs,* 110, 85-107).

BRIDGWATER A single grant was received in 1269 (*CPR*, 371). There are no remains, but the town records suggest that there were some kind of defences (ed. T. B. Dilks, *Bridgwater Borough Archives, Somerset Rec. Soc.,* 48, 53, 58, 60). Leland corroborates this, saying that there were four gates, but that the houses served instead of a wall (*Itinerary*, I, 162).

BRISTOL Murage grants form an almost continuous series until the end of the fifteenth century from 1232 (*CPR*, 483). Visible remains exist only at St. Nicholas' almshouses in King Street. Excavation has demonstrated the existence of a Saxon ditch (*Med. Arch.*, VIII, 265), which was later replaced by a stone wall, which was examined at Baldwin Street (*Med. Arch.*, II, 197). A further replacement is represented by the wall and bastion in King Street, probably constructed between 1250 and 1300 (*Med. Arch.*, VIII, 184-212). Bristol is one of the few towns where the protection of later suburbs was carried out, and the different lines of the defences should be seen in this light. (W. F. Whittard, *Bristol and the Adjoining Counties*, 1955, fig. 23.)

CRICKLADE Excavation of this Burghal Hidage town showed that it had been defended by a large bank fronted by a stone wall, but had never had a ditch (F. T. Wainright, *Wilts. Arch. Mag.,* LVI, 162-6).

DORCHESTER There is no documentary evidence to suggest that the Roman walls were maintained in the Middle Ages; excavation supports this. (R. A. H. Farrar, *Dorset N.H. and Antiq. F. C. Procs.,* 75, 72-83.)

EXETER The course of the medieval walls follows the line of the Roman defences, and can be traced easily. The remains are considerable, if not very impressive.

In the park to the north of Rougemont the wall stands to a height of twenty-five to thirty feet (7·62–9·14 m.). The masonry is very uneven in quality. Some is no more than rubble and may be modern repair work, but about halfway along this section there is some good work in squared ashlar blocks, regularly coursed. This may be re-used Roman stone. At much the same point a single chamfered base plinth becomes visible. Whether this also exists below ground level in the direction of the castle is not known, and it is possible that it was only constructed on the lower stretch to offset the effects of the slope of the ground towards Queen Street.

The wall crossed Queen Street, and another section, reaching almost to North Street, can be seen from Northernhay Street. The external face forms the garden walls of houses; the interior is visible from the car park. It shows signs of considerable alteration, but was originally built of large squared blocks regularly coursed, and similar to the masonry in Northernhay Park.

From North Street across Fore Street to a point opposite Stepcote Hill the wall now serves the purpose of a retaining bank, and houses have been built fronting onto the wall walk. It is not possible to comment on the original character of the masonry, which shows evidence of considerable patching.

The site of the West gate, at the foot of Stepcote Hill, is clearly marked by a wall plaque, but no details of the gate, which was destroyed in 1815, can be reconstructed architecturally. From this point until the south-west angle is reached the wall is now again only a retaining wall, standing to a height of about twenty feet (6·10 m.) with much modern repair work amongst older ashlar blocks.

From the south-west angle, where the Quay gate (a postern) stood, to the site of the south gate a substantial section of the wall remains. From the angle to Western Way the wall stands to a height of some fifteen feet (4·57 m.) on the outside, and along its length runs a single chamfered base course of uniform character. Above this level the character of the masonry is more diverse, and four easily distinguishable sections can be seen. Moving from the river eastwards the first two are both rubble work of uncertain date; the third shows the use of some large square ashlar blocks, though they are not well coursed; the fourth, a stretch of about thirty feet (9·14 m.) leading up to Western Way, is well built of oblong blocks of a porous stone, regularly coursed and facing a rubble filled core. The inside of this stretch has been much built against but it is possible to see a short section of the original rampart walk.

29. SOUTHAMPTON, *Catchcold and Arundel Towers.*

30. WINCHELSEA, *Landgate, interior face.*

31. WINCHESTER, West Gate, exterior.

32. CHESTER, *Bonewaldesthorne's Tower, exterior.*

33. (Left) *CHESTER, the Water Tower.*

34. (Right) *CAERNAR-VON, Tower 4, exterior, from the west.*

Between Western Way and South Street is another section of wall, standing to a height of about twenty feet (6·10 m.) on the outside, and about six feet (1·83 m.) on the inside. The chamfered plinth continues, and the masonry, though less easy to see under successive coats of whitewash, appears to be of similar character to that of the stretch immediately to the west. Both sections represent Roman work.

The site of the South gate (destroyed in 1819) is marked by a plaque and the next visible stretch of wall is that bounding the car park off Southernhay. This was originally both the city and the close wall and is in a better condition than other sections. Crenellations are visible, but may not be of medieval date. Alterations were made to this part of the wall during the seventeenth century, possibly in the Civil War, and excavation showed the wall walk was of this date.[1] This makes it possible that the crenellations also belong to this period. Between the top and the base plinth the masonry of the wall is very patchy, of large blocks irregularly placed. The two towers on this section are much more neatly constructed, but are not bonded into the wall. There is the possibility of seventeenth-century refacing and medieval foundations may be concealed beneath the present structures.[2] The more westerly of the two has no string course, and offers no evidence about the internal arrangements. The second, behind the municipal offices in Southernhay, was divided into three floors; the present entrance is clearly modern. The wall at this point stands to a height of about thirty feet (9·14 m.); on the inside, the wall is revetted by a sloping bank, reaching to the height of the wall walk, and possibly dateable to the period 1652-7.

The extant circuit is completed by a section of wall on the south side of Post Office Street. At the western end the wall stands on the outside to a height of about eighteen feet (5·49 m.), probably to the level of the original wall walk. The tower at this end is modern in appearance but may mark the site of a medieval bastion. The second bastion in this stretch, where the wall turns north, is clearly part of the original design, being bonded into the wall. It is paralleled only at Denbigh, and is five-sided, each angle being strengthened by a buttress reaching up about two-thirds of the total height. Internally it is semi-circular and is built of large ashlar blocks, not very regularly coursed except at the base.

N

Throughout the length of this section of wall the masonry on the external face is irregularly coursed, but of squared blocks, largely Roman work with medieval underpinning.[3] The masonry on the inside at one point, where the Roman blocks have been cut in half and re-used, may represent repair work done by Athelstan.[4] A plinth runs along the base, sometimes chamfered, sometimes merely a thickening of the wall, and it is not at a steady height from the ground. There is a slight slope, but not sufficient to warrant a stepped plinth.

From this corner bastion to the castle nothing now remains of the wall. The East gate was destroyed in 1784.

It is difficult to ascribe any date to the walls from architectural or archaeological evidence, but if we turn to the documentary evidence there is some indication that the walls were basically reconstructed in the thirteenth century, with intensive repairs and probably also some new construction in the early years of the fifteenth century. It seems clear that the line of the walls is substantially that of the Roman defences. The suggestion that near the West gate the Roman wall may lie behind the line of the medieval wall does not seem to have been substantiated;[5] and although William of Malmesbury states that Athelstan fortified the town with a wall and towers it seems almost certain that this refers to repair work done to the Roman defences, rather than to new work.[6]

The medieval builders had, therefore, virtually to start again. In 1215 the burgesses received 100 marks from the 1214 tallage towards the enclosing of the town,[7] and in the following year (1216) they were ordered to clear away houses built on the wall or in the ditch.[8] In 1218 the citizens received a further 100 marks from the tallage,[9] so it seems probable that the work of reconstruction began in the second decade of the thirteenth century.

The regular series of murage grants starts in 1224 with permission to levy murage for three years.[10] Licence was granted again in 1236[11] for a further term of three years, in 1257 for five years,[12] in 1261 for seven years,[13] in 1270 for four years.[14] In 1284, Edmund, earl of Cornwall, obtained on behalf of the citizens a further grant for five years,[15] which was renewed in 1290 and 1295, and in 1300 for a period of ten years.[16]

The next grant was not received until 1338,[17] and was renewed in 1340, 1341 and 1342.[18] In 1369 murage for five years was granted.[19] There seems to be no other grant enrolled on the Patent Rolls but the receivers' accounts suggest that the toll continued to be levied, possibly by that date being regarded as one of the rights of the city. In 1377 a commission was issued separately to both the bishop and the mayor of Exeter reciting that 'the King's enemies of France and their adherents with no small number of men at arms purpose to land in the realm and attack the city of Exeter'. It ordered both the ecclesiastical and the secular authorities to compel all residing within the city and having lands and tenements to contribute to the repairs, and empowering the mayor to take labourers within two leagues of the city to do the work.[20] A similar commission was issued in 1378 to the mayor alone.[21]

The building periods therefore fall into five fairly well defined groups: the early years of the thirteenth century 1215–39; 1257–74; 1284–1310; 1338–43; 1369–1410. It is difficult to determine what may have been achieved in the thirteenth century, but by the early years of the fourteenth century the grants were being misapplied. A commission of investigation was issued to Gilbert Knovill and Roger de Bello Fago in 1307 and was renewed in 1308 'on petition of the citizens of the city of Exeter to call before them the mayor and bailiffs, and to audit the accounts of the murage of Exeter'.[22]

It is only from 1341–2 that there is any evidence from the city archives. The sources here are of two kinds, firstly the receivers' accounts, a series continuous from 1331–2 which provides evidence for expenditure but only infrequently for receipts, and secondly a Miscellaneous Roll (M6) which contains a record of both receipts and payments for the later years of the reign of Edward III, and the building accounts for the North gate for an uncertain year sometime in the 1370s or 1380s. But although the documentary evidence for work on the defences is plentiful it is not always easy to use it for dating the surviving sections of the wall with any exactitude. Minor repairs to the gates appear in almost every one of the receivers' accounts, with more major work being undertaken on the North gate in the 1380s and in 1498–9; on the South gate in 1403–1404, 1408–1409 and 1413–14; on the East gate in 1361–2, 1376–7, 1403–1404 and 1460, and on the West gate in 1380–81 and 1388.

The accounts are relatively full of place-names, and it seems that most of the fourteenth and fifteenth century work was done on the south walls—an obvious step when the nature of the ground is taken into consideration. The fall of the ground from the castle along the line of the north walls to the Longbrooke valley, and to the River Exe on the west side, provided natural defences, and it was only on the southern and eastern sides that the wall rose from level ground, and was apparently given further protection by a ditch. Jenkins[23] states that there was one tower 'vulgarly called the Snaile Tower' on the western side fronting the river, and this is shown on Braun and Hogenburg's map. Jenkins also stated that there were five towers between the Castle and the South gate, only four of which can be seen on the Braun map. There are now extant only four towers on this stretch—two half-round towers in the car park off Southernhay and two in the car park off Post Office Street. In the accounts there are specific references only to three towers, that near St. John's Hospital; that by St. Peter's (1341–2) which is probably the same as the bishop's tower of 1376; and the tower next to that. The tower marked Bishopstrete is probably the other tower in this area. Of the Snail tower there is no mention in the accounts.

The other names mentioned in the accounts suggest that the repairs were to the south walls; the wall by the Friars Preachers whose buildings were north of St. Peter's church yard, the tower at South gate, the repair of the wall near the church of Holy Trinity, and by the church of St. John the Baptist. It may well be possible to link the different characteristics of the masonry of these walls with these scattered place references. It is unfortunate that the most impressive series of accounts, those for the six years between 1404 and 1410 provide only two place names—already mentioned —'*turris voc Bisshopstrete*' and the wall by Holy Trinity Church. In the accounts for the three busiest years of this period, 1404–1407, when the quantity of stone bought per week averaged one hundred loads over twenty-five, twenty-four and twenty weeks respectively, there are no place references, and one can only guess where work was going on.

ILFRACOMBE   A single grant of murage was received in 1418 (*CPR*, 172). There are no remains.

LAUNCESTON There are no murage grants, and the town records, although they are a nearly complete series from 1334, contain only occasional references to the gates and none to the wall.

The town is dominated by the castle whose bailey walls form a large section of the town defences on the east. They follow a natural defensive line, easily traceable although little remains of the fabric. From the south gate the wall ran along Madford Lane to Dockacre Road, across the end of Northgate Street; the western line ran inside St. Thomas Street and Dockey Street to the south gate. Of the original three gates this is the only one to survive. It is a plain rectangular structure, much restored. It stands twenty-seven feet five inches (8·36 m.) high, and consists of a single archway eleven feet three inches (3·43 m.) high, with five pointed ribs. There is no trace of a portcullis groove. Above the arch were two chambers eighteen feet six inches (3·51 m.) in length, fifteen feet two and a half inches (4·62 m.) in breadth (internal dimensions taken from drawings for alterations in 1887 deposited in the Lawrence House Museum). Originally the first floor was lit by a single three-light window in each face, the top floor by a two-light window. Each now has a square three-light window in each face, inserted in 1887. The wall walk ran through the first-floor chamber. The exterior face has two buttresses reaching to the height of the arch. The original string course divides the two floors. The crenellations and semi-circular coping stone were added in 1887 when the foot path was driven through the wall.

LYDFORD The town is assumed to be the site of the *burh* to which 140 hides were attached, mentioned in the Burghal Hidage. It is surrounded by a bank and ditch, most clearly visible across the neck of the promontory. Excavation has shown that the bank was built up from layers of turf; one tall square post, which had later been removed, was found. It might have been part of a palisade, or perhaps a support for a fighting platform. After its initial construction the front of the bank had been revetted with stone. (*Med. Arch.,* VIII, 232; *Ibid* IX, 170–71.) Three ditches lay in front of the line of the bank.

LYNG The Saxon defences consisted of a bank and ditch across the landward side of the spit projecting into the marsh on which the town stands. It runs south-east to north-west, and is clearly marked by a dip in the road. St. Bartholomew's church stands on the inner edge of the ditch (D. Hill, *Procs. of Somerset Nat. Hist. Soc.* 111, 64–6).

MALMESBURY   The town was fortified before the Conquest, and the system by which responsibility for the maintenance of the defences was allotted was recorded in the late thirteenth century (A. Ballard, *E.H.R.*, XXI, 98–105). Nothing remains, and there is no other documentary evidence.

MELCOMBE   A single grant of murage was received in 1338 (*CPR*, 63). A petition to parliament in 1379 was unsuccessful (*Rot. Parl.*, III, 70). There are no remains.

PLYMOUTH   A grant of murage was received in 1378 (*CPR*, 81), but there is nothing to suggest much activity until the receipt of two large grants in 1463 and 1485 (*CPR*, 269, 470). How much was achieved at this time only to be obliterated by the Elizabethan fortifications is not known. A plan of the later defences exists in B.M. Cotton Augustus I (i) 40 and 41.

POOLE   A single grant was received in 1433 (*CPR*, 298). A small part of the wall can still be seen in the yard of 5 Thames Street where a postern, stairs to the rampart and traces of crenellations remain. The external face of the wall contains corbel stones, perhaps to support wooden hoarding. The rest of the line has been lost, and it is possible that the defences were designed for the protection of the quay rather than the town.

SALISBURY   Despite thirteenth-century references to gates and bars, and Leland's statement that he thought the ditch was made in the time of Bishop Simon (d. 1315) (*Itinerary*, I, 259), it seems unlikely that much work was done to provide the town with a defensive, as distinct from a boundary, ditch until the late fourteenth century. A licence to crenellate was granted in 1372 (*CPR*, 220), but it seems unlikely that the work progressed beyond the construction of a bank. Part of the bank may have been additionally fortified by a wood palisade since there is a grant of timber to the townsmen in 1378 (*CPR*, 229). The work was still in progress in 1381 when part of the ditch and fences was broken down by evil-doers (*CPR*, 631). In 1455–6 Robert Warmell left £20 in his will for 'the making of bars about the said city for its defence and safety' (quoted from *Hist. Mss. Comm.* 55, 17th Rep. Var. Colls., IV, 203). The town was defended only on its northern and eastern sides, and part of the bank can be seen on the north-east of the town; the river formed the defence on the other sides.

TAUNTON   There are no murage grants, but early thirteenth-century references show that money was spent on the moats around the castle and the town, and on payments to carpenters working on the enclosing of the town and castle (ed. T. J. Hunt, *Somerset Record Society*, 66, pl. vii). Nothing further is known.

TOTNES   The first murage grant was received in 1264 (*CPR*, 312); a second, which was surrendered because nothing was being done, in 1355 (*CPR*, 243). Little remains of the wall, although its course is easily traceable in the modern street plan. It ran along a natural defensive line across the slope of the hill. Remains of the north gate lie close to the castle; it was a single-arched entrance, and probably had a chamber above since there is a flight of steps on the west side. Between this point and the east gate the wall serves as a retaining wall and houses have been built on its line. The gate has been much modernised; originally it probably consisted of two semi-circular towers flanking an entrance. The wall walk seems to have entered at the level of a first floor chamber through which it passed. From this gate to the site of the west gate the wall can be seen only at the top of a vennel leading to Tower Cottage. A semi-circular tower projects about five feet (1·52 m.) in front of the wall, with in internal diameter of six feet (1·83 m.). It appeared to be bonded into the wall, but it is difficult to examine. The west gate has been destroyed and the line of the walls to the castle is not certain.

WAREHAM   The Saxon defences on three sides of the town enclosed an area of eighty to ninety acres. The bank was fifty-five feet (16·76 m.) wide and is now about seventeen feet (5·18 m.) high;

there is a ditch in front of its line. The bank was later fronted by a stone wall (*Med. Arch.*, III, 120–39).

WELLS   A single murage grant was received in 1341 (*CPR*, 248). There are no remains.

NOTES

1 *Procs. of Devon Archaeological Exploration Society*, III, 1937–47, 136–9.
2 *Ibid.*, II, 1933–6, 64.
3 *Ibid.*, II, 1933–6, 60, 78–80.
4 I am most grateful to Lady Aileen Fox for this information.
5 *Procs. of Devon Arch. Exploration Soc.*, I, 1929–32, 123.
6 William of Malmesbury, *Gesta Regum*, I, 148 *(Rolls Series)*.
7 *Rot. Litt. Claus.*, I, 186.
8 *Rot. Litt. Claus.*, I, 268.
9 Pipe Roll 2 Henry III, Rot. 9a, quoted from T. Madox, *The History and Antiquities of the Exchequer in England*, 1769, 488.
10 *Cal. Pat. Rolls, 1216–25*, 495.
11 *Cal. Pat. Rolls, 1232–47*, 151.
12 *Cal. Pat. Rolls, 1247–58*, 592.
13 *Cal. Pat. Rolls, 1258–66*, 141.
14 *Cal. Pat. Rolls, 1266–72*, 456.
15 *Cal. Pat. Rolls, 1281–92*, 149.
16 *Cal. Pat. Rolls, 1281–92*, 375; *Cal. Pat. Rolls, 1292–1301*, 144, 512.
17 *Cal. Pat. Rolls, 1338–40*, 156.
18 *Cal. Pat. Rolls, 1340–43*, 44, 335, 562.
19 *Cal. Pat. Rolls, 1367–70*, 284.
20 *Cal. Pat. Rolls, 1374–7*, 476, 502.
21 *Cal. Pat. Rolls, 1377–81*, 3.
22 *Cal. Pat. Rolls, 1301–1307*, 544; *Cal. Pat. Rolls, 1307–13*, 86.
23 Alexander Jenkins, *History and Description of the City of Exeter*, 1806, 17–18.

PART VI

The Welsh Marches

This is an area which produces examples of fortifications of all periods. Two towns were Roman foundations, Chester and Gloucester; others belong to the spate of activity in the tenth century, Chirbury, Eddisbury, Runcorn, Thelwall, Stafford, Hereford and Worcester; two, Bridgnorth and Shrewsbury, may belong to this period or to a later date. The majority, however, were fortified for the first time only in the thirteenth century, because of the unrest produced by the Welsh wars. It is not always possible to connect the building of defences with a definite episode in the fighting, and much of the construction of fortifications was carried out after one attack, presumably in the hope of preventing further burning and looting. Many of the towns which received grants were small settlements, which in spite of the expense of walling, nevertheless did acquire stone fortifications. Others, although they clearly were fortified, apparently did not have grants, but perhaps received assistance from the lord.

ABERGAVENNY Grants were intermittent from the first, in 1241 (*CPR*, 178), until the late fourteenth century. There are now no remains, although part of the west wall was preserved between Baker Street and Nevill Street until 1961. The suggestion that the wall may date from 1087–1100, when the church and chapel of the castle were given to an abbey in Le Mans, together with land for making a 'bourg', does not seem probable from comparative evidence (D. Renn, *Norman Castles*, 1967, 84).

BRIDGNORTH A grant of timber was made in 1220 (*Rot. Litt. Claus.*, I, 421), and it was followed almost immediately by permission to levy murage (*CPR*, 239), a right renewed until the early years of the fifteenth century. Nothing now remains, but the probable line of the walls lies along Moat Street to Castle Terrace, and on the west side, parallel with but to the west of the High Street. The north gate, almost completely re-built in 1910, is now a two-storied building whose original central passage is now flanked by two side passages. The east and west gates have been destroyed, but sketches of the latter show it to have been a square single-arched structure (G. Bellet, *Antiquities of Bridgnorth*, 1856).

CHEPSTOW   There is no documentary evidence for the defences, but a wall 1,200 yards (1,123·35 m.) long defends the peninsula site of the town. It is built of undressed rubble limestone, standing about twenty feet (6·10 m.) high, and six feet nine inches (2·06 m.) broad. It was apparently planned as a whole, since the towers are bonded into the wall, and this is built on a low bank rising above the ditch, a feature best seen at the east end. A thin spur wall runs between the castle and the first tower, the only square one. In its face, as throughout the length of the wall, is a line of square holes, possibly the remains of constructional scaffolding, more probably the provision for the use of wooden hoarding. The other six towers all resemble each other. They are open-backed half-round projecting towers with a diameter of about twenty-seven feet (8·23 m.) and standing about twenty-five feet (7·62 m.) high; they are spaced at intervals of 200 to 250 yards (182·88–213·36 m.). The wall walk was carried continuously round the towers, although no flight of steps remains intact to make this clear. Crenellations remain in some places, but there are no arrow slits or gunports. The only gate still stands, though much restored; its square plan suggests a fifteenth-century date.

CHESTER   The first murage grant was received in 1249 (*CPR*, 49), and others suggest a concentration of effort in the late thirteenth and early years of the fourteenth century. A contract for building the Water tower in 1322 exists (B. M. Harl. Ms. 2046, f. 26v), quoted p. 48. Murage Books for the medieval period have been damaged by damp, but suggest maintenance in the fifteenth century. Except for one short section, the entire circuit of 1¾ miles is complete; it has, however, suffered continuous repair. The defences were originally Roman, and these were probably repaired, rather than extended, in 908; the present north and east walls are still on Roman foundations, but the south and west walls represent an extension, perhaps as early as the twelfth century (*Pipe Rolls, 7 Henry II,* 35; *ibid, 8 Henry II,* 20–21; *Antiq. Jnl.,* XXXIII, 22–32). The defences have been maintained throughout the centuries, and later work often makes the distinguishing of different periods difficult; there was considerable re-building after damage inflicted in the Civil War, and much of the structure dates from the seventeenth century. The north and east sides are the most interesting. The Phoenix, or King Charles', tower stands at the north-east corner of both the Roman and medieval defences; it stands about seventy feet (21·34 m.) high, rising on a battered base from the level of the ditch, now a canal, but originally cut during the Barons' Wars (*Cal. Inq. Misc.,* I no. 379; *CPR,* 1272–81, 104). The tower was almost entirely rebuilt in the seventeenth century, and all its external features are modern. Here, as elsewhere in Chester, the wall walk ran outside the tower. Pemberton's tower may originally have been a circular tower through which the walk would have run, but it was rebuilt in 1894 on its present plan, when it was graced with the inscription to commemorate the murengers, the officials responsible for the administration of the murage tax. The line of the wall beyond this tower represents the medieval extension; Bonewaldesthorne's tower marks the north-west corner; rising from a battered base, it was two storeys high, divided by string courses. It was probably not part of the original plan, but it became the means of access to the spur wall, which, ending in the circular Water tower, was the defence for the harbour, now the Roodeye. The tower stands some seventy feet (21·34 m.) high, and at each of its three stages was heavily defended, the roof also being equipped as a fighting platform. Its fitting out as a museum has obliterated the remaining internal medieval features, such as the window embrasures, but the octagonal vaulted roof of the lower chamber, and the latrine to the right of the entrance are still visible (D. F. Renn, *Jnl. of Chester and N. Wales Arch. and Hist. Soc.,* 45, 1958, 57–60). The west and south walls are devoid of features of interest, except for the base of the east tower of Bridge gate, the only part of the medieval gates, otherwise destroyed in the eighteenth century, to survive (plates 32, 33).

CHIRBURY There is no trace of the Aethelflaedian defences.

CLUN A single murage grant was received in 1277 (*CPR*, 249). There are traces of a ditch to the north of Newport Street, and on the south in Bridge Street. The eastern line of the defences could have been at Frog Street, the western being filled by the castle.

CRICKHOWELL A single grant was received in 1281 (*CPR*, 2). There are no remains.

EDDISBURY Excavation of the site showed that the levelled Inner and Outer Ramparts, originally of Iron Age date, were reconstructed by Aethelflaeda; the outer ditch was re-cut at the same time (W. J. Varley, 'Excavation of the Castle Ditch, Eddisbury 1935–58', *Trans. Hist. Soc. of Lancs. and Cheshire*, CII, 1–68).

GLOUCESTER The first murage grant was received in 1226 (*CPR*, 61), and they were frequent until the end of the fourteenth century. Four accounts are preserved in the City Record Office, which cover parts of the years 1298–1302, 1340, 1393–4, 1409–1410, but still little is known about the medieval walls. The Roman foundations were in part re-used by the medieval builders; the east wall runs along King Street; it has been partially excavated, and was found to stand six feet (1·83 m.) high (*BGAS*, 53, 272); it continues along Queen Street, after which its line must be assumed to lie inside Brunswick Road, with the south-east angle inside the junction with Parliament Street. Beyond the site of the south gate the line of the wall has not been found, but it may have extended beyond the line of the Roman walls (which turned north at the old castle) as far as the river, almost certainly the western defence of the town in the Middle Ages. The northern line of the walls is also confused; the cathedral was built over the north-west angle of the Roman defences, and in this area the town may have relied on the close wall for protection, utilising the Roman wall only in the north-east sector. None of the five gates remains. Speed's plan of the town in 1610 is of considerable value in plotting the course of the medieval walls.

HAY ON WYE   The first murage grant was received in 1232 (*CPR*, 477), and a second in 1237 (*CPR*, 178). Parts of the walls still remain; they overlooked the River Wye on the north-west, the Dulas brook on the south-east and connected with the castle at the centre of the southern side of the town. There were three gates and a postern, none of which remains.

HEREFORD   Murage grants are almost continuous from 1224 until the late fifteenth century (*CPR*, 473). Some accounts survive, the earliest of 1263–4; it suggests that the wall was largely completed in stone.

The sequence of defences is complicated; recent excavation has discounted Watkins' theory that the earliest line of defences was contained between the King's ditch and the castle, of which no trace has ever been identified (A. Watkins, *Trans. Woolhope Naturalists Field Club*, 1920, 249–58; F. G. Heys and J. F. L. Norwood, *Ibid.*, 1958, 117–25.) It is now suggested that the first line ran from the river along Victoria Street, turning along West and East Streets (known as Behind-the-Wall Street in the Middle Ages) and turning south to the river to include the castle; it is also thought that it was re-fortified, rather than created initially, by Harold, who is said to have defended the city with a deep, broad ditch, gates and bars in 1055 (*Two Saxon Chronicles*, ed. C. Plummer, I, 186). Even by the time of Domesday, however, this line was too small to contain the population, and burgesses living both inside and outside the wall were listed, and in the early twelfth century the defences were described by William of Malmesbury in terms of former greatness. At some date the fortifications were enlarged, so that the northern line can now be traced in the curve of Bowsey Lane, and crossing Widemarsh, Bye and St. Owen's Streets. On archaeological evidence the rampart which preceded the stone wall is not likely to have been constructed earlier than the middle of the twelfth century; it could belong to the reign of Stephen, but it might also have been constructed only a little earlier than 1190 when there is an allowance of £56 0s 8d to the sheriff of Hereford 'for the making of four city gates, and one gate at the castle' (*Pipe Roll*, 2 Richard I, 49). It is not certain that the eleventh-century defences had four entrances, and the Pipe Roll

reference may well date the extension of the defences comprising
Eign, Widemarsh, Byster and St. Owen's gates. Two of the gates
were still under construction in 1216, when the citizens were given
large timbers from the king's forest of la Haye to make two gates
(*Rot. Litt. Claus.*, I, 263). Prints of the gates show that they were
square structures, which might point to a date of construction
earlier than that of the half-round mural towers, but the construction of a stone wall did not lag far behind. The documentary
evidence suggests that by the time of the Barons' Wars the stone
defences had been at least partially completed; there are references
in the 1263–4 accounts to men working on the wall at
the back of the tenement of Matilda Hatchef. Some work was
also done on the ditch; when, in 1265, the citizens heard of the
coming of Sir Roger Mortimer they threw down houses to widen
the ditch between Friars gate and Widemarsh gate (*Cal. Inq. Misc.*
I, no. 391).

The remains of the circuit, which once measured 1,800 yards
(1645·92 m.) and included at least seventeen towers and six gates,
are not very considerable. Two bastions remain above ground.
One, now overlooked by the ring road on the west side of the town,
stand about fifteen feet (4·57 m.) high. It is built of large
ashlar blocks in regular coursing; one arrow slit remains. A second
stands in Victoria Street; it is in poor condition, but may have
resembled the first. Others have been excavated, and all were
similar in construction, being half-round. That in Blueschool
Street showed that it had been bonded into the wall, so that
the two had been built simultaneously. The front of the bastion
had been built about six feet down the face of the ditch, projecting about ten feet (3·05 m.) beyond the line of the wall.
Originally it had walls six feet (1·83 m.) thick, though now
much of the facing has been robbed. The inner face was twelve
feet (3·66 m.) in diameter. The pottery, from below the base of the
wall, appeared to be of early thirteenth-century date. A second
bastion was excavated in the Bath Street Car Park, built against
the face of the rampart bank. In the soil at the base of the rampart
the few rim-sherds which were found are thought to be of late
twelfth century date, and are presumably to be associated with the
extension. (S. C. Stanford, *Trans. Woolhope Naturalists Field Club,*
1966, 204–210; I am grateful to Mr. Frank Noble for information

about other excavation results, not yet published. F. Noble and R. Shoesmith, *Ibid*. 1967, 44–70).

KNIGHTON   A first murage grant was received in 1260 (*CPR*, 67), a second in 1277 (*CPR*, 249). Nothing remains to establish the line of the defences; on the west Offa's dyke may have been used.

LUDLOW   The first murage grant was received in 1233 (*CPR*, 35). The fourteenth-century building accounts suggest that although murage was being levied, it was not spent on the walls. The line of the wall departed from the south-west angle of the castle, but remains can be seen only on the south side of the town on the ridge above Ludford Bridge, where rough rubble walling stands to a height of about ten feet (3·05 m.), without surviving defensive characteristics. The one remaining gate, Broad gate, has been converted into a house, but was originally a single-arched entrance, flanked by semi-circular towers. The portcullis grooves can still be seen. The wall continues east along a modern passage, which turns north after crossing Old Street; it finally debouches into Tower Street, after which the line is lost until close to the north-east corner of the castle.

MANCHESTER   The Roman fort was re-used in the early tenth-century; nothing remains.

MONMOUTH   Two murage grants were received, the first in 1297 (*CPR*, 307), the second in 1315 (*CPR*, 297). The walls probably ran from the River Monnow along Nailer's Lane, parallel with Glendower Street, and then turned north to run along the bank of the River Wye. The north-east corner has been incorporated in the pub the 'Nag's Head' in St. James Street, and the north walls ran to the site of Monk's gate across the Hereford road and thence to the River Monnow. None of the four gates, placed at the cardinal points of the compass, remains. Further protection was afforded to the town by the fortified bridge over the Monnow, still surviving.

OSWESTRY   The first grant was received in 1257 (*CPR*, 609). There are no traces of the walls which ran from the castle along Arthur Street, Welsh Walls, English Walls and King Street. The four gates have been destroyed; pictures show them to have been single-arched square structures flanked by guard-houses (W. Price, *History of Oswestry*, 1815, 26, 27). Leland said that the walls were one mile in circumference and contained no towers (*Itinerary*, II, 73).

RADNOR The first grant was received in 1257 (*CPR*, 609). Traces of a ditch remain on the south and west sides of the town.

RICHARD'S CASTLE Footings of a wall and a semi-circular tower can be seen east of the church yard. There is no documentary evidence.

RUNCORN Nothing remains of the tenth-century *burh*.

SHREWSBURY The first grant of murage was received in 1220 (*CPR*, 238), and they were continuous thereafter until the middle of the fifteenth century. Bailiffs' accounts survive from 1256; they record in detail the sums collected, but are less informative about the work in progress. It seems probable that by 1256 most of the work had been completed, and only repair work was necessary.

The first defences were probably the timber ones of the Saxon *burh* of which no traces remain. The later stone wall can be traced for at least some of its path. It ran from the west side of the castle west of Bride Hall, and can be seen at Riggs Hall within the library building; it then went over to Roushill on a line parallel with Mardol. Excavation on this section showed that the wall had been built against a vertical clay face; it was four and a half feet (1·37 m.) wide, with a rubble core and sandstone facing. The chamfered plinth on the outside face had been twice stepped down to fit the contour of the hill (*Med. Arch.* V, 181–210). Beyond this point the wall abandoned the 200-foot (60·96 m.) contour line which it normally follows to secure Welsh Bridge, and then turned up the hill towards St. Chad's church along Claremont Bank, St. Chad's Terrace, Murivaunce, and Town Walls towards English Bridge; a square tower remains on this section. From Wyle Cop the wall returns to the castle, commanding the steep slope to the river. A ditch existed on the southern side. (I am grateful to Mr. J. T. Smith for allowing me to see his unpublished thesis on Shrewsbury.)

35. *CAERNARVON, the wall walk as it leaves the castle.*

36. *CONWAY, Upper Gate, exterior.*

37. *CONWAY, the latrines.*

38. *DENBIGH, Burgess Gate, exterior.*

39. *TENBY, the gate of the five arches, from the south-west.*

40. *Denbigh, Goblin Tower from the south-east.*

STAFFORD   A grant of timber was received in 1215 (*P.R. Soc.* 31 (NS) no. 46), and the first murage grant in 1224 (*CPR* 459). There are no remains of either the tenth-century or the later defences.

STOCKPORT   Remains of a possible wall were seen in 1893 (T. Kay, *Trans. of Lancs and Cheshire Antiq. Soc.*, XIV, 1896, 54–61). There is no documentary evidence, and nothing now remains.

THELWALL   The town was a tenth-century foundation which did not retain its military importance into the late Middle Ages.

WORCESTER   The town may have been fortified in the ninth century (V.C.H. *Worcs.*, IV, 377–8), although the town was not part of the Burghal Hidage system, nor is it generally recognised as one of the towns fortified by Edward and Aethelflead. The townsmen promised to pay King John £100 to avoid the destruction of the fortifications (*CPR*, 10). The first grant of murage was received in 1224 (*CPR*, 426), and others were frequent throughout the thirteenth century and intermittent until the late fifteenth century.

The line of the wall probably ran from St. Clement's gate in the north-west, along the Butts, across Foregate Street to Queen Street, then turned south along Sidbury, Bowling Green Terrace, where it stands to a height of about twenty feet (6·10 m.), thence through St. Peter's schools across Severn Street and thence to the river (*Trans. Worcs. Naturalists Club*, XI, 1956–7, 100–121). Excavation at several points has revealed a substantial wall of sandstone with a stepped base plinth (*Trans. Worcs. Nat. Club*, XI, 1956–7, 160–62; *Med. Arch.* IV, 150). None of the gates remains.

o

PART VII

Wales

The Welsh towns can be conveniently divided into two groups; those of the north and those of the south. Of the eight towns in the north, the defences of only two, Overton and Ruthyn, were built by private enterprise; the others were walled as a result of royal policy and by royal command. These towns enjoyed the benefit of a less limited budget than that at the disposal of most towns, as well as the services of professional architects. Mid-Wales too was protected by towns fortified by royal command, namely Aberystwyth and Montgomery. These towns were conceived as being military and administrative centres; those of the south were themselves centres of warfare and objects of attack. Many, however, were slow to avail themselves of murage grants, and had often been looted, and even burnt, before taking any steps to defend themselves. Their scant remains contrast sharply with the splendour of the fortifications of the northern towns, but it is significant that, as in the Marches, many small towns not only levied murage but also completed defences.

ABERYSTWYTH   The town was fortified by Edward I; work is said to have begun in 1277 (*Brut y Twysogion*, ed. T. Jones, 1955, 267), but the town was burnt in 1282, when the rampart round the town and castle was said to have been destroyed (*Ibid.*, 271). A survey of 1280 (P.R.O., C 49) noted the absence of locks, bolts or bars on the gates, and later £180 was allowed for work on the walls (P.R.O., C 62/56). The author of the *Annales Cambriae* remarked that 1283 was a year in which much repair was done (*Rolls Series*, 108). Three gates, sited at the bottom of Bridge Street, Great Darkgate Street and Eastgate Street, delimit the extent of the defences which connected with the castle. There are no remains.

BRECON There is no documentary evidence. Two of the original ten towers survive at the south-east extremity of an oval circuit based on the castle; they can be seen from Free Street and Captains' Walk.

CAERNARVON Preparatory work on the ditch and on the demolition of property on the line of the wall began in 1283 (P.R.O., E 101/351/9). By late 1285, when at least £1,818 is known to have been spent on the walls, much of the work must have been complete (P.R.O., E 372/131 rot. 26, 136 rot. 28, 138 rot. 25). In the revolt of 1294, however, the Welsh inflicted considerable damage on the walls, and reconstruction cost £1,024 18s 11½d, more than half the initial cost (P.R.O., E 372/146 rot. 24). Repair work continued through the fourteenth century, notably in 1347, when in the course of work on the towers the original wooden bridges were replaced by the stone arches, some of which are still visible.

The walls form a half circle, completed by the castle; much stands some twenty-eight feet (8·53 m.) high, with the towers rising ten or twelve feet (3·05–3·66 m.) higher. The wall stands on a bank, with the towers half-way down the bank into the ditch. In the circuit of 800 yards (731·52 m.) there are two gates and eight towers. Except for the north-west angle tower, which is three-quarters round, the towers are D-shaped open-backed structures. They were provided with three arrow slits at the level of an upper timber floor, which was reached by the same stone stair which provided access to the wall walk. Alternate merlons, which protected the wall walk, were pierced by arrow slits. The East and West gates were originally twin-towered single-arched structures; the East gate enjoyed the additional protection of a barbican on the further side of the ditch, while the West gate incorporated a small projecting barbican. Both structures have now been considerably rebuilt. Two posterns, at either end of Castle Ditch, have been destroyed. (A. J. Taylor, *Caernarvon Castle and Town Walls,* MPBW Official Guide; *King's Works; R.C.A.M.* (Wales) *Caerns.* II.) Plates 34, 35.

CARDIFF The wall is depicted on Speed's plan, but nothing now survives. There is no documentary evidence for the suggestion that the town was first surrounded by a ditch and embankment, replaced in the early fourteenth century by stone walls (W. Rees, *Cardiff, A History of the City*, 1962, 16).

CARDIGAN   The town was attacked in 1216 and 1233 (Lloyd, *History of Wales*, 644, 661) and received its first murage grant in 1280 (*CPR*, 371). There are no remains, but the walls, which were linked with the castle, formed a triangle; they were pierced by three gates, across Quay Street, High Street and St. Mary's Street.

CARMARTHEN   The town was burnt in 1214 and 1231 (*Annales Cambriae*, 71; Lloyd, *History of Wales*, 674). The first murage grant was received in 1233 (*Close Roll*, 199), and it was the only town in South Wales to levy murage in the first half of the thirteenth century. The original line of the defences, along Lower Bridge Street from the castle, north-west to Dark Gate, along Chapel Street and south to the castle was extended, perhaps after the receipt of murage for five years in 1415 (*CPR*, 308), east from Chapel Street along Wood's Row, south down Conduit Lane to Danybanc and the south-east corner of the castle (M. and E. Lodwick, *The Story of Carmarthen*, n.d. 33–5). Parts still stand behind Blue Street, Lower Bridge Street and Danybanc.

CONWAY   Work began on the northern section of the walls, parallel with Mount Pleasant and Town Ditch Road, in 1284–5, when £472 10s 4d was paid for part of the work (P.R.O., E 372/ 131, rot. 26). It probably included also the spur wall and the section on either side of Upper Gate. The Mill Gate section and the sea front were constructed between 1285 and 1287 (*King's Works*; A. J. Taylor, *Conway Castle and Town Walls*, MPBW Official Guide, 1961).

The wall is 1,400 yards (1,280·16 m.) long; there are twenty-one half-round open-backed towers and three gates. It is twenty-four feet (7·32 m.) high. The four towers and the intervening stretches of wall along the quayside have lost many of their defensive features. A spur wall, protected by a double line of crenellations, ended in a round tower since washed away by the sea, gave additional protection to the harbour. Its line was continued up the hill (Town Ditch Road and Mount Pleasant) to its peak. It included towers, each having similar features. On the east side a stone stair gave access to the wall walk and to the timber upper floor: from this the three arrow slits were used, the higher row being reached by a circular stair in the tower wall. The open gorge was bridged by a plank. The north-west angle tower is three-quarters round, with the lowest stage of solid masonry. The remaining towers in the section between this point and the castle resemble those already described. The unusual feature in this section is the twelve latrines, which have replaced the crenellations at a point where the walls were naturally protected by the slope of the ground (plate 37).

The gates, Upper, Lower and Mill were all double-towered; Upper gate was the strongest. A barbican stood in front of the draw-bridge, which could be pulled in to rest vertically against the face of the gate. A portcullis protected the wooden doors, and arrow slits commanded the intervening space; missiles could also be launched into it from an overhead timber platform. The rear of the gate was used as the porter's lodging, and was constructed in wood. Mill gate and Lower gate were less strongly defended, enjoying only a portcullis and wooden doors (*R.C.A.M.* (Wales) *Caerns.*, II.) Plate 36.

COWBRIDGE   The walls enclosed only thirty-three acres, lying on either side the main road through the town. Several stretches have been preserved, the best being from the surviving south gate to the south-west corner tower. There is no documentary evidence.

DENBIGH   The circuit of the walls remains almost complete. It enclosed a comparatively small area of nine and a half acres on a hill site commanding the Clywd valley.

Burgess gate, the only entrance to the town, stands roughly in the middle of the northern walls. In front of it was a ditch, crossed by a fixed bridge. The gate was built of green sandstone and stands about fifty feet (15·24 m.) high; the missing top courses and battlements might be expected to add another eight to ten feet (2·44–3·05 m.). It consists of a vaulted entrance passage, flanked by two projecting towers. On plan these appear as square projections, but the base of each tower is formed by a battered glacis wall reaching to first floor level, from which the circular towers rise about ten feet above ground level (plate 38). Although the round towers might have been equipped with arrow slits in order to give a more concentrated field of fire, in fact such provision was not made, and all defence must have been undertaken from the top of the towers. The only openings in the north face are a broad slit to provide light in the guard chamber on either side of the gate, and a small window with a hooded moulding above the arch.

Additional strength was given to the tower by the provision of a portcullis. In front of its grooves an arrow slit is found in each tower, and, also in front of its line, is a row of machicolations concealed by the line of the arch which takes the place of corbels. Between it and the wooden doors are two groined ribs, between which are murder holes, positioned over the centre of the passageway. There are also two slits, one on either side, to enable defenders to fire on any who had survived attack up to this point. Of town gates in Britain, Denbigh is amongst the best defended, and most nearly approaches the strength of a castle entrance. It has many similarities with the castle entrances at Denbigh. Moreover, on both gates there are decorative blocks of small white sandstone alternating with the darker sandstone, which are found also at the bastion tower. The explanation is probably that the building of the town defences formed part of the same operation as the erection of the castle, and the work may even have been carried out by the same men.

At ground level the guard rooms were entered by a door in the south-east corner of each. The rooms are almost identical in plan, and are lit by a narrow slit to the north and south, with a slit to fire on attackers in front of the portcullis and in front of the doors. The western chamber had a stair in the thickness of the wall leading to the upper floor, which extended over the whole of the gatehouse. It was lit on the south side by three large windows, and from it the wall walk could be reached from either the north-west or the north-east corner. The stair continued from this chamber to the roof.

The exterior of the south face is now faced in shale limestone. Although this could represent a medieval repair or refacing, it seems more probable that it is of more modern date, to protect the sandstone of which the greater part of the gate is built. This is clearly visible in the quoins and the mouldings of the door and window frames.

The wall has been partly destroyed up to the eastern side of Bull Lane.[1] It stands at this point to a height of about fifteen feet (4·57 m.); the wall walk is about four feet (1·22 m.) wide, and is protected on either side by a wall about eighteen inches (0·457 m.) wide. The top of the wall has disappeared. Small ashlar blocks coursed irregularly on the exterior face, but more regularly on the inside, cover the rubble core. The first tower on this section, the North East, is a half-round tower built at the point where the wall changes direction. The tower obviously commanded the section between Burgess gate and the Countess tower. It stands to a height of about thirty feet (9·14 m.), with a very slight batter at the base. The original arrangements have been obliterated. The lower chamber can be entered through a door in the angle of the wall, but there is no provision for defence at this level. At the level of the wall walk two windows in the wall of the tower probably represent enlarged arrow slits.

The wall turns south-east at this point and runs down the hill to the Countess tower. The tower consists of two angular turrets, to which some rooms were added in the angle of the wall at a later date. The tower was about twenty feet (6·11 m.) high, divided into two storeys from which it could be defended. It is at this point that the walls of the two building periods join. The earlier work turned south-west from the tower across the slope at a steep angle. It was built on a spur of rock and was probably not a very efficient line of defence since from the wall walk it would have been impossible to see straight down to the base of the cliff, and there was therefore a large area of dead ground. This was remedied after only a short time, possibly in 1294, when a second wall was constructed lower down the slope running from the Countess tower to the new Goblin tower. The section between the towers was provided with a double line of embrasures. The first could be used from ground level, the second from the narrow walk, clearly built for the purpose.

The Goblin tower is an impressive five-sided bastion projecting from the cliff (plate 40). It stands about seventy feet (21·33 m.) high from the battered base at the foot of the cliff, and was divided into two storeys. It is built of much larger blocks of stone than the work of the first period, and the quoins are of different stone. The main entrance to the lower storey was down a flight of steps which continued the line of the path from the Countess tower. From the lower level a narrow stair descended to the wall. The tower could be defended from both levels, each face being pierced by an embrasure, and probably also from the parapet walk.

Turning back up the hill this wall joins the earlier work at a postern, the drawbridge pit of which remains. The postern would seem to belong to the earlier work, and was perhaps an attempt to provide protection for the dead ground.

The wall continued north-west across the hill, but its remains are not considerable until the bastion tower is reached. This half-round tower marks a change in the direction of the wall, and commanded the south-east section of the defences. It stands now to a height of about twenty-five feet (7·62 m.), and has the checkerboard decoration similar to the Burgess gate. The wall continued to the half-round Postern tower on the south wall of the castle, and from there to the north-west corner the town and castle walls were the same. Clearly the plan used here was the same as that employed at Caernarvon, where the castle formed the fourth side of the town defences. The eastern side of the castle from the Red tower to the Green Chambers is of a later date than the western side, which forms part of the town defences.

From the Red tower, where the town wall again became independent, it ran along the crest of the hill to Ffordd Newydd, visible from the outside from Tan-y-Gwalian, and thence to Burgess gate. The wall has been largely built over by houses in this section.

There is no documentary evidence for Denbigh, but the walls were probably built between 1282 and 1294.

DOLFORWYN The attempt of Llewellyn to found a defended market town at his castle of Dolforwyn was thwarted by the English; even by 1330 all traces had disappeared (P.R.O., SC6/1206/2).

DRYSLWYN The castle was captured from Rhys-ap-Maredudd, in 1287, and the constable's accounts for 1287–9 include expenditure on the repair of the ditches round both the town and the castle (P.R.O., E 372/134, rot., 1).

HAVERFORDWEST The town was burnt in 1219–20, but obtained a grant only in 1264 (*Annales Cambriae,* 74; *CPR,* 248). There are no extant remains.

KIDWELLY The town was attacked in 1231, but waited until 1281 before applying for a murage grant (Lloyd, *History of Wales,* 674; *CPR,* 418). The only surviving gatehouse, with twin semi-circular towers, is probably of fourteenth-century date.

MONTGOMERY A castle was begun in 1221, but it was not until 1267 that the burgesses received a murage grant (M. Paris, *Chronica Majora,* III, 64; *CPR,* 106). There were intermittent grants subsequently until 1336. O'Neil thought that the building of a stone wall had probably been started *c.* 1230 (B. H. St. J. O'Neil and A. H. Foster-Smith, *Arch. Cambrensis,* 95, 219). Basing his argument on two entries on the Liberate Roll of 1279, Mr. A. J. Taylor wrote that *c.* 1279–80 a wooden palisade which had sur-rounded the town was removed to the castle, and a stone wall built in its place (A. J. Taylor, *Arch. Cambrensis,* 99, 281–3). Neither writer, however, mentioned the existence of the murage grants. Their existence must weaken O'Neil's thesis that a stone wall was built *c.* 1230, and it weighs against Taylor's conclusion that the palisade was removed and the wall built in one operation, 1279–80. The wooden palisade could have been constructed with the pro-ceeds from the earliest grants, and the levy continued to pay for the stone defences. The stone walls have since been robbed, but the course of the bank and ditch is still clear; from the castle it runs south along the top of the hill, turning sharply east down the slope into Kerry Street. The eastern line runs parallel with Church Bank, and turns towards the castle after crossing the main road. None of the four gates remains.

OVERTON A murage grant, obtained in 1300 (*CPR,* 505), is the only hint that the town was ever walled.

PEMBROKE The north-east corner tower, Barnard's tower, stands to a height of about thirty feet (9·14 m.), with a base battered to a height of about twelve feet (3·66 m.). Two other towers, shown on Speed's plan, stood on the south-west side. There is no documentary evidence for the erection of the defences, but on Leland's testimony, that the east gate was similar to the fortification of Tenby, a similarity of date may be presumed (Leland, *Itinerary in Wales,* 117).

RHAYADER   A town ditch may exist as the outer boundary of the burgage plots (M. Beresford, *New Towns,* 573).

RHUDDLHAN   The town may be the site of the Anglian *Cledemutha* (F. J. Wainwright, *Eng. Hist. Rev.,* LXV, 203–212; A. J. Taylor, *Rhuddlhan Castle,* MPBW Official Guide, 1965). The defences of the later town, established by Edward I, were constructed in 1281–2; a bank and ditch, strengthened by a timber palisade, surrounded the town on three sides. The north-west corner is still visible.

RUTHYN   A single murage grant was obtained in 1407 'because the town lies so open among the Welsh rebels' (*CPR,* 375).

SWANSEA   The town received two murage grants, the first in 1317 (*CPR,* 59), the second in 1338 (*CPR,* 6). There are no remains.

TENBY   There were originally three gates and twelve towers in the circuit; only one gate and six towers remain. Buildings, and more particularly garden walls on the cliff to the north and east of the town have obliterated much of the walls. Their line can, however, be plausibly reconstructed. Some parts have been destroyed since 1896.[2]

Today the walls are best seen on the west from White Lion Street, on the south from South Parade, and from the beach. Throughout its length the wall is built of undressed stone in blocks of irregular shape and size. There are signs of rough coursing in so far as the masonry was brought up to a level bed at three points in its height; just below the lower line of embrasures, just above this point and finally to accommodate the upper line of arrow slits and the crenellations. It seems possible that this may have been because the wall was built in three separate stages, and that the method of construction was similar to that employed at Yarmouth. The peculiar coursing is most noticeable between the first two towers, looking in an easterly direction. The sections of the walls still visible are remarkably uniform in character, and preserve a feature known in only a few places in England and Wales, namely a double line of arrow slits. These are placed in the wall at a more or less constant height throughout the remaining sections though not in the same relative positions. In the west wall in White Lion Street the slits are above each other and placed between the crenellations; to the east of the fourth tower the top slit is between the crenellation while the lower has been placed beneath the merlon, thus providing a wider field of fire. The upper slits were used from the wall walk, the lower from ground level. The wall walk was not bonded with the fabric of the wall, but was clearly a later addition. Much of it has disappeared, but it remains, for example, in the gardens of 'Katriona', Lower Frog Street, and in the Imperial Hotel.

The west wall, a stretch about fifty yards (45·72 m.) long, can be seen from White Lion Street, from the point at which the circuit has been breached by Frog Street. It stands about twenty-five feet (7·62 m.) high, and was built, like all the other sections of the wall, of undressed stone set straight onto the ground with no batter and no base plinth. The double row of arrow slits can be seen; those in the lower line are between five and six feet (1·52–1·83 m.) in height, and about ten feet (3·05 m.) above ground level; those in the upper line are only about three feet (0·914 m.) long and are about six feet (1·83 m.) above the lower ones. The slits have been placed directly above each other, and between the crenellations. On the inside of the wall the lower line is said to have been covered by a wall of masonry,[3] but this statement cannot be checked now because of the buildings which have been erected since it was made. The face of the wall gives no indication that this is the case.

The south-west tower is bonded into the wall. It stands about thirty feet (9·14 m.) high, on a slightly battered base. It is not possible to view the tower from inside, but the defensive arrangements suggest strongly that it was an open-gorged tower divided into three floors by timber staging. It appears also that the wall walk was carried round the tower on a corbelled parapet, which was protected by a crenellated wall, which on its eastern side probably stands to its full height. The tower could, therefore, be defended from this level or from the two levels of slits which are so placed as to give cover from every point of attack.[4] The tower marks the lowest point of the defences, and from this point the wall turns east to run straight to the cliff edge. Throughout this section it was protected by a ditch, now filled in and marked by the line of South Parade.

The wall between the first two towers, a stretch about one hundred yards (91·40 m.) long, exhibits to a marked degree the layers in which it was built. The stones differ only slightly in size in each layer, and suggest therefore, that the method employed was to build the wall in vertical sections, and that the work was done fairly quickly, rather than that it was spread over a long period of time. The method of construction would, therefore, resemble that followed at Yarmouth in the mid-fourteenth century where the accounts show clearly that the wall was built in two stages, and the same method was adopted at Conway in the late thirteenth century.[5] This section of the wall again shows the double line of embrasures placed directly above each other, and falling between the crenellations, and it shows a double line of putlog holes. One line runs at the level of the base of the upper slits, and the other, less regular, falls at the base of the lower row. It seems possible that these supported timber hourds for use from the wall walk. Laws said that on this section of the wall, although there were arches, they were not bonded into the wall and were slipping away from the wall.[6]

The second tower is half-round, standing to a height of about thirty feet (9·14 m.). It projects about twenty feet (6·16 m.) from the line of the wall, and was heavily fortified. Two arches were thrown out from the wall; they were connected to a third, and all three were filled in with masonry, though not to their full thickness. Unlike the first tower it is not open gorged, but had a solid back wall flush with the line of the curtain wall. It does not seem to have been bonded into the wall but to have been built before the adjoining curtain, and this is most easily seen on the western side where a straight joint in the masonry can be seen. There was clearly no access to the tower from the wall walk on this side, and indeed all traces of walk or arcades have disappeared. It was, however, a strongly defensible tower. There was a door into the ground floor chamber through the wall, which at this point is about six feet (1·83 m.) thick. Facing south is a large embrasure pierced by a slit. It is reasonable to assume that before the side walk arches were made there were also slits to the east and west through the much thinner walling. This chamber was a self-contained unit, and there seems to have been no access from it to the rooms above.

The upper floors were supported on massive semi-circular arches. These extended to the ground level on the inside, and were about six feet (1·83 m.) thick. They were protected by a thinner screen wall through which it is reasonable to suppose that arrow slits to east and west were originally pierced, to correspond with the embrasure to the south. These slits were destroyed by the making of the side walk arches in 1784. The upper chamber contained eight slits, covering every angle of attack. Above this was the wall walk from which the crenellated battlements, now largely destroyed, could be used. The chamber was reached through a door on the eastern side of the tower, perhaps from the wall walk, but it is not easy now, because of modern buildings, to reconstruct the original arrangements of the upper stages of the tower.

The wall between this tower and the south gate is about 130 yards (118·87 m.) long.

The South gate is an extremely interesting feature (plate 39). At first sight it resembles a half-round tower, standing to a height of about twenty-five feet (7·62 m.), and projecting about thirty feet (9·14 m.) beyond the line of the wall. Although it is now known as the tower of the five arches, only four of these are original, and only one of these, that on the western side, formed the entrance. It was about ten feet (3·05 m.) high and pierced a wall about eight feet (2·44 m.) thick. It was defended by a portcullis, the grooves of which remain. This was drawn up into a space between the exterior wall and the wall walk. There was then a pair of wooden doors. This, however, was only the entrance into the semi-circular tower which formed a kind of barbican to the gate, which is a single arch through the wall, about ten feet (3·05 m.) thick and further defended by three murder holes.

Attackers who overcame the first barriers were then trapped in the semi-circular tower, and could be fired on from the wall walk, and from three slits accessible from the passage way which crossed the arch of the main entrance. This same passage, the entrance to which was on the western side of the gate, ran round the barbican, and was the platform from which the eight slits could be used to fire on attackers beyond the ditch. The wall walk could also be used as a platform from which to fire on besiegers outside, since arrow slits appear in the merlons between the crenellations.

The arrangements for access to the upper storeys of the gate are complex. Guard chambers would have been superfluous in this kind of bent entrance to the town (the only example of such an entrance amongst the urban fortifications of Great Britain), and the stairways are therefore all external. On the western side a stair ascends from ground level to the level of the first floor passage way, which is presumably also the level of the wall walk, though this cannot be checked because of the presence of buildings. A second stair, passing over the entrance to the covered passage, rose to the level of the battlements. A corbelled projection to carry this stair can be seen from the inside of the tower.

The wall from the South gate to the next tower is sixty-three yards (57·61 m.) long. It may well have been re-built, at least in its upper stages, at the time of the Armada. There is a gun port inserted into the base of one of the arrow slits about ten yards east of the gate, and a plaque commemorating the work done in this section in 1588.

The third tower is a semi-circular tower, which now shelters a modern building.[7] It stands about twenty-five feet (7·62 m.) high, and projects about fifteen feet (4·57 m.) from the line of the wall. In its defensive arrangements it differs from the other towers, in that it has no corbelled parapet to support the wall walk. The crenellations, with arrow slits between the embrasures, remain, so that a walk carried round the tower is implied. It has only one arrow slit at first and at second floor level to the south, but two at each level which face east and west.

In the curtain wall, 105 yards (96·01 m.) long, between this tower and the fourth tower the disposition of the slits changes. Those forming the upper row continue to fall between the merlons, but the lower row fall between the crenellations, though at first irregularly. A clear difference is noticeable in the masonry, falling above the level of the lower row of slits. Whether this represents a change of plan within a fairly short building period or substantial reconstruction of the fortifications at some later date is not clear. The masonry higher in the wall is of larger blocks than those used in the lower layers. On the inside face of the wall two complete arcades remain. They can be seen from the gardens of 'Katriona' in Lower Frog Street. They stand about fifteeen feet (4·57 m.) high and ten feet (3·05 m.) wide; they are about eight feet (2·44 m.) in depth, separated by piers four feet (1·22 m.) wide.

The fourth tower, standing about thirty feet (9·14 m.) high, is the only square tower in the circuit. It probably belongs to the original plan since it is bonded with the wall, but it has undergone many changes, perhaps because its proximity to the sea made it suitable for changes in the sixteenth century. Originally there seems to have been one arrow slit of the type found in the other towers at both ground and first floor level in the east and west faces. Later, gunports of the keyhole type were inserted in each face about three feet (0·914 m.) higher than the earlier slits. Originally, therefore, there was probably timber flooring to enable the defenders to use the slits, removed when artillery came into use. The wall walk was carried on corbels, and was protected by a crenellated walk, with slits in the merlons. A corbelled projection at the junction of the wall and the tower at the south-west angle suggests that the stair had to rise fairly steeply from the wall walk.

The wall beween the fourth and fifth towers has been pierced by a modern arch. The fifth tower stands about thirty feet (9·14 m.) high, and has no corbels, though the crenellations remain. It has three slits to provide covering fire to the east, south and west. It may mark the south-east angle of the walls, which were later extended about twelve yards (10·97 m.) to the square watch tower, although there is no clear join in the masonry to mark this. The sixth tower stands about thirty feet (9·14 m.) high, and has no defensive provisions other than the wall walk, carried on corbels and protected by crenellations. On the inside of this section are tall arcades, bonded with the wall and standing about twenty-five feet (7·62 m.) high. They were clearly intended to carry the wall walk only, and do not link with slits in the exterior face of the wall.

Even the cliff face was defended, but the remains of the wall are very fragmentary. The best remaining section is that on either side of a tower, which can be seen from the beach, the best vantage point from which to view the defences.

The wall on the north side of the town has been destroyed by later building.

The documentary evidence for Tenby is very slight. It suggests that much of the work was done in the early fourteenth century, at much the same time as the construction of the walls of Norwich, Yarmouth and King's Lynn which the Tenby walls resemble. There is a murage grant for a term of seven years, received in 1328.[8] In 1457 Jasper Tudor issued a licence ordering the townsmen to repair their defences.[9] It has been suggested that it was at this date that the wall walk was constructed, but it seems more probable that this had been built earlier and is connected with the lower line of arrow slits.

NOTES

1 MPBW Official Guide, *Denbigh Castle and Town Walls*, 1943, describes parts of the walls.
2 E. J. Laws, *Arch. Cambrensis*, 5th series, XIII, 1896, 177–92, 273–89; cited as Laws.
3 Laws, 184.
4 A description of the inside of the tower is given by Laws, 185–6, which contains some differences from that given above. He had the advantage of being able to see the tower from the inside.
5 A. J. Taylor, *Conway Castle and Town Walls*, 30.
6 Laws, 186.
7 Laws described the internal arrangements, saying that three high arches were pinched into a semi-circle and filled with masonry. The tower was then divided into two chambers, 192.
8 *Cal. Pat. Rolls, 1327–30*, 245.
9 The grant is given in full in C. Norris, *Etchings of Tenby*, 1812, opp. p. 32.

Glossary

ALURE A walk or passage-way behind the parapet.

AMERCEMENT A fine.

ASHLAR Squared block(s) of freestone.

BAILEY A fortified enclosure forming part of a settlement.

BALISTA A military catapult.

BARBICAN A defended enclosure in front of, and giving additional protection to, a gateway.

BASTION Projection from a line of fortification.

BATTERED With the base or ground courses sloping.

BONDED Of the same build.

BRETASCHE Usually a removable timber structure projecting from the face of a wall and designed for its defence in war: sometimes a temporary palisaded enclosure.

BURH Saxon communal fortification.

BUTTRESS Masonry built against a wall to strengthen it.

CARCUCATE The amount of land which could be ploughed by one plough or team in a season. It was fixed only in 1198 at 100 acres.

CHAMFER Surface created by smoothing off the angle between two faces.

COURSE A level layer of stones.

CRENELLATION An opening in the upper part of a parapet.

CURTAIN Stretch of plain wall, connecting gates or towers.

DRUM TOWER A circular tower.

EMBRASURE A splayed opening in a wall either for a window or as the opening of a gunport.

FEE FARM A fixed sum or rent.

FOOTINGS Lower part of a wall, including the foundations.

HOARD, HOURD A timber structure supported on corbels in front of a crenellated wall and designed to further its defence.

MACHICOLATION An opening between corbels of a parapet or in a floor, for example a vault in a gateway, through which missiles could be projected.

MANGONEL Siege engine, the projectile end turning against a fixed stop.

MERLON Solid part of a parapet.

OYER AND TERMINER Commission to judges to hear and determine a criminal case.

PORTCULLIS A movable gate, suspended in grooves in front of a gate, let down for additional protection.

QUOIN Stone at the angle of a building.

RIB Raised moulding dividing a vault.

STRING COURSE Continuous horizontal moulding projecting from a wall face.

WALL WALK Passage along a wall top.

Appendices

APPENDIX A

The forms of Murage Grants

SHREWSBURY 1220

The king to the sheriff of Shropshire, and to all in the same county, greetings. Know that we have granted to our burgesses of Shrewsbury, to aid in the enclosing of the town and for the safety and protection of the neighbouring areas, permission to take once every week for four years

From every cart of the county of Shropshire bringing saleable goods for sale in the town, ½d.

From every cart of any other county bringing goods for sale, 1d.

From every load of saleable goods except a load of barley, ¼d.

From every horse, mare, ox and cow brought for sale, ½d.

From every ten sheep, goats or pigs brought for sale, 1d.

From every five sheep, goats or pigs, ½d.

From every boat coming to Shrewsbury by the river Severn bringing things for sale, 4d.

But after the four years have elapsed, none of these shall be levied. Once the term is complete, the custom shall cease and be completely abolished. We order you, sheriff, to proclaim this grant through out your bailiwick, and to cause it to be observed for its term, as is laid down.

LONDON 1315

A similar preamble preceded the following list:

For every weigh of cheese, unguent, tallow and butter 1d.

For a wey of lead ¼d.

For every hundred of wax 2d.

For every hundred of almonds and rice 1d.

For every hundred of grain 12d.

For every hundred of pepper, gulger, cetervale, cinnamon, frankincense, basil, quicksilver, vermilion & verdigris 2d.

For every hundred of cummin, alum, sugar, licorice, aniseed, turpentine, pione, gold pigment 1d.

For every hundred of sulphur, argoille, gall, resin, copperas and reed ¼d.

For a large 'frail' of raisins and figs ½d.

For a small 'frail' of raisins and figs ¼d.

For a pound of clove, nuts, muscatel, mace, cubebs, saffron and silk ¼d.

For a bushel of gingerbread 1d.

For a hundred of copper, brass, tin, ½d.

For a hundred of glass ¼d.

For a thousand of grey-work 12d.

For a thousand of red-work 6d.

For a thousand of rosekyn 4d.

For a hundred of coney-skins ½d.

For a timber of fox-skins ½d.

For a timber of cat-skins ½d.

For a dozen genette skins ½d.

For a hundred of sheep's woolfells 1d.

For a hundred lamb and goatskins ½d.

For a dozen of leather 1d.

For a dozen of bazin ½d.

For a quarter of woad ½d.

For a cask of honey 6d.

For a cask of wine 2d.

For a cask of beer for export 1d.

For a sieve of salt 1d.

For every measure at the mill 2d.

For a dozen handmills 1d.

For every mill *ad fabrum* ¼d.

For a cask of ashes and fish ½d.

For a hundred of board and oak imported ½d.

For a hundred of board and firpole imported 2d.

For 20 sheaves of steel ½d.

For every hundred of poumaundener 1d.

For every horse load of serges, woollen cloth, grey cloth and linen cloth 1d.

For a 100 ells of canvas imported 1d.

For a dozen wimples ½d.

For every cloth of silk or gold ½d.

For every samite and cloth worked with gold 2d.

For a dozen of fustian 1d.

For every refined cendal ¼d and for two other cendals ¼d.

For every pound of woven cloth imported 6d.

For every hundred weight of batterie [pots and pans etc.] viz. basins, dishes, pots and posnets 1d.

For every cloth of Flanders dyed and refined 2d.

For every Stamford from the same parts 1d.

For a dozen of hose from the same parts ½d.

For a hood 1d.

For every burel from Normandy or elsewhere ½d.

For every dozen of black or white monks cloth ½d.

For every bale of cloth coming to London for export 18d.

For every English cloth dyed and russet, except scarlet, coming to London to be sold 2d.

For every scarlet 6d.

For every summer cloth coming from Stamford or Northampton or elsewhere in England coming for sale in London 1d.

For a dozen blankets 1d.

For every pound of merchandise not mentioned above 4d.

For a ship-load of sea-coal 6d.

For a ship-load of turf 2d.

For a scout of underwood 2d.

For a boat-load of underwood 1d.

For a scout of hay 2d.

For a quarter of corn coming for sale by land or sea ¼d.

For two quarters of wheat, barley, mesline, pease and beans ¼d.

For four seams of oats ¼d.

For two quarters of grout and malt ¼d.

For every horse for sale, value 40s., 1d.

For a horse of less value ½d.

For every ox and cow ½d.

For six pigs ½d.

For ten sheep ½d.

For five porkers for sale ½d.

For ten gammons of bacon ½d.

For every burel manufactured in the city, leaving London, 1d.

For every cart laden with fish coming to London 1d.

For the hull of every big ship freighted with merchandise other than the above, for sale in London 2d.

For a smaller vessel 1d.

For every batel freighted ½d.

For a dozen salted salmon 1d.

For twenty-five melvel ½d.

For one hundred salted haddock ½d.

For a thousand of herring ¼d.

For a dozen salted lampreys 1d.

For a thousand of salted eels ½d.

For a hundred of coarse fish 1d.

For a hundred of salted mackerel ¼d.

For a hundred of sturgeon 2d.

For a hundred of stockfish ¼d.

For a load of sand-eels ¼d.

For a load of garlick ¼d.

For all other merchandise not here named, of the value of 20sh.—1d.

Letter Book E, 63–6.

APPENDIX B

Tables of receipts from murage and monies spent.

*Denotes possession of a grant.

YEAR	PLACE	GRANT	RECEIPTS (£ s d)	COLLECTED OVER	EXPENSES (£ s d)	SPENT OVER	REFERENCE
1262	LEICESTER	—	7 3 2	—	7 6 0¼	—	Bateson, 98[1]
1263–4	HEREFORD	*	—	15 wks	3 10 0⅛	8 wks	C/A
1279–84	FLINT	—	—	—	22 9 6½	—	Pipe Roll 131/26[2]
1280	NEWCASTLE	*	120 0 0	52 wks	—	—	Cal. Fine Rolls, 1272–1307, 132
1280–2	RHUDDLAN	—	—	—	250 17 5½	—	Pipe Roll 131/26
1280–1	ABERYSTWYTH	—	—	—	200 0 7⅞	—	Pipe Roll 125/2
1284–6	FLINT	—	—	—	171 7 5	—	Pipe Roll 131/26
1284–5	CAERNARVON	*	—	—	2,398 11 4½	—	Pipe Roll 131/26
1293–4	HEREFORD	—	18 13 0½	12 wks	149 16 11	—	C/A
1294–5	CAERNARVON	—	—	—	1,024 18 11½	12 wks	E 101/486/8
1295	CAERNARVON	—	—	—	—	—	Pipe Roll 146/24, 25
1297–8	HEREFORD	*	23 4 8¾	50 wks	15 12 8	—	C/A
1298	GLOUCESTER	*	13 6 0½	18 wks	0 15 10	9 wks	C/A
1299–1300	LUDLOW	*	6 8 5¼	39 wks	56 4 0	18 wks	C/A
1302	GLOUCESTER	*	29 16 3	4 wks	0 10 0	—	C/A
1306	OXFORD	—	—	—	5 15 10	—	Salter,[3] 255
1313–14	LUDLOW	*	20 2 3½	52 wks	0 1 5	—	C/A
1315–16	OXFORD	—	—	—	1 13 4	—	Salter, 258
1316–17	OXFORD	—	—	—	2 16 6	—	Salter, 259
1317–18	LUDLOW	*	9 2 4	—	0 0 10¾	—	C/A
1317–18	OXFORD	—	—	—	1 17 5	—	C/A
1317–18	LEICESTER	*	—	—	8 16 8	—	Bateson, 315–16
1319	LUDLOW	*	—	—	—	—	C/A
1319–20	HEREFORD	*	30 16 9	—	—	—	C/A

231

YEAR	PLACE	GRANT	RECEIPTS £ s d	COLLECTED OVER	EXPENSES £ s d	SPENT OVER	REFERENCE
1320-1	LEICESTER	*		—	0 10 8	—	Bateson, 326-7
1320-2	BRISTOL	*	93 0 0	3 yrs	93 0 0	—	Cal. Inq. Misc., ii, 408
1321	LEICESTER	*		—	0 6 0	—	Bateson, 338
1321-3	HULL	*		—	292 0 0	—	C/A
1323-5	BRISTOL	—	73 17 2	3 yrs	73 17 2	—	Cal. Inq. Misc., ii, 408
1326-9	BRISTOL	*	112 15 10	4 yrs	112 15 10	—	Cal. Inq. Misc., ii, 408
1325-6	OXFORD	*		—	0 17 2	—	Salter, 263
1329-30	OXFORD	—		—	0 3 1½	—	Salter, 265
1331-2	K's LYNN	*		—	3 16 7	—	C/A
1332-5	BRISTOL	—	96 6 3	4 yrs	96 6 3	—	Cal. Inq. Misc., ii, 408
1332	LONDON	*		—	40 0 0	—	Letter Book E,[4] 273
1335-6	LEICESTER	—		—	6 5 3¾	—	Bateson, 28
1335-8	BRISTOL	*	73 16 2	4 yrs	73 16 2	—	Cal. Inq. Misc., ii, 408
1336-7	K's LYNN	*		—	1 0 0	—	C/A
1337-8	YARMOUTH	*		—	40 9 10½	—	Swinden, 78-82
1338-9	YARMOUTH	—		—	39 2 3	—	Swinden, 83-7
1339-40	K's LYNN	*		—	4 1 10½	—	C/A
1340-1	K's LYNN	*		—	80 6 9½	—	C/A
1341-2	K's LYNN	*		—	3 6 9	—	C/A
1341-2	EXETER	*	31 19 4	—	28 2 6½	37 wks	C/A
1342-3	YARMOUTH	—	44 17 10½	—	72 3 9½	—	Swinden, 87-90
1343-4	YARMOUTH	—	30 6 1¼	25 wks	70 19 3¼	—	Swinden, 90-91
1344-5	YARMOUTH	—		52 wks	88 17 11½	—	Swinden, 91-2
1345	YARMOUTH	—	8 5 0	13 wks		—	Swinden, 93
1351-2	LEICESTER	—		—	5 12 4½	—	Bateson, 78-9
1355	WINCHESTER	—	17 17 7	18 wks	18 8 5	—	C/A
1357	WINCHESTER	—	8 7 3	16 wks	6 17 8	—	C/A
1357-8	K's LYNN	—		—	7 13 0	—	C/A
1359	WINCHESTER	—	4 10 3½	15 wks		—	C/A
1360	WINCHESTER	—	18 2 2	—		—	C/A
1360-61	EXETER	—	15 19 8	—	16 0 9	10 wks	C/A

YEAR	PLACE	GRANT	RECEIPTS (£ s d)	COLLECTED OVER	EXPENSES (£ s d)	SPENT OVER	REFERENCE
1361	LUDLOW	*	41 2 11	42 wks	60 9 2½	—	C/A
1361–2	K's LYNN	—	—	—	3 14 0	—	C/A
1361–2	HULL	*	48 9 6½	—	13 17 3	—	C/A
1362–3	OXFORD	—	—	—	0 0 9	—	Salter, 271
1364–5	K's LYNN	—	—	—	1 3 6	—	C/A
1367–8	K's LYNN	—	—	—	1 16 4½	—	C/A
1369–70	K's LYNN	—	—	—	8 17 9	—	C/A
1370–71	EXETER	—	45 19 5½	—	46 10 8	16 wks	C/A
1372	EXETER	—	8 17 9½	—	15 10 1½	9 wks	C/A
1373–4	K's LYNN	—	—	—	1 19 0	—	C/A
1376–7	K's LYNN	*	—	—	37 9 1½	—	C/A
1377	WINCHESTER	—	18 2 2	18 wks	40 0 0	—	C/A
1377–80	BERWICK	—	—	—	17 7 4½	—	E 364/15
1377–8	LEICESTER	—	—	—	—	—	Bateson, 165
1377–8	SOUTHAMPTON	*	202 10 0	52 wks	—	—	E 364/12
1378	WINCHESTER	*	14 4 1	14 wks	—	—	C/A
1377–9	LEICESTER	—	—	—	4 19 8	—	Bateson, 169–70
1378–79	LEICESTER	—	—	—	11 6 3	—	Bateson, 167–8
1384–5	EXETER	—	39 19 2¼	—	32 16 4½	12 wks	C/A
1384–5	NORWICH	—	—	—	4 8 6	—	C/A
1384–5	RYE	*	312 14 1	52 wks	427 5 8¼	—	E 364/31
1385–6	NORWICH	—	—	—	4 11 5	—	C/A
1386	CANTERBURY	*	—	—	619 11 10	—	*Cal. Close Rolls*, 120–21
1386–7	CARLISLE	—	—	—	80 0 0	—	E 364/26
1387	EXETER	*	61 15 0¼	—	68 17 11½	12 wks	C/A
1388–9	RYE	—	200 13 4	52 wks	336 7 9½	52 wks	E 364/22
1388–9	NORWICH	*	38 19 8	—	6 12 1	—	C/A
1388–9	DOVER	*	20 0 0	—	38 19 8	—	E 364/22
1389–90	WINCHESTER	*	—	—	20 0 0	—	E 364/24
1390	CARLISLE	—	—	—	139 3 10	—	E 364/29
1390–91	WINCHESTER	*	20 0 0	—	20 0 0	—	E 364/25

YEAR	PLACE	GRANT	RECEIPTS (£ s d)	COLLECTED OVER	EXPENSES (£ s d)	SPENT OVER	REFERENCE
1391	COVENTRY	*	7 9 0	—	7 10 3¾	16 wks	E 364/25
1391–2	BERWICK	—	40 0 0	—	40 0 0	—	E 364/15
1391–2	CANTERBURY	*	200 0 0	—	200 0 0	—	E 364/27
1391–2	WINCHESTER	*	20 0 0	—	20 0 0	—	E 364/26
1391–2	COVENTRY	*	24 0 0	—	24 0 0	—	E 364/26
1392–5	BERWICK	—	522 0 0	—	255 2 5	—	E 101/483/5
1392–3	WINCHESTER	*	20 0 0	—	20 9 2	—	E 101/491/24, E 364/27
1393–4	GLOUCESTER	—	18 0 7½	52 wks	14 19 7	—	C/A
1393–4	COVENTRY	*	24 0 0	—	24 0 0	—	E 364/28
1393–4	WINCHESTER	*	20 0 0	—	20 0 0	—	E 364/28
1394–5	WINCHESTER	*	26 0 0	—	26 0 0	—	E 364/33
1394–5	NORWICH	—		—	39 2 11	—	C/A
1394–5	COVENTRY	*	24 0 0	—	24 0 0	—	E 364/29
1395	WINCHESTER	*	11 14 7	16 wks	14 14 0	—	C/A
1395–6	NORWICH	—		—	60 0 0	—	C/A
1396	CARLISLE	*	16 11 0	—	16 11 0	—	E 364/30
1396–7	COVENTRY	*	26 17 4	—	26 17 4	—	E 364/30
1396–7	WINCHESTER	*		—	40 12 8½	12 wks	E 364/37
1397–8	WINCHESTER	*	11 14 8	16 wks		—	C/A
1398	OXFORD	—		—	0 2 6	—	C/A
1398–9	NORWICH	—		—	36 17 2½	—	Salter, 277–8
1398–9	SOUTHAMPTON	*	300 0 0	—	300 7 3	—	C/A
1400	NORWICH	—		—		—	C/A
1400–1401	SOUTHAMPTON	*	300 0 0	—	336 18 2	—	E 364/37
1400–1401	SOUTHAMPTON	*	300 0 0	—	303 17 4	—	E 364/36
1401–1402	CANTERBURY	*		—	1 7 2	—	E 364/36
1402–1403	CANTERBURY	*		—	11 0 2	—	C/A
1402–1403	SOUTHAMPTON	*	300 0 0	—	417 0 4	—	C/A
1403–1404	SOUTHAMPTON	*	300 0 0	—	345 2 0	—	E 364/36
1404–1405	EXETER	—		—	73 7 2	25 wks	E 364/39
1405–1406	EXETER	—		—	87 9 6	24 wks	C/A

YEAR	PLACE	GRANT	RECEIPTS			COLLECTED OVER	EXPENSES			SPENT OVER	REFERENCE
			£	s	d		£	s	d		
1406–1407	EXETER	—				—	50	10	3½	20 wks	C/A
1407–1408	EXETER	—	7	1	0	—	4	17	4	1 wk	C/A
1407–1408	WINCHESTER	—	8	4	8	—	20	5	6	13 wks	C/A
1409–10	GLOUCESTER	—	9	10	2	—	1	8	6	—	C/A
1409–10	GLOUCESTER	—				52 wks	5	6	6	—	C/A
1409–10	BEVERLEY	*				—	97	17	4½	—	Leach,[6] 26–37
1410–11	NORTHAMPTON	—	240	0	0	—	319	11	3	—	E 364/45
1413–14	NORWICH	—				—	6	13	8	—	C/A
1414–15	WINCHELSEA	*	56	13	4	—	80	1	4	—	E 364/57
1415	WINCHELSEA	*	79	19	11	—	43	16	0	—	E 364/54
1415–16	RYE	*	27	0	0	—	0	12	9	—	E 364/57
1416–17	WINCHESTER	—				—	12	1	3	—	C/A
1417–18	WINCHESTER	—				—				—	C/A
1418–19	WINCHESTER	—	4	14	11	16 wks	1	2	6	—	C/A
1418–19	NORWICH	—				—	9	19	7½	—	C/A
1419–20	WINCHESTER	—				—	100	0	0	—	C/A
1421	SOUTHAMPTON	—	100	0	0	—	1,069	9	8¼	—	E 364/25
1420–22	PORTSMOUTH	—				—	286	16	8¾	22 mths	For. Accts. 10 H. VI rot.-H
1422	CARLISLE	—				—				52 wks	E 364/61
1423	COVENTRY	*	84	3	2	—	56	13	8	—	Leet Book,[7] 65
1423–4	WINCHELSEA	—	56	13	4	—				—	E 101/491/12
1424	COVENTRY	—	84	3	2	—				—	Leet Book, 101
1425	COVENTRY	—	84	3	2	—				—	Leet Book, 109
1426–7	DOVER	*	4	10	10	—	2	8	6	—	Add. Mss. 29615[8]
1428	CARLISLE	—				—	80	0	0	—	C.P.R., 538
1428–9	DOVER	—	9	9	4	52 wks	1	11	8	52 wks	Add. Mss. 29615
1430–31	DOVER	—	9	0	6	52 wks				—	Add. Mss. 29615
1432–3	DOVER	—	10	19	1	52 wks	14	5	1½	52 wks	Add. Mss. 29615
1432–3	WINCHESTER	—	4	0	2	—	2	8	4	—	C/A
1433–4	DOVER	—	17	15	7	—	2	10	3	—	Add. Mss. 29615
1440–41	CHESTER	—	2	18	5	50 wks	4	15	7	52 wks	C/A

YEAR	PLACE	GRANT	RECEIPTS £ s d	COLLECTED OVER	EXPENSES £ s d	SPENT OVER	REFERENCE
1442–3	YORK	*	22 11 6½	—	16 18 3	—	C/A
1443–4	DOVER	*	5 9 6	—	1 16 10	—	Add. Mss. 29810
1445–6	YORK	*	26 8 9	—	22 17 9	—	C/A
1447–8	YARMOUTH	*	7 15 11½	—	—	—	C/A
1448–9	YARMOUTH	*	3 10 0	—	—	—	C/A
1449–50	YARMOUTH	—	6 16 7½	—	—	—	C/A
1449–50	DOVER	*	9 19 8	—	14 19 11	—	Add. Mss. 29810
1450	ALNWICK	—		—	17 17 2	—	Bates,[9] 21
1450	BRISTOL	*		—	55 0 0	—	Gt. Red Book II,[10] 127
1457–8	DOVER	—	2 12 3	—	0 1 10	—	Add. Mss. 29810
1457–8	YARMOUTH	*	20 0 0	—	20 0 0	—	E 364/98
1459–60	YARMOUTH	*	20 0 0	—	20 0 0	—	E 364/98
1459–60	NORWICH	—		—	2 0 6	—	C/A
1460–61	OXFORD	—		—	0 3 3	—	Salter, 287
1462–3	DOVER	*	1 6 9	—	0 3 11	—	Add. Mss. 29617
1462–3	SANDWICH	*	120 0 0	—	145 3 7	—	E 364/112
1463–4	SANDWICH	*	120 0 0	—	136 1 4	—	E 364/112
1463–4	NOTTINGHAM	—		—	4 2 9	—	Stevenson,[11] 373
1465–6	SANDWICH	*	126 13 3	—	142 3 4	—	E 101/468/28
1466–7	SANDWICH	*	26 6 2	—	28 3 4	—	E 101/468/28
1466–7	DOVER	—	6 2 4½	—	13 8 6	—	Egerton, 2090
1467–8	CANTERBURY	—		—	4 10 8	—	C/A
1468–9	SANDWICH	*	123 0 6¼	—	126 11 0	—	E 101/468/28
1469–70	SANDWICH	*	156 17 3¼	—	160 9 8	—	E 101/468/28
1469–70	CANTERBURY	—		—	1 5 5½	—	C/A
1470–71	CANTERBURY	—		—	3 5 3	—	C/A
1471–2	DOVER	*	5 4 0	—	2 4 6	—	Add. Mss. 29616
1471–2	SANDWICH	*	63 6 8	—	70 0 6	—	E 101/468/28
1472–3	SANDWICH	*	126 13 4	—	129 19 6	—	E 101/468/29
1473–4	WINCHESTER	—		—	15 11 8	—	C/A
1474–5	DOVER	*	8 9 8½	—	0 13 1	—	Add. Mss. 29616

YEAR	PLACE	GRANT	RECEIPTS	COLLECTED OVER	EXPENSES	SPENT OVER	REFERENCE
1477–8	WINCHESTER	—	—	—	13 16 2½	—	C/A
1478–9	K's LYNN	—	—	—	2 8 7	—	C/A
1479–80	CANTERBURY	—	—	—	3 10 4½	—	C/A
1481–2	CANTERBURY	*	—	—	3 18 1	—	C/A
1490–91	DOVER	—	6 14 7	—	1 18 4	—	Add. Mss. 29617
1497–8	DOVER	—	6 0 7	—	4 18 8	—	Add. Mss. 29617
1511–12	DOVER	—	4 2 7	—	1 4 6	—	Egerton 2092
1513–14	DOVER	—	2 16 0	—	0 2 6	—	Egerton 2092

1. M. Bateson, *Records of the Borough of Leicester*, 1899–1901.
2. Figures from J. G. Edwards, *Edward I's Castle Building in Wales*, 1944, 66–73.
3. H. E. Salter, *Munimenta Civitatis Oxonie*, 1920. Oxford Hist. Soc.
4. *Letter Books of the City of London*, ed. R. R. Sharpe.
5. H. Swinden, *The History and Antiquities of Great Yarmouth*, 1772.
6. A. F. Leach, 'The Building of Beverley Bar', *Trans. E. Riding Antiquarian Soc.* IV, 1896.
7. *Coventry Leet Book*, ed. M. D. Harris, *E.E.T.S.* Orig. Series vols. 134–5, 1907–1908.
8. Dover Accounts are amongst British Museum Additional and Egerton Mss.
9. C. J. Bates, *Border Holds of Northumberland*, 1891.
10. *Great Red Book*, ed. E. W. W. Veale, *Bristol Record Society*, 1931.
11. W. H. Stevenson, *Records of the Borough of Nottingham*, II, 1883.

APPENDIX C

The Distribution of Murage Grants.

Year axis: 1220 · 1230 · 1240 · 1250 · 1260 · 1270 · 1280 · 1290

Town	Murage grants (1220–1290)
ALNWICK	
ARUNDEL	
BATH	
BERWICK	
BRIDGNORTH	✕ ✕ ✕ ✕ ✕✕ ✕✕✕ ✕ ✕ ✕ ✕ ✕
BRISTOL	✕✕✕ ✕ ✕ ✕✕ ✕✕ ✕ ✕ ✕
BURY ST. EDMUNDS	
CANTERBURY	
CARLISLE	✕✕ ✕✕ ✕✕ ✕✕ ✕✕ ✕✕
CHESTER	✕✕
CHICHESTER	✕✕
CLUN	✕✕
COLCHESTER	
COVENTRY	
DOVER	
DUNWICH	✕
DURHAM	
EXETER	✕✕ ✕✕ ✕✕✕ ✕✕ ✕✕
GLOUCESTER	✕✕ ✕✕ ✕✕ ✕✕ ✕✕✕ ✕
GRIMSBY	✕✕ ✕✕
HARTLEPOOL	
HARWICH	
HEREFORD	✕ ✕✕✕ ✕ ✕✕✕✕✕ ✕✕ ✕ ✕ ✕ ✕✕✕ ✕✕ ✕ ✕✕
HULL	
ILFRACOMBE	
IPSWICH	
LANCASTER	
LEICESTER	✕
LEWES	✕✕
LINCOLN	✕✕ ✕✕✕ ✕✕✕✕✕ ✕
LONDON	✕ ✕✕ ✕✕ ✕✕ ✕✕✕✕
LUDLOW	✕✕✕ ✕✕ ✕ ✕✕
LYNN	✕✕
MELCOMBE	
NEWCASTLE	✕✕ ✕✕✕✕
NORTHAMPTON	✕✕✕ ✕✕
NORWICH	
NOTTINGHAM	✕✕ ✕✕ ✕✕✕
OSWESTRY	✕ ✕
OXFORD	✕✕✕✕✕✕✕✕✕ ✕✕ ✕✕ ✕ ✕
PENRITH	
PLYMOUTH	
POOLE	
PORTSMOUTH	
RICHMOND	
ROCHESTER	✕
RYE	
SALISBURY	
SANDWICH	
SCARBOROUGH	✕✕ ✕✕
SHREWSBURY	✕✕✕✕✕ ✕✕✕✕✕✕ ✕✕ ✕✕✕✕ ✕✕ ✕✕
SOUTHAMPTON	✕ ✕✕ ✕✕ ✕✕
STAFFORD	✕✕✕ ✕✕ ✕✕ ✕✕
STAMFORD	✕✕ ✕✕ ✕✕
TONBRIDGE	
TOTNES	✕✕
WARWICK	
WELLS	
WINCHELSEA	
WINCHESTER	✕✕ ✕✕ ✕✕ ✕✕ ✕✕ ✕✕
WORCESTER	✕✕ ✕✕ ✕✕✕✕ ✕✕ ✕ ✕✕✕ ✕✕ ✕✕ ✕
YARMOUTH	✕✕ ✕✕ ✕✕ ✕
YORK	✕✕ ✕✕ ✕✕✕✕ ✕✕ ✕✕

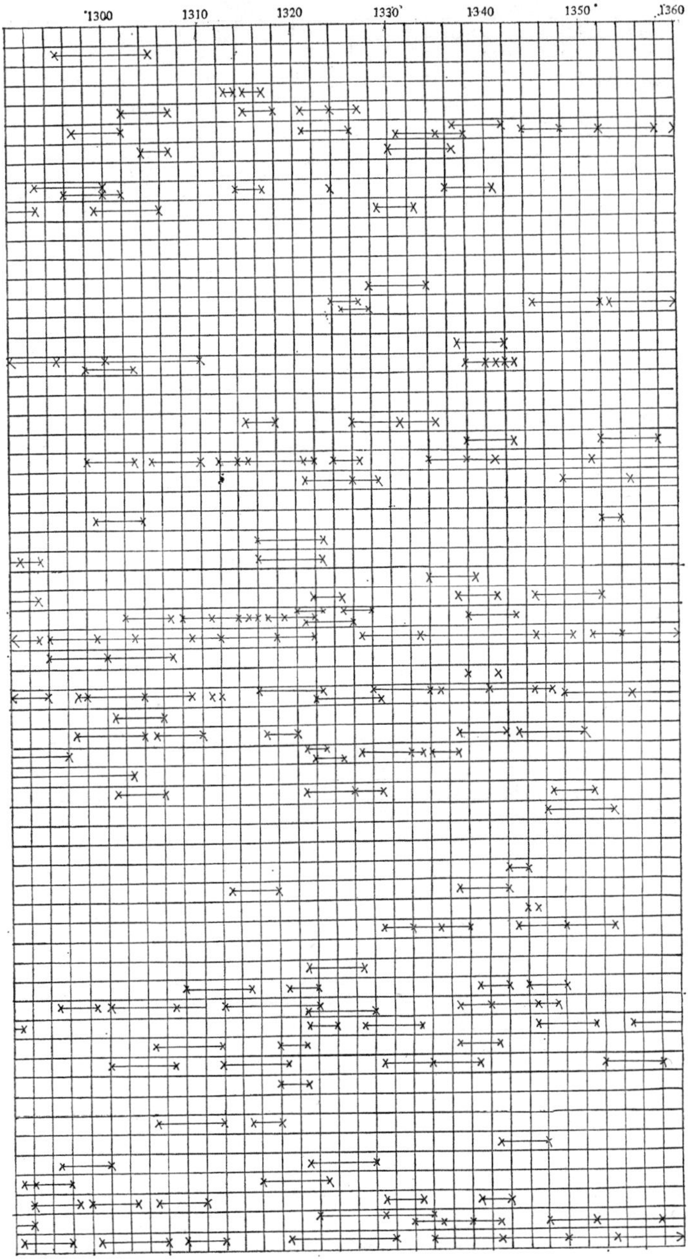
1300
1310
1320
1330
1340
1350
1360

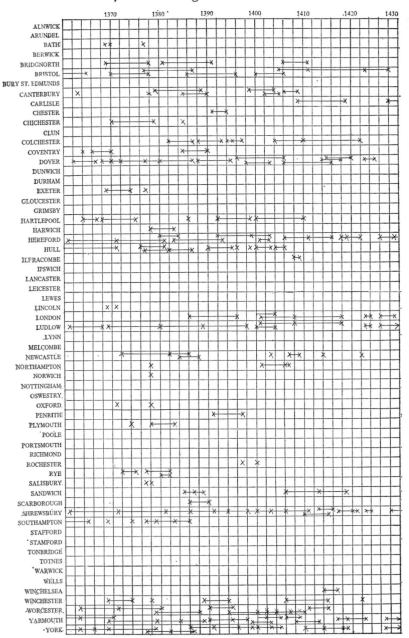

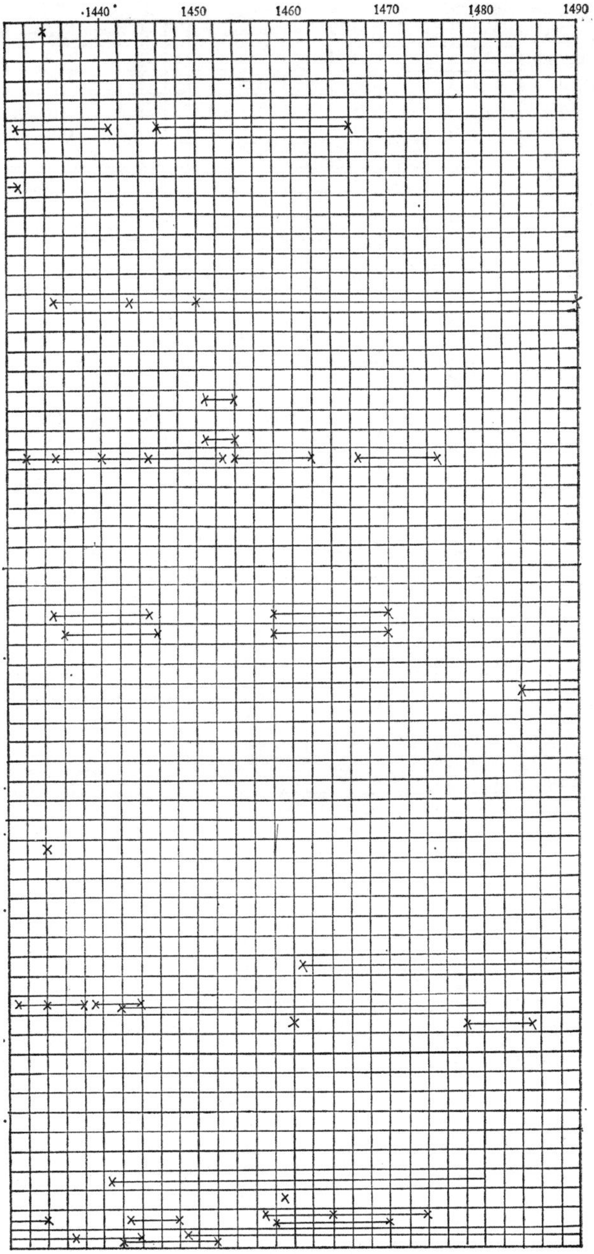
1440
1450
1460
1470
1480
1490

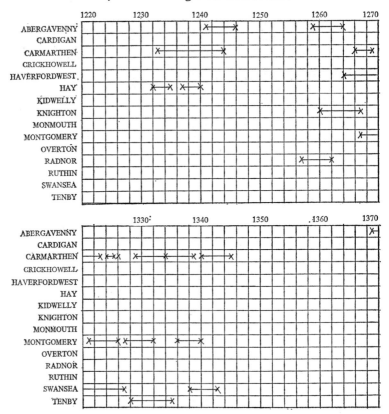

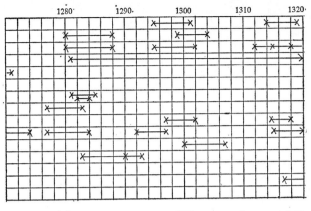

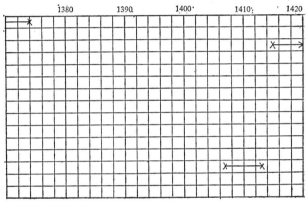

Index

ROMAN fortifications, re-used,
20, 21, 25, 53, 111, 113, 119, 125,
148, 154, 156, 158, 181, 191, 203,
204

SCOTS, 78, 79, 97, 99, 100
Supervision of works, 49

TOWNS (attacked)
Canterbury, 21
Colchester, 20
Gloucester, 77
Hereford, 21
in Wars of Roses, 80
Lynn, 77
Northern England, 78
Rochester, 77

Southern England, 80
Worcester, 77
Towns (besieged), Carlisle, 78–9

WALLS
against disease, 88
alignment of, 55–7
compared with castle, 55, 71
features of, 57
length of time to build, 50
linked with castle, 55
non-defensive uses, 87–9
police uses, 88
portrayed, 92
Wall walk, 61–5
Watch and ward, 83, 84
Welsh, 75, 210, 211, 212